UNTOUCHABLES

*My Family's Triumphant Journey Out of
the Caste System in Modern India*

~~~~~~

Narendra Jadhav

SCRIBNER

New York   London   Toronto   Sydney

SCRIBNER
1230 Avenue of the Americas
New York, NY 10020

Originally published in Marathi in 1993 by Granthali as *Aamcha Baap aan Amhi*
Revised and translated into French in 2002 by Librairie Arthème Fayard as *Intouchable*
First published in English in 2003 by Penguin Books as *Outcaste*

Published by arrangement with Librairie Arthème Fayard and Narendra Jadhav

SCRIBNER and design are trademarks of Macmillan Library Reference USA, Inc.,
used under license by Simon & Schuster, the publisher of this work.

For information about special discounts for bulk purchases,
please contact Simon & Schuster Special Sales:
1-800-456-6798 or business@simonandschuster.com

DESIGNED BY ERICH HOBBING

Text set in Stempel Garamond

Manufactured in the United States of America

1   3   5   7   9   10   8   6   4   2

Library of Congress Cataloging-in-Publication Data
Jadhav, Narendra, 1953–
[Aamcha baap aan amhi. English]
Untouchables : my family's triumphant journey out of the caste system in modern India /
Narendra Jadhav.
p.   cm.
First published in English in 2003 by Penguin Books as Outcaste.
1. Jadhav, Narendra, 1953– 2. Economists—India—Maharashtra—Biography.
3. Monetary reformers—India—Maharashtra—Biography. 4. Dalits—India—
Maharashtra—Biography. 5. Dalits—India—Social conditions—20th century.
I. Title: My family's triumphant journey out of the caste system in modern India.
II. Title.
HB126.I43J3313 2005
305.5'688'092—dc22   2005044166

ISBN-13: 978-0-7432-7079-3
ISBN-10: 0-7432-7079-7

To
the vision of my blind grandma,
the genius of my father, who never went to school,
and
Sonu, my mother, who killed her hunger to keep us alive,
and
all those anonymous men and women
everywhere in the world
who stood up for human rights

CONTENTS

UNTOUCHABLES

INTRODUCTION

Every sixth human being in the world today is an Indian, and every sixth Indian is an erstwhile untouchable, a Dalit. Today there are 165 million Dalits (equal to more than half the population of the United States) and they continue to suffer under India's 3,500-year-old caste system, which remains a stigma on humanity. However, Dalits are awakening. We are struggling against caste discrimination, illiteracy, and poverty; our weapons are education, self-empowerment, and democracy.

Hindus believe that God created the caste system. The sacred Rig-Veda, the earliest literary source in India, dating back to around 1000 B.C., describes how human stratification came about: a cosmic giant, Purusha, sacrificed parts of his body to create mankind. His mouth became the Brahmin, the priestly class; his arms the Kshatriya, the warriors and landowners; his thighs were made into Vaishya, the merchants; and from his feet were born Shudra, the servants. This fourfold division of society is called the Four Varnas (Chaturvarna). The untouchables have no place in the Chaturvarna, and are placed even below the lowest Shudra Varna.

Ancient Hindu law books such as *Manu Smruti* and *Gautama Dharma Shastra* did not allow Shudras and Dalits to possess any wealth other than "dogs and donkeys." The doors of education were closed to them. This is what the law books prescribe for untouchables who dare approach the sacred texts:

1

If he listens intentionally to the Vedas, his ears shall be filled
   with lead.
If he recites them, his tongue shall be cut out.
If he remembers them, his body shall be split in twain.

In the Indian epic Mahabharata, dated around 1000 B.C., there is a
celebrated fable about Ekalavya, a tribal boy and an outcaste.
One day Ekalavya saw a group of young boys listening to the
famed guru Dronacharya. He tried to befriend them but was surrounded by four armed guards, who roughed him up. The princes
were learning the art of archery and warfare, and if Ekalavya
was ever seen again in the vicinity, they warned, he would be
killed.

But curiosity got the better of Ekalavya, who began rising at
dawn to furtively watch the training of the young princes. He
would strain to hear everything that was taught. By night, in the
moonlight, he would practice, reciting the instructions he had
heard the guru utter. He soon mastered the art of archery.

One day the guru saw Ekalavya shoot a deer that was bolting at
lightning speed. Amazed at the precision of a young boy dressed
in rags, the guru questioned him, and was shocked when he realized that this boy was a tribal outcaste.

Ekalavya wanted to offer *guru-dakshina*—the traditional gift
offered to a teacher in gratitude—so he offered himself as the
guru's slave. Instead, the guru asked Ekalavya for his right thumb.
Ekalavya was caught off guard. In his right thumb rested all the
prowess of archery. But Ekalavya calmly said that a guru is equiv-
alent to a god and he would gladly do as the guru wished. So
saying, he severed his thumb and laid the bleeding stub at
Dronacharya's feet.

Every Indian child hears this mythological story about guru-
bhakti—devotion to the teacher. "Great are the disciples as dedicated
as Ekalavya. See, his name lives on forever," children are told.

But I see the tale in a very different light. For me, Ekalavya is an outcaste—a Dalit—who was denied an education by the guru Dronacharya, who embodied the highborn. Dronacharya was protecting his knowledge and power as well as perpetuating a social order that was inherently unjust.

For me, the moral of the fable is simply that power will remain the guarded possession of the highborn, striving to ensure that an outcaste remains a lowly outcaste. Paralyzed by the system, the outcaste will never dare to question it.

Ekalavya was cornered into sacrificing his strength, and as consolation, his devotion was glorified and his silent consent transformed into a myth that promotes submission among the disempowered.

The 3,500-year-old caste system in India is still alive and violently kicking. In cities they will tell you, "The caste system is a thing of the past, it now exists only in villages." Go to the villages, and they will tell you, "Oh no. Not here, maybe in some other village." Yet open the matrimonial section of any newspaper and you will find an unabashed and bewildering display of the persistent belief in caste and subcaste.

Untouchability was officially abolished by the Indian Constitution when the country became a republic on January 26, 1950. Mercifully, today the untouchables are no longer required to place clay pots around their necks to prevent their spit from polluting the ground. They are no longer required to attach brooms to their rumps to wipe out their footprints as they walk. But while caste discrimination may have changed form, it has not disappeared.

When you meet a person in India today, even as you introduce yourself, your caste will quickly be assessed from your family name. Consciously or subconsciously, Indians, whether in their own country or abroad, still make judgments based on caste. Over the years, the caste system has taken on sophisticated dimensions; it has become subtler, though no less pernicious.

*   *   *

The fourfold Chaturvarna and the untouchables are divided into more than three thousand castes and subcastes, with mind-boggling differentiation built into the hierarchy. Every individual is believed to have been predestined by his or her fate into a caste. The caste is the defining factor in determining the course of a life. The place from where he drinks water, whom he dines with, whom he marries, and whether he becomes a scholar or a scavenger—all depend on his caste.

In this system of graded inequality, the Dalits were so inferior that their mere touch was believed to pollute others. They were denied human rights and were forced to scrape together a living from denigrating chores such as carrying human manure and removing the carcasses of cattle. They were powerless to change their caste-based social status. There was no scope for a revolt. How could mere mortals challenge a structure ordained by God himself? Social and religious sanctity had ensured unquestioning perpetuation of the age-old system.

The untouchables themselves were indoctrinated in the theory of karma, which stated that they were burdened with demeaning tasks only because of their own misdeeds in past lives. Their dharma—duty—now was to perform their tasks assiduously with the hope of redeeming themselves and aspiring to a better life in the next incarnation. A person belonging to a sweeper caste had to dutifully carry human excrement on his head with the hope that he could look forward to bettering his lot in another life.

Nirvana is the ultimate attainable bliss in human existence. In this state, the atma—the soul—is released from its path through a preordained cycle of 8.4 million births. The only salvation for humans is a life that follows prescribed devotion to the assigned caste-based duty; following it unquestioningly will lead to nirvana.

Certainly, revolts against the caste system did take place—the most notable being the one by Gautama Buddha in the fifth century B.C., which questioned and discarded the Chaturvarna and the caste system arising from it. Buddhism gained prominence over a large part of India and spread to other countries such as China and Japan, and to Southeast Asia, from the fourth century B.C. to the sixth century A.D. However, Buddhism's influence in India declined in the seventh century and virtually disappeared as a widely practiced religion before the arrival of Islam in the tenth century.

The fourteenth century saw the emergence of a religious revival and reformation similar to the sixteenth-century Protestant Reformation in Europe. It took the form of the anti-orthodox Bhakti movement, which included women and untouchables. At its helm were saints, poets, and philosophers—who came mainly from the lower strata of society—potters, gardeners, tailors, barbers, carpenters, and even untouchables.

The Bhakti movement established equality before God; its followers believed even untouchables shared the grace of God. As they reach God, they cease to be distinguished: as salt becomes one with the ocean, the untouchables become one with God.[1] However, the inclusiveness of the Bhakti movement was confined only to the religious sphere. Even the compassionate saint-poets tended to uphold the divisive caste system in the social realm. While the Bhakti movement raised awareness, it was not radical enough to challenge the social system in day-to-day life.

With the advent of the British Raj in the early nineteenth century, education, once the privilege of the upper castes alone, gradually became accessible to castes lower down the hierarchy. Knowledge brought with it the desire to be recognized and respected; it strengthened the resolve to struggle against discrimination.

In a historic event in 1873, Jyotiba Phule, a teacher in a Christian school who came from the gardener community, established the first non-Brahmin social organization that emphasized education for the masses and advocated reduction of Brahmin ritual power. Phule educated his childless wife, Savitri, who started a school for women. Over the years, Jyotiba established many schools for untouchables and women. In the 1870s, Jyotiba's campaign for education of the traditionally disenfranchised laid the groundwork for massive social change. Even today most Dalits see education as the panacea for their problems. Indeed, literacy rates among Dalits have been improving faster than those among non-Dalits.

When the Prince of Wales visited India in 1889, he was greeted with signs:

> *Tell the grandma we are a happy nation.*
> *But 19 crores are without education.*[2]

This was the beginning of a revolution.

Among the many erstwhile untouchable Dalit castes, the Mahar caste is the single largest in Maharashtra, a progressive province on the west coast of India, with Mumbai (Bombay) as its capital. Mahars are found in almost every village of Maharashtra, constituting around 10 percent of its population. Their quarters, called the Maharwada, are invariably set outside the village boundaries.

Traditionally, the Mahar's duty in the village, as classified by British administrative manuals, was that of an "inferior village servant." The Mahar was the "watchman and guardian of the village and the living chronicler of its concerns." Apart from arbitrating in boundary disputes and guarding the village, their duties also included carrying death notices and messages to other villages, bringing fuel to the cremation ground, mending the village walls, summoning landowners to pay land revenue in the chavadi (village hall), escorting those conveying the government treasury, sweeping the village roads, serving government officials, tracking thieves, and removing the carcasses of cattle from the village.[3]

These traditional duties of the Mahars came to be known as Yeskar duty, and were performed by every Mahar family in a village on a rotation basis. This duty, which came to be seen as a birthright by Mahars, was compensated by the village in the form of baluta—entitlements in kind, such as grain and the meat and skin of dead cattle—besides a small amount of land known as watan.

There is a Mahar legend about how these birthrights came to be granted.[4] A handsome Mahar warrior named Amrutnak was in the service of the sultan of Bedar. He volunteered to rescue the sultan's queen, abducted during a hunting expedition. Before proceeding on his long journey to Kabul in Afghanistan, Amrutnak presented a small box to the king for safekeeping.

After many adventures, he succeeded in bringing back the queen. However, he was met not with gratitude but hostility because of the days and nights he had spent with her. When questioned, Amrutnak simply smiled and reminded the king about the "small box." The box contained the ultimate proof of his loyalty. In return for his self-castration and bravery, Amrutnak was granted his demand of fifty-two rights for his people, the Mahars.

The legend of Amrutnak is one of loyalty and self-sacrifice, which became a part of the Mahar psyche. However, the so-called rights included nothing more than a de facto right to begging, a claim to the clothing of the dead, and the like.

Mahars did find an outlet from their traditional village duties by serving as guards in the hill forts or enlisting in the military. The consolidation of British rule in India led to the Mahars' entry into the British Indian Army and paved the way to their awakening. The British Army provided the Mahars with more than a decent job. The army established compulsory education for Indian soldiers and their children, both male and female. Until then, women in general, and all untouchables, had been denied the right to learning. Education for the untouchables in the army gave them a new vision and a new sense of self-worth. They realized that the low esteem in which they were held was not an inescapable destiny but a stigma imposed on them by the priests. They felt the shame of it and were determined to get rid of it.

*   *   *

Then, in 1891, came the birth of someone who would lead the revolution for equality in India. This man, a son of a Mahar schoolteacher in the British Army, was Dr. B. R. Ambedkar, affectionately known as Babasaheb.

Babasaheb was the great leader of the Dalit movement in twentieth-century India. It was he who organized, united, and inspired the Dalits to effectively use political means toward their goal of social equality. He was highly educated—a Ph.D. from Columbia University (1917), D.Sc. from the London School of Economics, and Bar-at-Law from Gray's Inn, London (1923). These achievements, spectacular by any standard, were simply incredible for an untouchable.

Dr. Ambedkar wrote books on economics, history, law, sociology, politics, and comparative religion. He published *Mooknayak* (Voice of the Dumb), the first of many newspapers for Dalits. He led numerous protests and in 1935, when he felt that there was no way to change the Hindu caste system, he declared he would "not die a Hindu," setting in motion a movement that eventually resulted in conversion of about five hundred thousand untouchables to Buddhism in 1956. He established a chain of hostels, schools, and colleges primarily for Dalits. He founded political parties that successfully politicized the Dalits throughout Maharashtra and, in due course, all over India.

Dr. Ambedkar submitted a concrete program of action called "A Scheme of Political Safeguards for the Protection of the Depressed Classes in the Future Constitution of a Self-Governing India." This document constituted the Declaration of Fundamental Rights for Dalits. It called for equal citizenship for Dalits, abolishment of untouchability, and the banning by law of discrimination. It demanded adequate representation for Dalits in public service and the establishment of a Public Service Commission for recruitment and enforcement. Most important, it demanded adequate Dalit representation in the legislatures and the right of Dalits to elect their own representatives through separate electorates.

Dr. Ambedkar often crossed swords with Mahatma Gandhi. Yet it was at the insistence of Gandhi that Dr. Ambedkar was chosen as chairman of the Drafting Committee for the Indian Constitution. In that capacity and also as law minister in independent India's first cabinet, he played a significant role in creating contemporary India's legal system. He was posthumously awarded India's highest civic honor—Bharat Ratna, the Jewel of India.

On India's independence in 1947, untouchability was abolished by law and an affirmative-action program against caste-based discrimination was put in place. This policy has had some success, and Dalits continue to gain political and economic strength.

On the political front, representation of Dalits in the political decision-making institutions at local, provincial, and national levels is commensurate with their population share. However, a united countrywide Dalit political force has yet to be established.

A strong Dalit middle class is emerging, but there is much that remains to be done. Past exclusion and discrimination has impacted Dalit access to capital assets and employment opportunities. This has meant a greater incidence of poverty and deprivation among Dalits.

Following an unprecedented macroeconomic crisis in 1991, the Indian government has adopted a new economic policy based on liberalization, privatization, and globalization. As a result, the Indian economy has emerged as one of the fastest-growing in the world. On the flip side, however, the rate of job creation has slowed down. This has led to a debate on the affirmative-action policy, which in India has been confined to the public sector. Presently, Dalit groups have been demanding extension of the policy to the large and growing private sector as well, but this is being opposed by corporate interests. The struggle of Dalits goes on.

The movement spearheaded by Dr. Babasaheb Ambedkar continues, decades later, to gather momentum. His message to Dalits to "educate, organize, and agitate" has been reaching far and wide.

Dalits, once rendered untouchable, are finding their voice. Indeed, they are mounting a slow but steady rebellion.

Dr. Babasaheb Ambedkar touched the lives of millions of Dalits. One of them was Damu—Damodar Runjaji Jadhav. Damu was an ordinary man, but he did an extraordinary thing: inspired by Dr. Babasaheb Ambedkar, he stood up against the tyranny of the caste system. This is the story of Damu, my father, and Sonu, my mother, as told to me. In their lives and times, you will find my story as well.

PROLOGUE

July 1948. Damu has made up his mind to go to a well-known school in Mumbai to seek admission for his son.

On seeing Damu, who was poorly dressed, the gatekeeper stopped him and asked, "What business do you have here?"

"I am here to get admission for my child," Damu replied.

The gatekeeper looked him up and down contemptuously and said, "What makes you think you can walk in here at any time and get admission? Don't waste my time. Get lost."

Damu was annoyed. He was not going to let anybody stop him from enrolling his son in what he thought was a good school. Hiding his irritation, Damu took a fifty-paisa coin from his pocket and pressed it into the gatekeeper's hand. The gatekeeper's entire demeanor underwent a change. He pocketed the money quickly and not only did he let Damu in but also showed him the way to the headmaster's room.

Damu walked up to the room and knocked. On getting no response, he pushed open the door and looked in. He saw a man sitting at the desk, writing something. Damu cleared his throat and asked if he could enter.

The man looked up and asked, "Who are you? What do you want?"

Damu stepped into the room. He replied, "Saheb, I am Damu. I work in Mumbai Port Trust Railways. I am here to get admission for my son."

"This is now the month of July," the headmaster replied. "All admissions to the school close by May and the academic year begins in the month of June. There are no vacancies now. You can try for admission in the month of May next year."

So saying, he looked down and continued to write. Damu's enthusiasm waned. He had come with such high hopes only to be brushed away so lightly. All this talk of terms and academic years had bewildered him. His only thought was to ensure his child's education in a good school and nothing further. He tried again.

"Saheb, I am a poor man. If my child is well educated he will not have to lead a life like me, doing hard manual labor. Please, saheb, my son is an intelligent boy. He will do whatever you tell him to do."

The headmaster was irritated. "Did I not tell you that there is no vacancy? I can do nothing to help you. Please go away and try again next year."

Damu felt helpless. He had not anticipated such a problem. He had thought that all he had to do was go to a school of his choice and have his child admitted. He felt his dream slipping away. Never before had he felt such helplessness and frustration. The only thing he could hear was Babasaheb Ambedkar's voice urging his people to educate their children. Education was the only way to ensure a life of dignity. And here was this man nonchalantly telling him to come back and try again next year. Damu's feeling of utter helplessness erupted into anger.

He flung himself onto the floor in front of the headmaster and announced, "I am not going to budge from here. Do what you want. Call in the police if you wish. But I am not leaving this room till you admit my child. I will go on a hunger strike till you give me what I want."

The headmaster, completely taken aback, was embarrassed and amazed by Damu's determination. He also felt a grudging admiration for this man.

"Get up and go home. There is no need to create such a spectacle. Come back tomorrow with your son and I will see what I can do for him."

Damu looked at him suspiciously and remained where he was. The headmaster was amused.

"Damu, get up. I told you that I would do my best for your son. Go home now and return tomorrow. Don't forget to bring eleven rupees and twenty-five paise."

Slowly Damu walked home, wondering whether to believe the headmaster. That night he slept fitfully. He was up early and impatiently waited outside the school. When the headmaster arrived he was surprised to see Damu and his son waiting. He called them to his room and asked the school clerk to get the required forms. The clerk then duly filled out the forms and Damu was asked to sign them. When the formalities were over, the headmaster asked the clerk to lead the child to his classroom. Damu, too, got up and followed them. Only the sight of his child sitting down in the classroom soothed his mind and put to rest all his doubts.

All his life, Damu refused to define himself by circumstances and aimed at shaping his own destiny. He steered his children to educational heights and inculcated in them the spirit of excellence.

After retirement in 1970, Dada—as we called him in the family—had a lot of time on his hands. With his penchant for fixing things, this barely literate, rugged man turned his attention to "repairing" all the gadgets in the house, including those in perfect working order. Out of a desire to keep him from being a nuisance, I persuaded him to write his memoirs. At the beginning he was reluctant, but writing soon caught his fancy and he continued the exercise for many years, until poor health forced him to stop.

After Dada's death in 1989, I edited and reconstructed his diaries, written in rudimentary Marathi, and added to them from oral recollections of others, including those of my illiterate mother and accomplished elder brothers, sisters, and sisters-in-law. Published in 1993 as the memoirs of a Dalit family entitled *Our Father and Us*, the Marathi original was widely acclaimed and went on to become a bestseller. It is being translated into several Indian languages, including Hindi, Punjabi, Gujarati, Kannada, Tamil, and Malayalam. This edition has been adapted from the Marathi original.

I

UP AGAINST BONDAGE

March 1, 1930

It was an unbearably hot afternoon in the village of Ozar. Damu was barefoot, running as fast as he could, soles burning on the scorching ground. The mamledar, a senior revenue official, was visiting the village for a routine inspection and Damu had to herald his arrival. Outpacing the mamledar's horse, he ran until he felt his legs would give way. He ran singing the praises of the mamledar, alerting the villagers that an honorable person was arriving. This was his Yeskar duty.

Later, Damu patiently waited outside the house of the patil, the village headman, to escort the mamledar to another village. He could hear loud laughter echoing from inside. Hours later, they came out. By the time Damu had led the mamledar back, he was tired and hungry. Walking home slowly, he was looking forward to some hot tea and bhakris, homemade millet bread, when a policeman came looking for him.

"Eh, Damu Mahar, I have been looking everywhere for you. Where have you been wandering, you son of a bitch?"

The constable was flustered; a dead body had been found floating in the broken well by the mangroves.

"You will sit guarding the body till the fauzdar and the police party come to inspect the scene and write a report," the constable ordered. "Nobody is allowed near the well. Remember, if anything happens to the corpse, your body too will end up in the well."

Damu told him that he had not eaten since he had met the mamledar's tonga—horse carriage—that morning and that he would be back in no time, but the constable would not listen.

"Do you see my baton?" he asked, brandishing it. "I'll stick it up your ass and you will see it come out of your throat. I'll beat you up so badly that you'll forget the name of your father."

Damu ran, stopping only when he reached the mangroves.

It was quiet by the well. Damu looked all around but there was no one in sight and no sound except for the crickets.

Gathering all his courage, Damu hesitantly approached the well and peeped inside, only to turn back in revulsion. It was a ghastly sight—the body of a woman in white garb, disfigured and swollen, a shoal of fish nibbling at her limbs.

It was getting dark and the stars were beginning to come out. There was no one around, he thought, and it was a corpse after all. What harm would it do if he went home for a quick bite? He was sick with hunger and had not been home since sunrise. It was already midnight; his wife would be worried. Soon, however, he was glad that he had not moved from his post. The constable had come to check on him.

"Damu," he yelled, "I am going home. Be sure to keep a watchful eye and don't let me catch you asleep. The fauzdar is expected to arrive by morning to make his report."

"Saheb," Damu said humbly, "I have not gone home since sunrise . . . my wife will not take a sip of water without some word about me."

The constable's face took on an angry expression. Damu faltered; no words could form and he stood open-mouthed.

"So what, you bastard? Do you want me to go feed her while you are away?"

Damu cringed; yet without realizing that his voice had taken a sharp edge, he persisted. "Can you at least let my folks know that I will not be home till this body is cremated?"

"Let my folks know, you say. Look at this lout's arrogance! Do you think we were born as messengers for you lowly outcastes? Your woman is not going to die if she does not eat one night. And if she does, who cares?"

Soon, dawn was breaking and the villagers were beginning to come to the fields for their morning ablutions. Damu sat by the well, unseen by anyone. He could hear them as they started whispering. All kinds of rumors were afloat.

"Why did she commit suicide?"

"How do you know it was suicide? She might have been pushed into the well."

"What would you expect when a widow from a high caste gets pregnant, eh?"

"Arre, she was a loose woman. Don't you know her husband died of tuberculosis some three years ago? She must have been in heat and gone under whoever was available."

They all burst out laughing.

"Let the dead lie dead. Who knows, her spirit may be roaming around here and will haunt you in the night."

"Who knows what the truth is? She is dead now, bless her soul. Let's not talk ill about her."

"Why this sudden affection for her? Had she granted you some special favors?"

"That has nothing to do with what I am saying. Why blame the poor woman for being with child? Why don't you talk about the man who committed this act? Is it not his responsibility too? But no one talks about him. . . ."

Damu kept awake by pacing up and down. He drank water to quell his hunger and continued to wait for the fauzdar. The police would draw the body out, the report would be written, and the dead woman would be handed over to her family. Then he could go home after the body was cremated.

Hours passed and the sun was overhead and yet, there was still no sign of anyone official. As Damu looked up at the sun, he felt dizzy. Then he saw someone walking toward him. It was Namya, one of his cousins, clutching a small basket.

"Arre, Damu, everyone was worried about you. Sonu did not sleep last night. You should have at least come home to inform us, or sent word." He handed over the bhakris sent by Sonu. "Sit by that tree and eat."

"No, I cannot eat now. They will arrive any moment. If they catch me eating, they will beat me." As they were talking, the policemen arrived. One of them struck the ground with his baton.

"What's this fellow doing here?"

Another saw the basket and gave it a blow. It flew out of Damu's hands and the bhakris scattered on the ground. Namya scrambled to collect as many as he could. Damu sat near the well on his haunches and whispered to Namya, infuriated, "Why should I have to be the one to sit around without a meal since yesterday, when everybody else has his belly filled?"

Namya tried to pacify him. "Arre, Damu, these are big people . . . how can they go hungry? That is for people like you and me. That is the way life is . . . just accept it, what else can we do?"

Then, feeling sorry for Damu, he whispered, "Come, stand behind me and quickly eat one bhakri. You will feel better."

Damu refused to eat while hiding behind Namya as if he were doing something wrong.

"Why should I hide? Am I any less human than they are?" Damu asked Namya.

The clip-clop of hooves grew louder, and the crowd stood at attention. The fauzdar rode in, cracking his whip arrogantly. He dismounted, tossing the reins to one of the constables, who rushed forward. The constable tied the horse to a tree and ordered Damu to fetch hay and water.

The fauzdar circled the well, intent on his inspection. He stood looking at the broken structure. He went to the side where there were steps leading down. A few stones had come precariously loose and those farther below were covered with green moss.

The sides of the well had sprouted bunches of weeds and grass and the algae on the surface of the water glowed fluorescent in the light that filtered through the thick foliage above.

The well was deep but had been abandoned for many years. The fauzdar noticed that the constable and patil were talking animatedly. He went toward them and they conferred for some time.

Suddenly the constable approached Damu and bellowed, "Eh you, Damu Mahar, why are you sitting and gaping at everyone? Do you think the fauzdar has nothing better to do than wait for you to get the body out?"

Damu watched him, bewildered.

"Come on, move!" he shouted.

"Saheb, we are poor Mahars. Our duty is to guard the dead. I have done that. How can I get the corpse out? The dead person belongs to the high castes. It would be sacrilege if I were to touch the high castes," Damu mumbled.

The fauzdar approached him, twirling his whip.

"Are you talking back to me? Did you not hear what he said? Don't waste my time, get the body out."

Damu bent down as much as he could and spoke with utmost reverence. "Maay-Baap, I was just saying that I will draw the wrath of the dead one's relatives if I touch the body. It is one thing if no one had come to claim the body and disowned it, but—"

"You motherfucking son of a bitch, do you see this whip?" the fauzdar thundered. "Do you want to see it lashing across your mouth and getting at your tongue? You have my orders. Do as you are told."

The abuses struck at the core of Damu's heart. But he swallowed his anger and pleaded, "Sarkar, have pity on me, a poor helpless Mahar. You have given orders but what will happen when you go away? Once you go, I will have to face the wrath of the entire village."

The fauzdar was in no mood to listen. He cracked his whip on Damu, who fell to the ground.

He raised his head and stared at the fauzdar. "No," he said, his voice barely audible.

"What did you say?" the fauzdar yelled.

"No," Damu said clearly. "I am not going to do it."

Namya rushed to Damu's side, trying to pacify him. He held his hand across Damu's mouth to prevent him from saying anything.

"Damu Dada, don't take these things to heart. This has been the way of our village. You should respect the fauzdar saheb. We are dependent on them for all our needs. Even if they get angry with us and beat us, we have no choice but to obey them."

Damu pushed his hand away and yelled, "Whoever wants to claim the body will come and worry about getting the body out. No matter what, I am not going to do it."

Cursing, the fauzdar struck him with his whip again. "You want to defy my orders?"

Damu had a strong impulse to grab the fauzdar's whip and beat him. Instead, he curled his palms into tight balls.

The fauzdar lashed out again. "I know the reason why you lowly creatures are suddenly meeting our gaze and talking back to us. It is all due to that Mahar Ambedkar. He thinks that just because he has read a book or two, he will suddenly become a high-caste Brahmin from a Mahar. And you listen to his talk and start thinking that by talking back to us, you can get away with it."

Damu suddenly stood up and gripped the half-raised whip, giving it a jerk. Not expecting this, the fauzdar lurched forward. He let go of the whip, lost his balance, and fell. A few of the onlookers could not help laughing.

"Wait until I break your jaws!" Damu roared. Namya rushed forward, yelling at Damu to shut up.

The fauzdar was enraged. He screamed at the constables, "Arre, motherfuckers, what are you looking at me for? Catch him and skin his hide!"

At these words, all hell broke loose. Fury tore at Damu's guts. His senses urged him to flee but he stood still as the constables bore down on him. Damu lay jerking and convulsing at every blow and whiplash landing on his body until, with all his might, he cried out, "I will die but I will not bow down before you. Come on, beat me all you can and kill me. Let the world know that a helpless Mahar was killed doing his duty. See, the entire village is witnessing your atrocities."

The beating stopped immediately. The patil rushed forth, shocked at Damu's bloodied state. He stood in front of Damu, preventing anyone from hitting him further and pleading with the fauzdar, asking him to forgive Damu.

"It seems Damu has become insane," the patil reasoned, saying it was not worthwhile paying attention to his blabbering. Then, turning to Damu, he said, "What have you done, Damu? Do you want to be killed?"

He told Namya to take Damu home. "Go; take him away before it is too late. I will see what to do about getting the body out."

Namya helped Damu up. Damu could tell that even the patil was angered by the fauzdar's behavior. But he seemed helpless. All he could do was to tell Damu in a kindly voice to go home and tend to his wounds.

As Damu staggered away, he heard the patil call out to the family of the dead woman: "Why are you ashamed to come forward? Have you already disowned the poor woman? God bless her soul!"

At home that night, Damu cried out in pain. His throat had gone dry but he refused to take even a sip of water. His wife, Sonu, took an old rag, dipped it in oil, and gently dabbed at the welts on Damu's back. Raghoji, the eldest of his cousins, was angry. "You have tarnished the Mahars' reputation for loyalty," Raghoji growled. "You think you can come back from the big city and behave according to your whims and fancies? You have broken our tradition. Have you no brain? No one in his right mind questions the authorities. And look at you—you had the audacity to insult him."

Sonu, sobbing uncontrollably, tried to pacify Raghoji.

"Big brother, please forgive my man. He has committed a grave mistake. Forgive us, big brother. Please overlook our mistake. I assure you we will abide by every tradition."

Damu looked around with some effort and found the rest of the family watching accusingly. He shouted at Sonu to shut up. This was a matter between men. A woman had no say in this.

"What kind of a tradition is this that treats Mahars worse than cats and dogs?" Damu yelled. "I spit on these inhuman traditions. I am not going to abide by such traditions. I am a man of dignity and I will not go from house to house begging for baluta. What will you do? Kill me?"

Damu's cousins were shocked. Raghoji growled, "Arre, let me see how you will abandon your duties. In the sixty years of my existence, and from all that I have heard from our forefathers, no Mahar has ever refused or left his Yeskar duty halfway. As long as I am alive, it is not likely to happen."

He looked at Sonu and said, "Put some sense into your man's head. It looks like the whipping has affected his brains. It is late now, we will talk it over in the morning."

Eventually all was quiet, everyone asleep. Silent tears escaped Sonu's eyes as she caressed her man's forehead. He was struggling to sit up. When he managed to get to his feet, he pulled at her hand and led her out of the hut. Scared that someone would wake up, Sonu did not make a sound of protest, or even ask him where they were going. A little distance away, Sonu shuffled to a halt.

"We are leaving this place at once," Damu said angrily.

"In the middle of the night? Where will we go?"

"Yes. Right this moment. We will go to Nashik and look for a ride to Mumbai."

Sonu hesitated. He looked so fiercely determined that she was afraid to say anything. Finally, she said, "Perhaps we should wait till dawn breaks . . ."

Damu let go of her hand and started walking away, without a single word. Sonu ran after him, horrified that he would leave her. He halted in his tracks and turned around. He gave her a penetrating stare and asked just one question: "Are you going to walk shoulder to shoulder with me?"

"Of course! But—"

"There are no buts if you have agreed," he said. "Let's go."

It was only when Sonu begged and pleaded that he agreed to wait for a few minutes by the banyan tree.

She ran back home, fear clutching at her heart. What if someone woke up and caught her? What if someone caught her man standing by the tree? What if her man left without her?

Lost in her thoughts, she stumbled against the water pot and sent the pail flying. Her sister-in-law woke up and asked who it was. She hastily replied that she was fetching some water for her man.

She quickly grabbed a few onions and whatever bhakris were left over, tucked a couple of saris and her man's dhotis under her arm, and stealthily left the hut, afraid that her heart would burst. She tied the clothes into a bundle and, holding her breath, ran back.

Together, they started walking toward freedom.

II

TOWARD FREEDOM

SONU

We walked endlessly on the soft mud road. My feet assumed a will of their own, heedless of fatigue. Whenever we heard the bells of an approaching bullock cart, my man would hastily pull me into the bushes. We dared not ask any of the cart owners to let us ride with them.

I walked in constant fear through fields and riverbeds, paths lined with huge trees forming a canopy over us. I imagined wild animals or bandits attacking us. The moon hid among the clouds, shrouding us in darkness, and then darting out just long enough to light up the path.

We could tell that we were approaching a village when we heard dogs barking. A few of them then followed us for some distance. After a while, when we walked on without looking at them, they went away.

I was exhausted, but how could I complain to my man? It was an effort for him just to continue walking. He would whimper from time to time, then stride along without a word or a look at me. In the beginning, I tried talking to him, asking him where we were going. His only answer was silence.

I wondered who we were to make plans when life willed otherwise. I dreaded going back to Mumbai. It was barely a month since we had left for Ozar, my husband's village, for the Yeskar duties. Around that time, both my man and Sasubai, my mother-in-law, had lost their jobs. In Mumbai, there were four mouths to feed, but no money even for the rent of our small room, and soon we ran out of money for food. Fate had turned its fury on us.

This turn of events had taken its toll. I had never seen my man so crestfallen. I talked endlessly, trying to raise his spirits. Nothing seemed to work and his spirits sank lower each day. At times, he came home tired from a day's hard labor that paid a pittance. At other times, he had walked all day with no luck.

He came home tired, hungry, and frustrated. I kept dinner ready for him—but the meager serving of thin bhakris, with only a raw onion alongside, heightened his sense of failure. To make matters worse, Sasubai had begun taunting him.

But at night, my man soothed me when I cried.

"Remember, Sonu, it takes both rain and sunshine to make a rainbow," he would say.

I had not seen Aaee, my mother, for years and I missed her terribly. I was married when I was about ten years old, and I had lived with my husband for nearly five years now. Nothing had worked out. I had come to Ozar in the hope that I could visit my parents for a few days. My village was only three hours away. How I wanted to lie in Aaee's lap like the carefree girl I was just a few years ago. Growing up is never easy. . . . Aaee! I recalled the desperation of our lives in Mumbai. I felt as if a dam had burst open, and all the grief I had stashed away in the corners of my heart broke loose.

In Mumbai, I had prayed desperately for some change—any change would be better than facing my dejected husband each evening. Soon enough, my prayers were answered. Word came from my husband's village that it was his turn to perform the Yeskar duty.

Traditionally, the head of every Mahar household took turns performing this duty for three months. As a village servant, my man would go from house to house, bearing news of the village. He would announce deaths, and tend to the carcasses of cattle. He would be running in front of the carriages of government officials, singing their praises and announcing their arrival. In return, he would be given a handful of grain and be allowed to go begging from house to house for leftovers.

When my man was called upon to do his duty, he was upset that his uncles and cousins still expected him to carry out such a humiliating task.

"How dare they expect me to go accept the ghongdi?" he had said. The ghongdi, a black woolen blanket, and the staff that the Yeskars carried, were passed on ritually for generations. Though these were mainly symbolic, the blanket covered the Yeskar in cold or rainy weather and the staff gave him some protection against wild animals in the forests.

I could not understand what was so bad about taking our turn as Yeskar. It was a good chance to stay in the village for a few months. After all, scores of generations had done this duty; what was making him so angry?

"Soney, you will remain foolish forever. Can you imagine me going from house to house, knocking the ground with the jingling stick, and begging for baluta? Can you see yourself eating the stale, half-eaten food doled out as baluta?"

My man began pacing up and down, his voice rising with every word he said.

"Do you know what the upper castes say when they throw the baluta? '*Aamcha anna ghe. Aamchi eeda ghe. Aamchi peeda ghe.*'" (Take all our evils away as you take this food. Go, take the food away . . . better in your stomach than in the garbage, if you will take our perils with it.) "We would probably treat dogs with more dignity."

My man's voice quivered with emotion as he asked, "How can I participate in Babasaheb's movement to reclaim dignity for our people and support these inhuman traditions?"

Sasubai intervened. "Why are you yelling at her like a madman?" she screamed at him. "Have you gone out of your mind? Do

you think you have become so clever listening to those speeches of
Babasaheb that you no longer care about our tradition?"

They argued back and forth. Sasubai maintained that Damu had
to stand up to what was expected of him. My husband, however,
would not bend.

"Arre, Damu, do you have any shame?" Sasubai shouted. "Do
you want to tarnish the name of our family? At least think of your
father. Until today no one has ever refused the ghongdi. A true
Mahar would die before shirking his responsibility."

She broke down and started crying.

"If you refuse, it would amount to a slap in my face. Did I give
birth to you in order to hang my head in shame, that too, when I
have become so old?"

There was no way he could refuse his duty after that. Finally, it
was decided that we would go to his village for three months. I was
so excited that we were going to Ozar. I put together a few of our
clothes and daydreamed of how we would stay with his cousins.
My man would do the village duties and I would work in the fields.
We would no longer have to worry about getting a good meal.

The first time I saw him walking from house to house asking for
baluta, I felt terrible. I realized why he was so averse to being a
Yeskar. The proud, self-respecting man I had known looked for-
lorn and defeated. He was almost unrecognizable with the thick
black ghongdi on his back. He bent into the staff and knocked it on
the ground every few steps so that the tiny bells on it jingled to
alert people that an untouchable was passing.

The upper-caste folks gave out the food, standing as far away as
possible from him. They were careful not to touch the Mahar or
any of his belongings.

Late in the evening, he returned and handed the food over to me
without a word. He flung off his ghongdi and the staff, drank some
water, and lay down. I tried talking to him several times and asked
him what the matter was, but he would not say a word.

I sat next to him massaging his head and after a long while he asked me for something to eat. I could not hide a smile as I fetched the bhakris.

"I can't take it anymore, Soney . . . I can't take it." He broke down. "We must have self-respect. We must have dignity. How can I take to begging from door to door? Baluta is our right, they proudly claim! My foot! Have you seen how they throw the food? I don't want rights as a dog. I want my human rights."

I tried to reason with him: "Calm down now, will you? How does all this matter? Soon all this will be behind us and then we can go back to Mumbai. Already your cousins think badly of you. We should not upset them anymore. At least we don't go hungry here."

He was furious; his body trembled and he almost raised his arm to hit me.

"Soney, are you no different from a dumb mule? If we just think about filling our stomachs, how are we any better than animals?"

I was hurt and could not sleep, worrying about what he had said.

My heart was crushed when his cousin brought him home badly beaten, bloodied, and raging with fever. All along, I had seen his frustration, his anger and his helplessness, after taking on the duties of a Yeskar. But I had not seen this coming. I had not understood why he was not willing to conform to tradition. I kept thinking that it was simply a question of a few months, but now I realized that my man needed to be true to himself, to his thoughts and beliefs.

No, it was not a question of a few months; it was a question of his identity—our identity.

DAMU

I lost count of the number of times I relived the incident. Each time I thought about the fauzdar, anger surged within me like a hissing snake. The long walk ahead would do me good. It would help me cope with the storm raging in my mind.

As I walked on with Sonu trailing behind, I wondered if I had done the right thing.

I had tried to reason with the fauzdar and then pleaded with him against my will. All I got in return was abuse and a show of highborn authority intended to make us—the untouchables—cower.

Was that really I who challenged the fauzdar? In front of the entire village, the fauzdar and the patil, I had emphatically refused to go down the well and get the corpse out. I could not believe it.

Never would they have imagined that a Mahar would have the temerity to stand up to them. Gradually, the magnitude of what I had done dawned on me. The more I thought about it, the more I knew that I had not acted on impulse. My actions were true to the teachings of Babasaheb.

No, I had not done anything wrong. Perhaps I should not have waited so long to do the right thing.

I longed to talk with Tau Master. He was the one who had initiated me into the movement led by Babasaheb Ambedkar. I remembered the first time I met Tau Master.

*   *   *

In 1924, after years of struggle in Mumbai, I got my first regular job in the railways. I was a young boy and my mother insisted that I visit Tau Master and seek his blessings.

"Go and sit with Tau Master for a while. He is the only educated Mahar from our village and the only elder of our clan here in Mumbai. Go and get his blessings before you start your new job," she had said.

Grudgingly, I agreed. I always felt intimidated by Tau Master. Those days, anyone who had graduated from high school was addressed as "Master," and Tau Master taught at a municipal school. Tall, well built, and fair-complexioned, he resembled highborn gentry. He was known to be a strict disciplinarian and a stickler for cleanliness.

That Sunday morning when I visited him, Tau Master was busy cleaning the house. He was polishing some brass lamps, his hands messy with black grime. Yet, he was dressed in a crisp white dhoti and kurta, and as I sat before him, I became conscious of my own shabby clothes.

Asking about the well-being of my family, he looked me in the eye and said, "Damu, you are doing well for yourself, I hear. Soon you will settle down in your job and then into matrimony. When are you going to think beyond yourself?"

I squirmed under his penetrating stare. All I could do was gaze at him uncomprehendingly.

"Isn't it about time that you thought about bigger issues, like doing something for our community?" he asked, and then was silent for some time. As the silence stretched on, I grew more uncomfortable.

"We need young energetic people like you, Damu," Tau Master said finally, just as I was about to leave. "There is a meeting tomorrow evening at Narey Park. Meet me outside Parel Station at six."

He then shut the door before I had a chance to say anything.

*   *   *

"Educate, unite, and agitate," was the slogan chanted at Babasaheb Ambedkar's rally that day. Excitement ran through my veins. I was instantly taken with Babasaheb. I knew we untouchables had finally found a savior and before I realized it, I had been drawn into the vortex of the social movement.

In late 1926, perhaps in October, I got married. Sonu was too young then to join me, so I returned alone to Mumbai from my village. I heard in a gathering around that time that a Dalit meeting would take place in Mahad, a town near Mumbai.

For hundreds of years, untouchables were prevented from collecting or drinking water from any of the points where the upper castes did. In 1926, the government of Bombay Province adopted a resolution abolishing such discrimination. In its wake, the Mahad municipality had passed a resolution to allow untouchables full access to all village waterfronts, including the largest reservoir, the Chavdar Lake. However, under the hostile eyes of the upper castes, this resolution had remained only on paper, and the untouchables, who worshipped the same Hindu gods and who belonged to the same religion, were not allowed to take even a drop, even though Muslims and Christians could. Babasaheb decided to hold the meeting at Mahad, where the untouchables would exercise their rights en masse. The idea of rebellion was thrilling.

March 19, 1927. I arrived in Mahad. I could not believe my eyes. Tens of thousands of people had assembled. People of all ages, mostly wearing rags and carrying bhakris wrapped in cloth bags, moved about, charged with anticipation.

When Babasaheb spoke, everyone listened. He urged the untouchables to rebel against the humiliating and enslaving traditions of village duties.

"It is utterly disgraceful to sell your rights for a few crumbs of bread," he said.

"We will achieve self-elevation only if we learn self-help, regain our self-respect, and gain self-knowledge," Babasaheb said.

What touched me the most were his thoughts about raising a family.

"There will be no difference between parents and animals if they do not desire to see their children in a better position than their own."[5]

Then came the great event. Everyone was to march to the disputed Chavdar tank, the water reservoir from which untouchables were banned. Babasaheb led the procession. We marched in a disciplined manner, in rows of four, shouting, "Educate, Unite, and Agitate!" The sun was shining brightly and the water sparkled. The square reservoir was surrounded by the houses of Brahmins on all sides. Every door, window, and terrace of those houses was full of shocked people, who looked on helplessly at the huge, determined crowd gathered around their tank, "polluting" its sanctity. Babasaheb glanced around and walked down the half-dozen steps with firm resolve. He paused for a few seconds, and looking at the thousands of expectant followers, calmly bent down, cupped some water in his palms, and drank. The crowd roared and let loose cheers of "*Jai* Bhim" (Glory to Bhim—Babasaheb) as everyone took a symbolic sip of water.

I was exhilarated by this rebellious act but I did not understand how drinking water from that tank would help our community's advancement. We were not going to die without that water.

Then Babasaheb proclaimed that we were asserting our rights as human beings. We were making history. Indeed, we had defied the arrogance of the tyrants who boasted that their religion treated even animals with forbearance.[6]

"But we have done it!" he said as a loud cheer went up. Realization suddenly dawned on me. What we had done was to claim our equal rights to the water. We were equally human after all. Why should our touch pollute the water? We had cupped the water in our palms and sipped it.

*   *   *

Most of the delegates had scattered in small groups throughout the city. Some were busy packing and some were eating their meals before dispersing to their villages. Suddenly a large crowd of upper-castes armed with bamboo sticks gathered at the street corners, catching us unawares. A rumor was afloat that the untouchables were planning to forcibly enter the local temple. This docile and conservative town was in ferment. They said religion was being threatened and God was being polluted. The rowdies charged at our delegates, who fled. They spared no one—men, women, or children—knocking our food into the dirt and pounding our utensils. At first we were paralyzed but soon we began to run helter-skelter trying to save ourselves.

I feared that Babasaheb would be attacked and I rushed to where he was. Many others had done the same, and hundreds of young men had gathered, impatiently awaiting Babasaheb's orders.

We were screaming with rage, itching for retaliation. A word or signal from our leader and Mahad would have turned into a battlefield. To my surprise—and disappointment—Babasaheb appealed for peace and discipline. He said that our struggle was to enforce the law, not to break it.

We returned to Mumbai only to learn that the orthodox highborn of Mahad had the Brahmin priests "purify" the "desecrated" reservoir by pouring into it 108 pots of curd, milk, cow dung, and cow urine amid loud religious chants.

The symbolic march to the Chavdar tank had kindled in us untouchables the flame of dignity and self-respect. It was the beginning of our awakening.

On August 4, 1927, the Mahad municipality revoked its earlier resolution granting untouchables access to the water tank. Babasaheb took this as a challenge and announced that we would intensify our struggle by holding another protest meeting in Mahad in December.

December 1927 saw an even bigger meeting in Mahad, where Babasaheb challenged the authority of all Hindu scriptures. He told the highborn that just as they were Hindus, we too were Hindus.

"If you say your religion is our religion, your rights and ours must be equal. Is this the case? If not, on what grounds do you say that we must remain in the Hindu fold?" Babasaheb asked.[7]

In the conference, Babasaheb denounced the *Manu Smruti*. This book, compiled around fifteen hundred years ago, had traditionally governed the law and life of Hindus. Revered by the so-called upper-caste Hindus, it was reviled by the Dalits, as it directed that molten lead be poured into the ears of untouchables if they heard or read the Vedas. Babasaheb felt that the *Manu Smruti* was a charter of rights for the so-called upper-caste Hindus but a bible of slavery for the untouchables. He condemned it as a symbol of tyranny among the Hindus. He then gave a call to publicly burn copies.[8]

That evening, the *Manu Smruti* was placed on a special pyre and ceremoniously burned amid cheers from the untouchables.

I had not done anything wrong in defying the fauzdar's authority. Babasaheb had inspired us to stand up and reclaim our dignity. I had done just that.

I thought of my mother. Perhaps she was right in her own way, expecting me to live up to the family name and to honor tradition. She would probably blame me forever, saying that I had tarnished our name and ensured that we would never again be welcome in our village. Even she would be shunned if she visited the village.

The thought of facing my mother when I reached Mumbai troubled me. She would surely blame this on Babasaheb's speeches.

I should not have agreed to go to Ozar for the Yeskar duty in the first place. It was done, however, and it was good that I had gone. I had proved to the entire village that we untouchables did not have to accept everything handed out to us. We could fight back against injustice.

Didn't Babasaheb say it is in our hands to reclaim our dignity?

SONU

I looked at my man walking beside me. I could not see his face as we walked in the dead of night. Yet, I saw him in a new light. I was beginning to understand him. His determination had surprised me. It also scared me. There was no turning back—I was going to walk with him.

The first time I had seen the man I was to marry was when we were halfway into our wedding ceremony. I was exhausted with hours of waiting through rituals, sitting decked out in my cumbersome sari and all the beads and bangles. After a long wait, my uncle came forth, gave me a garland, and walked me toward the canopied wedding platform.

I was asked to stand on one side of the antarpaat, a cloth curtain held up at face level. On the other side of the curtain, I could see a tall man, holding a garland. My heart jumped at the realization that I was being married off to him. As I stood on the platform, my hands trembled and I tightly clutched the garland of sweet-smelling jasmine flowers, afraid I would drop it.

The priests chanted mantras, and then began singing the mangalashtak. At one point, all of a sudden, the curtain was drawn apart and the man garlanded me. Everyone started clapping and throwing auspicious rice confetti on us. Then I was asked to garland him, but he was so tall and I was so tiny that I couldn't reach him. Everyone was waiting expectantly. I raised my eyes only to

43

realize with a shock that I was looking at him. I was overcome with shyness and fear. I could feel my eyes clouding with tears, and just at that moment, he bent his head before me.

That was the first time I saw him. I thought he was a great big wall, a rough-hewn mountain, like the one behind our hut—tall, dark, and rugged.

My eyelids dropped with fear of this unknown being, bending down and waiting to be garlanded. My hands froze in midair, and I could not raise them. One of my tears escaped. He softly whispered, "Don't cry." I mustered all my courage and garlanded him.

No sooner had I done so than the drummers broke into a crescendo. We were pronounced man and wife amid loud chanting of *Savadhaan*—caution; you have entered the bonds of matrimony. I had become a wife. The wife of a big towering man.

There was little space in his family's one-room home in Mumbai and I knew little about what marriage entailed. All I knew was that marriage was a ceremony where they gave a lot of gifts and clothes, and after that I would have to go stay in a new house with another family. Had my mother not done the same?

On my first day in Mumbai, after dinner, my mother-in-law closed the door that was usually left wide open. That stopped the neighbors from peeping in. "Now," she declared, "it is time to sleep. We need to get up early."

Najuka, my sister-in-law, unrolled the straw mats. In one corner, she covered them with a thin quilt of old rags. Then my mother-in-law tied one end of a string to the windowsill and the other to a nail in the opposite wall. She hung a thick old sari across it to curtain off the area. Najuka lay down on one of the straw mats with my mother-in-law by her side. I sat down next to her, unsure how I would sleep in the tiny place. My mother-in-law smiled at me.

"Sonu, you are no longer a child to sleep next to me. You are a grown woman now and your rightful place is next to your husband." She then called out to her son, "Damu, come, take your wife away . . . take her with you."

Overcome with embarrassment, I felt tears rush into my eyes.

"You want me to go sleep near . . . near . . . umm . . ."

I did not know how I was supposed to address my husband. My mother-in-law patted me on my back and said, "Don't be afraid. My Damu is a tenderhearted man. Go, make him happy."

I could not understand what she meant by "make him happy." She asked me what advice my mother had given me before I left. I told her that she had asked me to obey my husband and do as he asked me to.

"Good," is all my mother-in-law said.

I heard my husband call out my name from where he was sitting behind the curtain. Hesitantly I stood, my feet unwilling to move. Najuka was half asleep and she complained about the light. I put out the light and groped my way. He asked me to lie on the quilt beside him. I stood there dumbfounded and shocked.

All through my childhood and especially since I had started bleeding, I was warned to avoid physical contact with any male. Even if it was Aba, my own father, I had to be very careful around him. And now this man was asking me to lie next to him! For all I cared I would remain standing or I would go sleep out in the open, but next to this stranger, never!

He tried persuading me three or four times but I had my gaze fixed on the floor. I did not even look up. To my dismay, I soon heard him snoring, fast asleep. I was even more annoyed that he was sleeping peacefully while I, a newcomer at his house, was standing without a place to lie down.

I remained standing for a long time. Finally, exhausted beyond caring, I lay down as far away as possible from him. Very early in the morning, when it was still dark, I heard the kerosene lamp being lit. I heard the rattling of pots and pans and the quiet mumbling of my mother-in-law. The door of the room was open.

I scrambled to sit up but could not. My husband's dark, hairy hand lay across my body. I pushed it off with a jolt and rushed past the curtain.

The next night, my husband went to meet his friends after dinner. We had finished all the chores, and Sasubai and Najuka were getting ready to sleep. I had no choice but to go behind the curtain and arrange the quilts. I did so grudgingly, hoping that my husband would never come home for the night.

I tossed and turned but sleep evaded me. I was dreading his return. I recalled the way I had woken up that morning sensing the dead weight of his arm, heavy across my breasts. My face burned with that memory. I was sure if my mother ever found out, she would have the choicest words for me in a long talk on proper behavior for chaste women. Why, then, had Sasubai pushed me to sleep next to him and what did she mean by "Go, make my son happy"?

The thought of Mother made me nostalgic. How I missed our village! I thought about our river and my favorite peepul tree. I would spend hours daydreaming under that tree, watching the serene water flow past. I longed to be back there in familiar surroundings. Yet, it was only my second day in my new home. The thought really shook me and I started crying. I tried to smother my face in the pillow to quiet my sobs. They continued uncontrollably and I began to choke. I imagined Aaee's hand soothing me and I missed her even more.

Meanwhile, my husband had returned, for I felt him take my hand and gently pull me toward him. I resisted all I could and lay all bundled up in the corner. He came and lay beside me. I felt embarrassed, thinking of Sasubai and Najuka lying on the other side of the curtain. The tall, dark mountain wall lying beside me prevented me from looking pleadingly at my mother-in-law through the curtain. The tears did not stop. The big, dark, hairy hand gently rubbed my back and wiped my tears. I don't know why but I began to sob even more. Perhaps his gentleness reached somewhere deep inside my heart.

"It's all right," he said. "You are tired. Go to sleep. Don't spoil your pretty face."

He kept rubbing my back and soon I felt soothed and dropped off to sleep. When I woke up the next morning, I was shocked to discover that I lay trapped under one long leg thrown over my hips and one arm encircling my waist. I struggled to get out of his entrapment. To my horror, he was awake.

"My fair little bride, how come you got a rough, dark bumpkin like me?" he whispered. "You are so pretty and I want to be close to you. Soon . . . soon enough . . . Aaee wants us to go worship Lord Khandoba first as a couple . . . and only then. What an agony to see you so pretty, so close yet so far away."

I struggled to rearrange my sari, which had come undone. It was so cumbersome to sleep ensconced in its folds. I rushed out as quickly as I could, saved by the hustle and bustle in the corridor.

I looked at my man walking ahead, as lost in his thoughts as I was in mine. He did not glance back even once to see if I was there. I longed to rest for some time and catch my breath but I did not dare ask him. This was a man who could be so tender when he wanted, and so aloof when he was possessed by some idea. He had been so understanding back then . . . I felt a smile tugging at me as I recalled the night when he made me his woman.

We had returned from our worship of Lord Khandoba at the town of Jejuri. Sasubai and Najuka had stayed back in Jejuri for the annual fair. He had gone off to work and I was all by myself. I sat in a corner for a long while, thinking of the past few days. Unwillingly, I got up and went about the cleaning and cooking chores, methodically, as my mother had told me.

Lakshmi kaku, our neighbor, came knocking and invited herself over for a cup of tea. She was a kindly woman who asked me all about my village and my parents, and my wedding day. She then told me about her village and she had tears in her eyes when she spoke of her mother.

Then she came and sat next to me and patted my back.

"Damu said you are just back from worshipping Lord Khandoba as a couple," she said with a coy smile on her face. She added, "Today is a big day for you, Sonu. Have a bath in the evening after you finish cooking and change into a clean sari. When your husband comes home, give him tea and let him freshen up. Then tell him that you will obey him, as he is older and wiser. Tell him that you know he will take good care of you and that you want to make him happy." She looked at me strangely and said, "Did you understand what I said?"

I merely nodded. "But . . . how do I know what will make him happy? He never even talks to me."

She smiled and said, "Give it time and you will know. Where will you go without him, and where will he go without you?"

I was still perplexed.

"It's a bond that will unite you," she said, patting my back. "Your husband is your god. You are tied to him forever. Now you will leave his side only when you die."

She slurped her tea, and continued, "Accept your husband. That is the reason why we have been given our long, flowing padar for the sari. It is big enough to accommodate all the shortcomings of our men, and long enough to cover them with the shade of our understanding."

She started weeping quietly. "I don't know why, but as I tell you all this, I feel I am saying this to the daughter I never had." She gulped down her tea, and left.

That evening, what Lakshmi kaku had said kept going around in circles in my head. It made no sense to me, but was similar to what my mother had told me the day I left my house. I should obey my husband. I should serve him nice, hot meals. He would then be happy. It was simple.

I waited for him, freshly bathed and cleanly dressed. As soon as he arrived, I made myself busy in the kitchen, brewing tea for him. He went to the washing area and emerged fresh.

"Hmm . . . I smell tea," he said.

I gave him his cup of tea and stood quietly at a distance, shy and unsure of what to say or do.

"This is what I call tea," he said, sipping loudly. "Tea should be strong and taste like real tea."

He came into the kitchen looking for me, and asked me why I was not having tea with him. I said I had not made any. He took my hand and led me out and made me sit next to him. He poured some tea into a saucer and gave it to me. I had one sip, and made a wry face. The tea had no sugar in it!

I had tears in my eyes. Was this how I was going to make my husband happy? The first time I make tea for him, I give him bitter tea, and he does not even complain. My rugged husband seemed to have a kind heart.

He wiped my tears and pulled me close, holding me there. Time passed slowly as he sat holding me close, stroking my back. Strangely, I felt at peace, as if this huge sturdy mountain had gently enveloped me. I felt as if there was no danger to me from anyone or anything in the world as long as my man was by my side.

I sat massaging his head, but soon he pulled me toward him. I began sobbing. And, at some point, his hands began to stroke my body all over and he pulled me even closer.

"Don't cry, Sonu," he kept repeating, wiping my tears. "You are making me very happy."

I felt his entire weight shift atop my body and, for a moment, I thought I would die of suffocation, if not embarrassment. I was scared stiff and, despite the darkness, I had my eyes tightly shut. I had the foreboding that something terrible was going to happen but I was surprised to find that I could take his weight effortlessly.

I was sobbing by now, but he did not seem to notice anything, only sighing and crying out my name. He was saying over and over again, "Oh Sonu, you are so beautiful! How I have waited for this moment from the time we were married!"

I could only think that I had brought great shame upon my family. Everyone had told me to obey my husband and make him happy, and I wondered if this was what they meant.

"Come, let us sleep. It is late," he said after a long time, re-arranging the quilt to cover me as I fell asleep, exhausted and confused.

The next morning when I woke up, I found myself entangled with him. Quietly, I tried to draw myself out from under him. My movements awoke him. Hurriedly, I pulled the corner of my sari to cover my face in shame as I recalled what had happened the previous night.

I turned on my side with my back toward him and felt his arms encircle me. We lay quietly, basking in the warmth of our bodies. I was surprised to find that I was in no hurry to detach myself from my man. I lay quiet and unmoving for a long time. I knew that I had arrived.

"What are you smiling about?" my man suddenly asked me as we continued walking. Startled out of my reverie, I felt blood rushing to my face. I glanced at him from the corner of my eyes, hoping he could not read my mind.

But he had caught the look in my eye. I averted my gaze and hoped desperately that he would change the subject.

DAMU

I dreaded to think about my mother's reaction. Surely, she was going to curse me for defying tradition. It was not going to be easy to explain to her. Even my cousins who knew about the brutality of the fauzdar had not been able to comprehend my rebellion.

The implications of my action were becoming painfully clear. Perhaps my family in Mumbai would be cut off from the village forever. There would be no going back. There would be nothing to go back to. The bond was severed. Recalling my own childhood in Ozar, it hurt me to think that my children might never know the joys of village life.

My father and uncle lived next to each other, in mud huts with thatched roofs. The floor of the hut was uneven, sloping down in odd places. The entrance was very small and the low, mud-brick walls of the hut meant we had to stoop every time we went in or out. Only one wall was high enough to allow a person to stand. The other wall was barely four feet in height. An adult had to bend to walk around the cramped hut. There was no door as such. My father had made a makeshift door of reeds and branches to keep out stray animals. We had to lift the lidlike door to move it.

The only source of light inside the hut was a little oil lamp near the cooking area. Around the lamp, the mud wall was blackened and greasy and the floor underneath was sticky with dripping oil. In the corner, we kept our long, sharpened knives for skinning cattle. The mud stove and the stone grinding wheel stood near the high wall.

We had a small plot of land, but it was too small to provide enough food for our family. We often had to go hungry. At times, we were lucky to get some grain like wheat or millet. Then Mother would happily grind it into flour, singing, just as her mother had, interweaving all our names in the verses as she sang. Early in the morning, pretending to be asleep under our coverlets, I listened to her sing.

Aaee would make bhakris by kneading the flour into dough, and then beating it out flat and round on the palms of her hands. Crouching over the fire, she would bake them on a flat iron skillet. My job was to gather twigs and kindling from the nearby woods.

We had very meager possessions. In one corner of our hut were our gods, Mariaai and Khandoba, tiny brass statues handed down from generation to generation. Every day after her bath, Aaee performed the puja—reverence. I found it amusing that when things went bad for us, or when someone was ill, she would scold the gods.

Our hut kept us dry for most of the year except during the monsoons. One rainy season, clouds had hidden the sun all day long, and it felt like night. As we ate our bhakris that night, there was no respite from the rain and I could sense that my father was very worried. Aaee was praying fervently to her gods to make the rain stop, but they seemed deaf to her pleas.

She poured water on the cinders of the stove to douse the fire and pushed our few iron pots and pans aside to make room for us to sleep. She began laying our beds on the floor, covering it first with old empty sacks. We curled up on the floor under our rag quilts, huddled together, sharing our body warmth.

Aaee did not sleep. She sat weeping in front of her gods. I knew this was a time to be quiet, as the slightest provocation would surely get me a tanning. I had just fallen asleep when it started to pour heavily and water gushed down from the roof, soaking us all. I was drenched and I moved to a dry spot, but in a few minutes that was wet too. Soon there were puddles of water all around me.

All summer long, Aaee had nagged, and then yelled at my father to thatch the roof. He hardly had any time to look after his own house and family, though. He kept putting it off until the next day, and that day had never come.

Now they desperately tried to collect water in the few large pans we had. I helped them, shivering all the time. As soon as one pan was full, it was emptied outside and placed back under the leaky spot. When I went to pour the water outside, the goats we kept under the awning in front of our hut were bleating pitifully. I felt sorry for them and brought them in. They were shivering in the cold so I dried them with a rag. They huddled together, following me around the tiny hut. One of them began peeing, and Aaee cursed them.

By now, Aaee had started cursing the gods as well, threatening them that if they did not make the rain stop, she would place them outside our hut, submerged in the knee-deep water. One moment she was prostrating before them, and the next moment she was actually threatening them!

The rain stopped after a long time. The idols were still intact, and stood exactly where they were. Aaee wrung out all the soaked rags and sacks and spread them out on the chool, our mud stove. Fortunately, the hearth was still dry. My eyes were getting heavy with sleep. The last thing I heard was Aaee telling Baba, "Tomorrow, the roof . . ."

In our village, the untouchable castes included mainly the Mahar, Chambhar, Dhor, and Mang. As elsewhere, each caste had its own hereditary communal duty. Chambhars and Dhors processed raw hides of animals and made them into shoes and other leather products. Mangs twisted hemp into ropes and made baskets. We

Mahars were the village servants. We did not have traditional duties and survived on doing odd jobs for the high castes.

The untouchable castes also had a strange internal hierarchy of their own. The musicians who accompanied wedding processions, coming from the Chambhar caste, would never play at Mahar weddings. How could they? They considered themselves a higher order than the lowly Mahars. The barber community did not mind shaving the buffaloes but they could not bring themselves to give a haircut to a Mahar.

Each Maharwada had a chavadi—a village hall and meeting place. Mahars gathered there to exchange news and discuss local issues. Meetings of caste councils were also held here.

Ozar had only two temples back then. One was the temple of Hanuman. Untouchables were never allowed into the temple. Even our shadows were not supposed to fall on the temple, and we had to pray standing far away. The other temple was our own, that of our goddess Mariaai. Except when there was fear of an epidemic, none of the other castes worshipped Mariaai, whose temple was traditionally located within the Maharwada, where the Mahars lived.

Once there was a long dry spell. For three years in a row, Ozar did not have a good monsoon. That was the beginning of a famine. We had no reserves of grain and no crops in our fields—there were no peanuts, no pulses, and no wheat. We were starving and there was no work to be found in Ozar. A few elders of our family decided to go to Nashik, the nearest city, to look for work.

My parents and cousins found work in a limestone quarry. Only Punjababa, my old, ailing uncle, and I were left behind. Though men and women were all given the same work of breaking huge boulders into gravel, men were paid four annas per day, but my mother was paid a mere two annas. Sixteen annas made a rupee, and they had to work for three days to get one rupee. Grain and rice were being sold at a much higher price than usual due to the shortage, and they barely managed to survive after buying extra food to send us.

As if this was not enough, bubonic plague swept through the region after the famine. Death was stalking us. Every family was burying its dead. Families had abandoned their village homes and moved to their farms. They built makeshift straw huts on the farms and lived there, waiting for the plague to wane. Our family did the same but it did not help. Death had already marked us out.

One day my cousin Shankar caught the chills. He was burning with fever and everyone thought that it would be wise to send him back into the village with his mother. However, no one had the heart to send them into the plague-affected village. They stayed with us, but in another hut a few feet away. Soon my cousin died, and about twenty days later, his mother passed away too. Our family was plunged into sorrow and fear. We felt that it was the end of our world.

Shankar had been the clever one in our family. He had bought a broken sewing machine from the village tailor and repaired it to working condition after much tinkering. I was very proud of him when he sewed a new shirt for me on that machine, a shirt made of layers of paper glued together. He had made me very happy. Once when my uncle had his turn as a Yeskar, he received a bolt of the white cloth used to drape the dead. I was thrilled to have a new shirt made of actual cloth! Now with Shankar's death, I felt as if a part of my own body had gone.

Punjababa had become blind in his old age. He was no longer the feisty, ill-tempered, towering presence who bullied everyone, and living around him was not as terrifying as it used to be. I felt sorry for the poor old man, knowing how proud and domineering he had been just a few years ago.

What little food we had was kept in the hut. We had two sacks of wheat, one sack of millet, and one and a half pots of jaggery that we had carefully preserved. We also had one sickly rooster, four or five hens, and two goats. We divided all the chores of cooking, cleaning, and looking after the animals between the two of us.

Since Punjababa could not see very well, he would sit grinding millet or wheat on the grinding wheel. I hated making dough out of the flour, as it would get all sticky and runny. Punjababa was good at this, and made the dough in no time. He beat the dough between his palms into bhakris, and put them on the griddle. I would roast the bhakris to a golden brown, and serve them to Punjababa along with watery curries. While he ate, I would quickly make one for myself and join him before he finished off the curry.

There were no lights in our hut. We did have a tin lamp, but the wick had burned out and there was no oil in it. After sunset, our lives were engulfed in darkness. One evening, I thought Punjababa had placed a bhakri on the sizzling hot griddle. I pressed it hard with my bare hand to roast it, but the griddle was bare and I was left with a roasted palm instead. I was in agony all night long and yelled in pain, calling out for my mother. Punjababa bandaged my hand with rags after gently applying a few drops of oil to soothe it.

Another time, thieves broke into our hut in the dead of night. Mahars like us, they stole all our wheat, most of the jaggery, and a few of the hens. One of them sat on blind Punjababa's chest and held him down while the other ransacked our hut and collected the booty. I saw everything from where I was huddled in a corner, but I was too frightened to stir. I even recognized the thieves, but was too scared to tell anyone later.

A few days afterward, we left the hut on the farm and went back to stay in the Maharwada. By then, Mother had found a job in Ozar. All day long, she shelled tamarind pods, removing the hard covering. For this she was paid two or three annas a day, depending on how much she got done. Even Punjababa and I tried to get some work in the village but no one would hire us. I could understand that Punjababa was old, but I looked strong and able, yet no one wanted to hire me.

Four seers of wheat cost three annas while millet cost two,

with jaggery being the most expensive item on our modest list of needs. Whenever the monsoon was exceptionally good, there were plenty of things available in the market. Only, we had no money to buy them.

Sometimes Mother was able to bring home a few tamarind pods, and this was a great treat. Four sivarais made one anna and, with great difficulty, we would manage to buy one sivarai's worth of jaggery and somehow make it last for two days. Mother would cook the pods for us, peel them, and smear them with jaggery. We would all sit around her, with our mouths watering, eyes glued to the pot, to find out who was given how much of a share. The sweet-sour taste would make our faces pucker, and weeks later just the memory of the pods would make our mouths water again.

One day, my father came home, threw his blanket on the floor without a word, and lay down on it. He didn't eat anything. Soon he had a raging fever that kept rising. By evening, his head was drooping and he was muttering incoherently. Everyone was terrified. They had watched people die of the plague. Now to see my father in the grips of the disease was nerve-shattering. We were left with a feeling of helplessness and fear of the outcome. By the next morning, he was dead. The whole household broke down, wailing and howling our laments. All the villagers gathered around, offering soothing words. A few village elders had taken me aside and explained to me that I was now the man of the house and the head of the household. I was reeling.

In the afternoon, my father's body was taken to the crematorium. As was the custom, water from the holy river had to be poured into my father's mouth. I was sent to the canal to soak a rag in water. The canal was deep and its bank sloped steeply. I slithered down the sides, dipped the cloth in the water, and was about to climb up when I found a one-anna coin lying on the edge of the canal. I thought it was a sign. My father had blessed me with the anna.

*   *   *

A few days went by and the village elders decided to build a new temple in Ozar. Workers moved around in a flurry of activity, piling up bricks and mortar. They dug up the foundation and set up the basic framework. We were called in to work on the days that the regular workers were absent. Madhav, a cousin, was working on one of the walls and I was helping him. He kept asking me to do things, one after another, and before I could finish, had already barked out another order. He yelled at me to go fetch water. Because I didn't bring it quickly enough, he began beating me with a cane. Aaee saw this and came running, pulled me close to her, and started weeping, caressing my back. "My poor boy, look at your plight," she wailed. "Just because your father is dead, look at how our own people get away with ill-treating you."

The very next day, Aaee, Najuka, and I set out for the village of Akrala, where my grandmother lived. Najuka was married when she was just five, but she used to stay with us since she was too young to be sent to her in-laws' house. We set off on foot. The sun was scorching hot and the ground beneath us felt as if we were walking on burning coals. Najuka began crying as we walked. Then Aaee searched by the wayside and found some rags and strips of cloth. She tied them tightly around our feet; only then could we walk on the hot ground. We flanked her on either side as she held our hands all the way to Akrala, telling us stories of kings and queens.

Aaji, my grandmother, was very happy to see us. Tears welled up in her eyes when she saw our burnt feet. Hari mama, my uncle, at once bought slippers for us. In those days, adult-sized slippers cost about nine or ten annas, and for children, they cost about three annas. This was the first time I had ever worn slippers. I was overjoyed and put them on every day when I took the cattle out to graze. I was so thrilled when the other boys enviously asked me if they could try them on. Aaee stayed with us for a few days and then returned to Ozar. I stayed on in Akrala.

In Akrala, I was enrolled in the local school. Every day I went with a broken piece of slate in my pocket. The school was in an old hut, a single room with a broken chair as the only furniture. We sat on the floor, away from other high-caste boys and girls, waiting for our teacher, Genu Master. He came from a neighboring village. As soon as he entered, we jumped up from the floor and greeted him by calling out "Ram Ram" in a singsong manner.

Genu Master was covered in boils, his skin clear only from the neck up. Behind his back, everyone called him Mr. Lizard. He roared in response to our greetings, "Those who are smart raise your hands."

The first day I raised my hand, not knowing what he wanted. He called a few of the students who had raised their hands and asked, "Do you know where to find good cow-dung cakes?" We nodded.

"Whoever brings me good cow-dung cakes will always be favored by me."

We wandered through the woods all morning, picking dried dung. Each of us delivered a sackful to him and then went home for our midday meal. When we returned for the afternoon school, Genu Master said, "Show me a sample from your sacks." He then removed his shirt, sat on the chair, and made us massage his back all over with the dried dung. The rest of the students watched.

Such was our school. When Hari mama found out about this, he stopped me from going to school.

Sometimes I accompanied Hari mama to Konkan. We filled the carts with hay and sold it in the surrounding towns. If the hay was of good quality, we earned about fifteen or twenty rupees. Hari mama used to take his bullock cart to many towns to fetch hay. I began going with him and assisting him with odd jobs. We carried enough bhakris to last us for the week-long journey. At night, we slept on sacks in our bullock cart. On the way, we saw other bullock carts, and then we traveled together in a group of six or seven. Many people in the surrounding towns knew Hari mama well and respected him. Because of Hari mama, they treated me as if I was special. I loved it when they addressed me with respect and asked about my well-being.

Once, late at night, our cart was the last one in line. A part of the yoke had broken. Hari mama had gone into one of the carts ahead to smoke his chillum and to chat with others. I was alone in our cart. I saw a man walking near our cart but did not suspect anything. I did not see him creep under the cart.

After going quite a distance, we stopped the carts. We freed the bullocks from the yoke and gave them fodder. Then we started looking for our sacks of bhakris but they were nowhere to be found. Hari mama thought they had fallen off because the yoke was broken. A fellow traveler said he had seen a man running away. We did not know what to do. Our animals were munching their cud contentedly, but we were ravenous. Our fellow travelers gave us a few bhakris and we ate them, pulled our sacks over us, and fell asleep.

The next morning we hitched the animals to the carts. The road was good and skirted the mountain. By the time we reached the peak, it was dark, so we decided to rest and freed the animals.

It was winter. We shivered out in the open. We could burn dung cakes and get some heat, but couldn't see to find them in the dark. So we used our feet. We picked up anything we felt might be cow dung, collecting enough to light a fire. In the warmth, many of us dozed off. Soon, I was fast asleep. In the early dawn, when the sun was just beginning to rise, we awoke and began looking for our cattle. But none of our animals were in sight. We didn't know if someone had stolen them or if a tiger had made off with them.

Leaving me to guard the carts, the others went in search of the cattle. I sat by the bullock cart, munching on the few peanuts left. I drank water from a nearby stream. Soon the peanuts were gone and I had nothing more to eat. Whenever I was thirsty, I drank water. Whenever I was hungry, I drank water. All day long, I waited and drank water.

It began to grow dark but still no one returned. I stared anxiously, my eyes not leaving the direction in which Hari mama had gone, praying that he would return. Soon it was dark. I had eaten nothing. I was terrified, alone out there in the open, but I could not leave the carts. As my eyes wandered over the mountainside, I saw a movement a few hundred feet away. A tiger was on the prowl. I was petrified. Shaking with fright, I untied the sheaves of hay, made a tunnel, and burrowed into it, pulling the hay around me, trying to remain as still as possible, a tight knot of fear inside me. Soon, the tiger came. I could see him through the hay. From my hiding place, I watched, not moving, not daring to make a sound, clenching my jaw, afraid my teeth would start chattering. The tiger circled the cart two or three times, then went and sat under a nearby tree. I did not see him leave the place, and feared he was waiting for me to come out.

After a very long time, Hari mama and the others came back with the bullocks. They brought the news from a nearby village that a tiger had attacked their cattle. After much discussion, Hari mama hitched our bullocks to the cart and we returned to Akrala.

After three months, I grew restless and longed to be with my mother. Every day I asked Hari mama when I could go home to see Aaee. He would just grin and say this was my home now, and that I was no longer a little kid to whine for Mother. I realized that he wanted me to stay there and work for him and that if I wanted to get home, I would have to outsmart him.

One day as we were walking behind the grazing animals, we came upon a broken, abandoned well next to a crumbling hut. I started walking toward the well to see if it had any water when the boys with me started screaming.

"Come back, turn around. . . . Are you out of your mind? . . . Don't you know that place is haunted?"

I ignored them and walked on toward the well and suddenly started wailing, as if some invisible thing had struck me. I ran back and flung myself on the ground. They took me home, where I lay listless, occasionally jerking my limbs. Soon, Hari mama summoned Saeebai, a woman in the village who reputedly had visions.

I was now terrified that my plan was going to backfire. Saeebai arrived, looking ferocious with her hair loose and vermilion covering her forehead. Glancing at her, I fled, with all of them running behind me. I ran ahead, climbed atop a mango tree, and managed to shoo away a vulture that plunged down toward me. Saeebai started screaming. "Look, look, he has unleashed a vulture on us . . . he is possessed! He will bring doom on us. Send him away."

Immediately, I was sent back to Ozar.

SONU

It had been a long time since I had seen my man smile. I mustered up courage and asked, "What are we going to do now? In Mumbai . . ." I trailed off, dreading even the thought of going back there.

"We will go to Mumbai and I will get a job. We will have a life of dignity, earning a respectable bhakri," he said, forcing enthusiasm into his voice as he managed a weak smile.

"Why is fate determined to treat us so badly?" I asked, emboldened by his response.

"Fate is what we make of ourselves. It is entirely up to us," he said indulgently.

Usually, he never had any patience with talk about fate or destiny, but he must have known how scared and confused I was and so we talked.

"How can I make my fate myself?" I persisted. "I happily came to Ozar thinking we would go visit my parents for a few days . . . but you decided otherwise."

Silenced for once, he had nothing to say.

"You are my fate ever since the day you made me your woman." I smiled shyly.

"My fate is following Babasaheb's teachings and fighting to claim dignity for our community. Did you see how they treated us in the village? We are not called by our names but simply as untouchables, the outcastes, and the lowly people who do not matter at all." His voice had taken on a high-pitched note.

"Calm down now, will you?"

"Soney, have you ever wondered whether we are born untouchables or are made so by society? Tell me, when did you first realize that you were being treated differently? Did you have to be told? No. It must have come to you slowly but surely, that you were different."

"How did you know?" I asked.

"One day, my father was called by some people in the village to chop wood for them. I kept insisting that I wanted to go along. At first, he refused, saying that the sun was too hot, but I was adamant. He then took me along, probably hoping they would give me something to eat.

"We walked some distance and I began to regret my stubbornness. My eyes were smarting under the glare of the sun and my throat was parched. I wanted to go home but did not dare ask my father. We came across a huge, blossoming tree. Someone had left a large vat of water under it. The water looked cool and inviting.

"'Baba,' I said to my father, 'I want to drink water.'

"Baba looked scared. He looked around.

"'Just wait,' he said. 'Someone will come soon.'

"I didn't understand. 'But why do we have to wait?' I whined. Just then, a man came by.

"'Johar, Maay-Baap,' Baba greeted him with the traditional reverent greeting of the low castes.

"'Please, my son is thirsty, can you let him have a drink of water?'

"'Are you trying to scorch him to death in this heat?' The man smirked.

"'He followed me without my knowing,' said my father fearfully. 'I'm on my way to cut some wood.'

"The man was dark and his clothes were dirty. He went near the water and picked up an iron tumbler lying near it. A dog was resting under the shade of the tree. The man kicked the dog aside and dipped the tumbler in the water. I looked at him expectantly, but he drank it himself. Some of the water spilled, glinting in the dark hair on his chest. He washed his face, and then wiped it off with the end of his mud-streaked dhoti. Then he dipped the tumbler again and turned to me.

"'Eh boy, come here!' he barked. 'Sit there!'

"I squatted on the ground and stretched my hand out for the tumbler.

"'Son of a bitch!' the man screamed at me. 'How dare you try to touch this? You think you can take this from my hand?'

"Baba pleaded with the man. 'Forgive my ignorant boy, Maay-Baap. What does he know? He is still a child.'

"Baba turned to me. 'Now, cup your hands like this, my boy, and drink only the water you get in your palm.' He cupped his own hands and showed me. I sat down again with my hands cupped. The man poured water into my palm. Some of the water trickled through. Without realizing it, I raised my hands closer to the water.

"'Down! Get your hands down,' the man shouted again. I lowered my hands, dipped my face in my palm, and drank.

"When we were walking away, I asked, 'Baba, he drank water straight from the vat. Why can't I?'

"'Arre, little one, we are Mahars. We can't touch that water. If we do, we will be punished because the water will get polluted . . . and then no one else will be able to drink from it.'

"I didn't understand. But Soney, when I looked back the dog was lapping up the water from the same vat! That was the first time I wondered if it was better to be born a dog than a Mahar."

"Even in our village, Taru Kherda," I said to my man, "we were treated as outcastes—as untouchables. I realized this when I was still a child. We were never allowed to use the river water upstream like the others did, and I couldn't understand why, but I realized there was something wrong with me, with our community.

"You know, whenever there was a wedding feast at our land-lord's house, we would all be summoned to help with odd chores such as plastering the floor with cow dung, collecting twigs and dry branches for firewood, or grinding wheat on the stone wheel.

"At one such wedding, I was waiting to be given some work to do. Well-dressed girls from the bride's family were carrying plat-ters full of sweets. I had nothing to do so I thought I would help them. I picked up one of the platters to distribute around. No sooner had I started offering sweets to the guests than Heerabai, our landlord's mother, shrieked.

"'Eh you bloody Maharin, what do you think you are doing?'

"'I have not done anything. I have not eaten anything from here, I swear,' I managed to say.

"'Not done anything? You have polluted all our auspicious food, you fool. Who is going to make good for this, that one-eyed father of yours? You scoundrels, your caste will never change—give you an inch and you grab a mile.'

"I could not understand what I had done to make her so angry. I raised the platter as if to give it to her. She suddenly exploded.

"'Now you have the audacity to touch me? Wait a minute. I will show you what it means to touch me.'

"Making sure none of the important guests was around, she caught hold of my ear and yanked me to one corner. I yelped in pain, and before I knew what was happening, she had pushed the platter from my hands and it landed with a loud, crashing sound. The food scattered all around.

"'Your shadow has contaminated the food. It is not fit for eat-ing,' she said with a contemptuous look on her face. I stood rooted to the spot, crying softly.

"All the other girls from my neighborhood, who had been called to work, came running. While I stood dumbfounded, they fought like cats and dogs to grab the food. One of the girls, who had managed to grab more than she could hold in her hands, came toward me and offered me a ladoo.

" 'Don't cry. Here, eat this . . . because of you, all of us got the sweets.'

"I merely shook my head, disgusted that they had picked up the food greedily, even when Heerabai had sneered and said it was not fit to be eaten.

"I could not figure out why the food was contaminated. Just because I had touched that platter, the food was contaminated?

"I could never understand who had decided that things should be this way. Like you, I often wondered if we untouchables were worse than animals. I would assume that as they said, I must have committed a terrible sin in my last birth to be born as an outcaste in this life."

"Don't you see?" my man said. "This is a clever trick played by the highborn. This is what they have told us through the ages so that we would take it quietly and not challenge them. But as Babasaheb says, we have to organize and agitate."

We had come to a small river. I looked longingly at the water and my man sensed that I wanted to rest awhile. Soon, we were sitting on the edge of the bank, our feet soothed by the cool gurgling water. My man had finally opened up after the long silent spell.

"You know, Soney, if it weren't for a few women working in the fields who had heard my cries, I would long past be dead . . . I would no longer have been sitting here next to you . . . as your husband."

I hastened to silence him by putting my palm across his mouth.

"Don't talk about such things," I said.

"Why not? I am only telling you how I was saved," he persisted.

"As a baby, Aaee carried me bundled in her sari when she worked in the fields. This way she could feed me while picking the crop. One day, when I was about three, my mother left me playing under a tree while she picked groundnuts with a few other women. After a while, I became restless and started exploring my surroundings. I found a tumbler and decided to go to the river to fetch water.

"The river was inviting. I kept walking, attracted by the ripples and the butterflies flitting above the water. Before I knew what was happening, I lost my balance and fell in, the current sweeping me away. I tried to breathe, and started choking as I gulped in water through my nose and mouth.

"I could not cry or even make a sound. Some women saw me floating away and raised an alarm. They screamed, rushing to the water's edge. One of them jumped in and swiftly pulled me out. I was bloated because of all the water that I had swallowed. Aaee came running and grabbed my feet, held me upside down, and twirled me about rapidly. Water gushed out of my nose and mouth. I was still unconscious and my mother wrapped me in a rag and ran home, wailing. In the village, she tied me to a potter's wheel and spun me around rapidly. More water gushed out and with a bout of coughing, I finally gained consciousness."

In Mumbai, my man and I hardly had any opportunity to talk openly. It would have been a sign of disrespect to the elders, like my mother-in-law. Now, my man seemed anxious to share his childhood with me. He continued talking even as we resumed walking.

"You know, when I was a child, we gathered every night near the house of a neighbor, Tulsirambaba, for storytelling sessions, settling around a huge banyan tree. One night, while we were engrossed in a story, there was a tremendous burst of light over our heads that lit up our neighborhood in the Maharwada. We looked up and saw a ball of fire racing across the sky. Frightened to death, we scattered in all directions. I darted into Tulsirambaba's large house and jumped into an empty urn, one normally used to store grain.

"Women ran to the scene, screaming and calling out to their children. I heard Aaee's wailing as she called out to me, but I was too scared to come out of the urn.

"Tulsirambaba's daughter heard some scrambling noise and she peeped into the urn with a lantern in hand. Seeing the top of my head, she pulled me out by my hair.

"'Rahee kaku, Rahee kaku,' she called out excitedly to my mother. 'I found your son.' My mother, who was beating her breast thinking that I was lost, rushed inside, held me in her arms, and took me home. Years later, I learned that the ball of fire was a meteor.

"Let me tell you another funny thing . . ."

Now there was no stopping my man.

"You know my cousin Madhav?" he asked. I nodded.

"Madhav's wedding was arranged. It caused a lot of excitement. There would be a feast. Although we were very poor, they somehow managed to arrange a good wedding ceremony. According to the custom, we had to give the groom a long white tunic. Moreover, after the wedding, as I had nothing else to wear, I began wearing his tunic.

"One day, I went to the farm wearing the tunic. Darkness fell as I was returning home. As I walked, I could see two of my friends coming along the road. I waited for them on a boulder outside the cremation ground. The oversized tunic covered me from top to toe. When they came close, I stood up to greet them. Seeing a white-robed figure suddenly rise up in front of them outside the cremation ground scared them so much that they ran away, dropping all the jaggery they were carrying, which I polished off.

"The next day, I was out with the cattle, wearing the same clothes. They saw me and realized what had happened.

"'Were you on the cremation grounds last night? We thought you were a ghost so we ran away.'"

"I am sure you were a very naughty boy," I said, leading him on.

"That is nothing," he said. "Right outside our house in Ozar, there was a crumbling skeleton of a hut where an entire family had died. The village children were scared to death of this place. On the wall at the far end of this house was a huge beehive, full of mouth-watering honey. We longed for it, but were too scared even to approach it.

"One day, all the boys made a collective dare: whosoever succeeded in gathering honey alone would become the undisputed leader of our group.

"No one took up the wager, and before I knew it, I had volunteered. As the boys spurred me on, I felt compelled not to let them down. They all escorted me to a shady grove close to the treasure. A few of them patted my back, while others threatened me that if I returned empty-handed, they would beat me to a pulp.

"I kept cursing myself. There was no turning back now. I gingerly climbed up the tree and stretched my hand toward the beehive, thinking about my triumphant return with the fresh honey. The next thing I knew, I had fallen to the ground with an angry swarm of bees stinging me repeatedly. I retreated quickly, wailing and scratching. Seeing my friends, I started screaming even louder for fear that they would begin to beat me up. Some of the boys raced to alert my parents. When I returned home, Aaee, who had intended to give me a sound thrashing, ran toward me with a cane, but one look at me and she dropped it in alarm, pulling me close to her as I howled in agony. She quickly ground some roots and leaves and applied the cool soothing paste all over my body. In a few days the swelling was gone with only a few telltale scabs."

My man looked charming telling stories. His eyes twinkled and his gestures grew livelier as he became absorbed in his narrative. Slowly, I grew bolder and asked him more questions, drawing out more tales of his childhood.

"As I grew older, I began taking our animals out to graze. One day, I took out the cattle along with a few other boys. While the animals grazed by the side of the road, we played. Nearby, a few workers were building a new road. Suddenly, we heard a loud rumbling noise. People around us began shouting, 'Elephant! The elephant has come!' We ran in the direction of the shouts but we were terrified when we saw the gigantic beast coming our way.

"Just then a few of the village women came by. They carried copper pots and lemons on a copper plate, as if going to a temple for worship. They sprinkled water on the elephant, and put the sacred vermilion on its forehead. We watched fascinated. Was this a god? We could not take our eyes off the beast. Each woman prostrated herself in front of the elephant, lowered her head to touch its feet, and then left. Strangely, this beast had no feet; instead, it had three wheels. A man was sitting perched high on the elephant. We talked about this strange creature for many days.

"Sometime later, while in Akrala, Aaji took me with her to a pilgrimage to Nashik. Many sadhus had gathered there. It was Sinhastha Parvani, a rare sacred occasion for Hindus. There I saw these holy men for the first time. I was terrified of their long beards and the strange ash marks on their foreheads, and clung to Aaji's waist. I saw one man sitting on a huge animal that had a long hanging nose. Aaji told me the animal was an elephant. So this was a real elephant! I remembered the iron elephant I had seen in my village and burst out laughing. Years later in Mumbai I learned that what I had seen in the village was a road roller!"

"In our house we always had a shortage of food. Every year something would go wrong," my man said wistfully.

"There would either be too much rain or too little, and all our crops would be lost. When I was about six or seven, I was playing with my friends and we wandered into the grocer's lane outside the Maharwada. We caught the aroma of sweets cooked in pure ghee.

"'Hmm, looks like there's a wedding feast,' one of the lads said. We watched as cooks fried jalebis in ghee and stirred large cauldrons on the open fire.

"'Let's play here,' one of us suggested. 'They will surely give us some leftovers.'

"We waited until evening, but no one offered us anything to eat, though they threw away lots of uneaten food on the garbage heap. We were utterly disappointed as we returned home, tired and with a roaring appetite whetted from all the tempting smells. Worse was to come. Our worried parents had searched everywhere for us. When I reached home, hungry and tired, I was given noth-ing to eat; on the contrary, I received a good hiding. Even after Baba had stopped, Aaee continued beating me with a cane. Finally, Baba pulled her off me. Aaee said, as a punishment, I would have to go without food for the next two days. Quietly, Baba brought me some roasted lentils. I ate them, drank lots of water, cast an angry look at Aaee, and took my sack to the field. I slept under the canopy of stars, trying hard to swallow my anger. You know, Soney, I swore to myself that when I was older, I would not treat my children this way."

I smiled to myself at the thought that my man had already thought about how he would deal with his children when he himself was just a child.

He continued, "Looking back, I now wonder whether Aaee's endless fasting rituals to appease the different gods were aimed more at making the meager grains last all week.

"The days Aaee fasted no food was cooked. She subsisted on watered-down milk and sometimes a boiled potato. I would then sneak off with the boys to the river. After a nice long swim, we would catch a few crabs and fish. I was an expert at building a slow fire of twigs on stones. We would enjoy a repast of roasted crabs and fish. I would then head homeward with a small tired face, pre-tending to have gone hungry the whole day. Aaee would take one look at me and her heart would melt. 'My poor lad,' she would say, and serve me a large helping of sweet potatoes or ragi rice that she had made.

"Sometimes, there would be special occasions when word came that some cattle or sheep were dead. That was the most longed for news. Then we would all excitedly rush to grab the best cuts of meat."

"Yes," I said, "even in our village, if there was a cull, the meat would last us for weeks."

"Do you remember the culls too?" he asked. "You were so young when you left the village after our wedding."

"Oh yes, I remember a little."

His voice picked up excitedly. "Whenever an animal in the village died, the news would spread like wildfire in the Maharwada. Everyone would run to the wasteland, even the children, women, and the old ones, for every hand was useful in getting some meat for the family. As soon as we heard of a cull, we would grab any container we could find in the house—pots, pans, buckets, baskets . . . Some people carried back meat even in the folds of their dhoti or sari if they could find nothing else."

"Or if they had already filled their basket and pot!" I rejoined.

He smiled. "What a fight there would be! The men and women carried knives, axes, machetes, and sickles. We used to wait impatiently for the Mahars on Yeskar duty who had first right to take their cuts. Hardly breathing, mouths watering, bodies tensed to go, we watched, until they took their share. Then, as they moved back and shouted to the others, a roar would go up from the crowd, and we would all fall upon the carcass.

"I saw people run screaming, children scrambling to pick up the smaller pieces that fell to the earth. The little ones like me were cautioned to stand back. We had the important job of pelting the dogs with stones to keep them at bay.

"Vultures, crows, and kites waited in the trees. They cawed and screeched continuously, until you thought the noise would drive you crazy! Every now and then, they swooped down to steal a morsel from the baskets or pots. As the men and women hacked and tore away, they had to keep an eye on the bloody, heaped-up treasure. Usually the stones and sticks kept the dogs away, but when the kids ran out of ammunition, the dogs came close, snapping at the heels of the adults, trying to slink through the melee and reach the carcass."

"In no time the huge bull or cow was just a skeleton," I murmured. "Bones cleaned of every bit of flesh."

My man nodded. "Not only did we scrape off every morsel of flesh, but the smaller bones, the gristle off the bigger bones, the knuckles and tendons were also juicy tidbits. When the people were through, the scavenging animals fell upon what was left.

"And what a procession made its way back to the Mahar-wada—men, women, children, all bloody and loaded with the spoils of their fight. But this was one fight that did not leave them tired. There was a spring in their step, a smile on their blood-smeared faces, as they anticipated the feast. People walked laden with baskets, troughs, and pots on their heads; one hand clutching the container, while the other flapped and hit out at persistent birds.

"Oh, it was so difficult waiting—we could barely wait for the meat to be cooked. I remember sitting, watching the huge cauldron bubble and simmer, but when I went closer to look, Aaee shooed me away. Even my father would sit impatiently on the threshold, waiting for the pot to be taken off the fire."

My man licked his lips at the remembered feast. "Usually, Aaee cooked enough to last us for a few days. Those were happy days. But there was more happiness in store. Whatever meat could not be consumed quickly before it got spoiled, she dried in the sun. After a few days of drying, the sun turned the meat into thin, crackly strips. These chanya were so delicious. Aaee would roast them in the fire for us to eat, and for many weeks, we would beg her for the treat. Nothing like chewing slowly on roasted chanya. It makes me hungry even to think of it . . ." My man trailed off, again lost in childhood memories.

DAMU

We walked on, lost in memories of that excitement. I mused aloud, "But sometimes the cull didn't turn out as usual. And there was no food."

"What do you mean? You didn't get the meat?" Sonu asked.

"Well, one summer that was longer and drier than most, there was a cull. A huge bull belonging to the patil had died. It was a big, healthy animal that died suddenly one night. A boy came running to the Maharwada early in the morning, yelling, 'The patil's bull is dead! The patil's bull is dead!'

"The animal had died in its pen the previous night, and two of the Mahars had already dragged it to the wasteland. As we arrived there, we saw the bloated carcass lying under a thorn tree, but there were no signs of the men who had brought it. The birds were perched on the trees around, and occasionally the crows flapped down and circled the bull. But the dogs were nowhere around. That was really strange, and the crowd skidded to a halt a few feet from the dead animal.

"A strange hush fell. Where were the men who had the privilege of the best cuts by virtue of their Yeskar duties? Who should make the first move?

"As the sun climbed higher, and hunger gnawed, people grew tired of waiting. They debated on what should be done, how long to wait, what was wrong . . . The women muttered and complained, yet sensed something was amiss. But the children ran toward the bull, to stare at its glazed eyes, its mouth lined with dry foam, trying to touch the stiff tail. The elders shouted at us to keep away, and a few of us got whacked soundly.

"Finally, we fell to it with the usual gusto, forgetting the initial unease, and the mad scramble for the largest quantity of meat followed. Already all eyes were bright with visions of pots full of piping-hot meat curry; there was a lot of lip-smacking in the midst of all the fighting. Soon, all that was left was a heap of bones, and there was a collective sigh of happiness. And we trudged back, arms full because this had been a huge, young animal."

"What happened then?" Sonu asked.

"Wait, let me finish. There were no crows or kites to fend off that day, for none followed us. The elders looked worried as the children skipped ahead excitedly. Most people were quiet, except for occasional murmurs and worried whispers. They were subdued and their steps were slow. Some of the older kids sensed something was wrong, but when I asked Aaee what happened, she told me to shut up and mind where I was walking.

"We reached home and deposited our loads, but Aaee made no move to wash the meat. Soon, our neighbor came running. She ran into our hut, and we heard her screaming, 'Curse that rat! May he rot in hell! Don't eat the meat. Don't touch it! Would you believe what those good-for-nothing scoundrels did—poisoned the bull to get back at the patil!'

"Aaee struck her palm to her forehead. 'Oh God, what bad luck! What are we to eat now? Why did they do it? And who was it?'

"Soon it was all over the Maharwada that a man named Khandu had poisoned the bull, to get back at the patil. He had been whipped by the headman the day before, and this for him had been the last straw in a string of humiliations. So he and his friend had dug up some poisonous root in the forest, ground it, and mixed it with some flour.

"Then they mixed the balls of dough with the fodder. The poison was known to work quickly and quietly, and by dawn the strong young animal was lying dead in its pen."

"Were they caught?" Sonu asked.

"No. They disappeared from the village for many days after that. But it was terrible to watch the whole Maharwada get rid of all the food. They dug a deep pit in the ground and everyone dumped the meat into it. There were those who wanted to hold on to the meat, hoping to find some good parts from it and ward off hunger at least for a day. But the elders went around from house to house, and warned, cajoled, or bullied everyone into throwing away the meat.

"Everyone was disappointed. The elders sat around listlessly and when we pestered them for food, the beatings we got were more severe than usual."

Sometimes the people who were ill-treated, abused, and beaten by the higher castes could take it no more, and killing a valuable farm animal was a good way to get back at them.

It didn't do much good in the end because there would be a lot of anger and resentment from the rest of the Mahars. Besides, the higher castes would be out to catch the culprit and hand out severe punishment. Nevertheless, a man can bear only so much, and when his suffering has crossed all limits, no one could predict if he would break or explode. Both of us knew this and we walked on quietly.

Another event of great excitement was our village jatra. Someone would offer a sacrificial animal and the main attraction would be the meat curry. One year it was our turn to host the jatra.

The day of the jatra dawned after much anticipation. A tent was erected near the chavadi, which looked festive with sunbursts of bright marigold flowers and auspicious, lush green mango leaves.

We were all excited. Two buffaloes were to be sacrificed that day by Shankar and Bhagabai, who lived in the village. Shankar had promised one as a penance last year when his daughter suffered an epileptic fit. Bhagabai, childless for nine years, had at last conceived after endless prayers to Mariaai. Bhiku, her husband, was not willing to make the sacrifice. The high-caste village priest had advised him to name the baby Kacharu, meaning dirt, so the devil would stay out of sight and the baby would thrive. Raging fights had ensued, with Bhiku trying to dissuade Bhagabai from slaughtering the buffalo, but she had remained adamant.

Strong young men led the two sacrificial animals to the stream and scrubbed them until they glistened a shiny black. The animals seemed content to remain in the muddied water and resisted when the men began pulling them out. Bands from different villages were ready. Children, men, and women danced to the reverberating beat of huge drums in a procession that led the animals through the Maharwada. With oil lamps lit in copper jars, the women waited excitedly for the procession to come to their doorstep. They garlanded the animals with strings of oleanders and mango leaves and applied vermilion to their horns. Everybody then joined their hands in prayer and bowed before the animals.

Each household had prepared a sweet as an offering to Mariaai. This was one occasion when the women could deck themselves in their finery. Almost all had preserved their wedding saris—their most prized possessions—to wear on this special day. Their neatly combed hair was adorned with flowers. They guarded a variety of pots and pans containing sweets for the goddess from the greedy eyes of the children, who whined hungrily. Every household joined the procession as it arrived at their door, eager to worship Mariaai with fervent music and dancing, but I was too impatient to wait and joined the procession early on. We moved from house to house. As we neared my house, I rushed in and urged my people to come out quickly and join. Nimba Mahar was an expert who would kill the buffaloes. He took off his shirt, hitched his dhoti neatly between his legs, and caressed a razor-sharp knife as if to assess its sharpness. With folded hands, he bowed before Mariaai and let out a thunderous full-throated cry, "Mariaai *ki jai!*"

Others picked up the chant. Nimba raised his long knife and slit open the buffalo's neck with one stroke. Blood spurted out and the men rushed forth to collect it in brass buckets. The poor animal let out one pitiful bellow. And then there was silence. Then Nimba used his curved scythe and severed the animal's head from its body.

Shankar, who had made this offering, was given the severed head. Placing an oil lamp of cupped wheat dough on the animal's head, he laid it as an offering at the feet of Mariaai, singing her praises. He then pulled forth Rakhuma, his young daughter saved by the goddess. The little girl was terrified of the piercing eyes in the dead buffalo's bleeding head. Shankar made Rakhuma prostrate before Mariaai. The other animal met the same fate, and it was Bhagabai's turn to make her offering.

Suddenly, some Mahar women began swaying and gyrating as if possessed. Their eyes were shut but they were moving back and forth in perfect harmony with one another. Everybody watched excitedly, waiting for the women to foresee the future. It was believed that the spirit of the goddess would momentarily pervade them.

The villagers began questioning them, seeking answers to problems ranging from when their daughter would find a suitable match, to where a well should be dug.

Some of the Mahars were called potraj, the servants of Mariaai. They had the special honor of leading the procession. The potraj tortured their bodies as a penance to worship the goddess. They also had the honor of being the first to collect the blood that spurted out of the slain buffaloes. Partaking of this blood, I was told, had made them extremely robust and gave them the grit to bear the extreme pain of physical penance.

The potraj women were dressed in dark green saris, symbolic of fertility, and their foreheads were smeared with vermilion. They carried brass statuettes of the goddess atop their heads. The women were dancing to the cymbals and drums played by the little boys of their family.

The potraj men moved about topless, with worn-out animal skins tied around their waists. Their ankles were adorned with bands of tiny brass bells. With the slightest movement, the bells resonated. These men were huge and able-bodied, and their backs glistened with sweat as they danced. They carried a thick, serpentlike rope of coiled hemp, with a handle at one end made up of a wad of tightly wrapped rags. The whip was long and tapered into a thin cord knotted at the tip. This made the end of the whip slightly heavy and it hit right on target.

As they led the procession, dancing in blissful abandon, the men would crack their whips across their own backs with immense force. The whips would uncoil in the air and crackle crisply before descending on their bruised backs with a resounding smack. The raw, exposed flesh on their backs bled as the whips cut through. But the potraj danced on happily as if unaware of any pain. They believed their purpose in life was to offer penance on behalf of all Mahars, for all their sins and wrongdoings.

Every year the month of Vaishakh brought spring and our biggest celebration, an occasion to thank Mariaai, or cajole and plead with her, and a time to forget suffering amid great celebration. People used this occasion to meet their near and dear ones, and to look out for eligible matches for their sons and daughters.

One of the big attractions for me was the cockfighting competition. People traveled long distances with their aggressive roosters, hoping to become the new champion. The winner got the defeated rooster as a prize, which was then roasted alive in front of its owner with a lot of jeering and mocking.

Everyone would secretly wait for midnight. The men would drool, imagining the tamasha dancers clad in shimmering saris and decked in jewelry, dancing with provocative gestures. At the stroke of midnight, the wait would finally be over and the folk dances and drama performances would begin. In a little while, the children and women succumbed to sleep, and only the men stayed awake. They would hoot and boo the performers, calling out to the raunchy tamasha dancers playing to the gallery. Special requests were entertained, if accompanied by rupees. There were repeats of popular sequences until the early hours of dawn, when the dancers were ready to drop.

During the jatra, representatives from each village were elected to compose a caste tribunal. A lot of bickering and fighting with some horse-trading ensued but, finally, a committee was set up. For two whole days, there were heated parleys and discussions about the arrangements for hosting so many people, and other important issues concerning the Mahar community. What should the arrangements be, who would stay where, and who was making an offering? These were among the main topics of discussion.

The caste tribunal also made decisions as to who should be honored, and who ought to be penalized. Deaths, diseases, births, marriages, and disputes made for juicy bits of gossip and were discussed with great gusto.

Sometimes an entire village community was ostracized as punishment for failing in its duties. The number of years of ostracism depended on the gravity of the offense. They were made outcasts among outcasts. They were not allowed to mingle or even eat together with the rest of the Mahars. No one would marry a girl from such a village, and no one would let their daughter marry into that village. There was to be no social interaction, no communication with the ostracized Mahars.

The village elders got together each evening to discuss local matters. Often, when they were chatting, I sat quietly nearby, listening to what they were saying. I never opened my mouth when I was among the elders. I did everything they asked. I ran and fetched them water, got them matches or bidis to smoke. When I was told to run an errand, I was fast on my feet and eagerly did their bidding. Often, they would give me peanuts and roasted gram to eat.

I remember those days so clearly. One man used to say that no one in the country would be happy as long as wild cactus, three tufts, and ruddy mugs flourished. The three tufts were the Brahmin priestly class, and the ruddy mugs the British. I didn't know about the priests and the British, but the red cactus was surely flourishing. It had grown wild all around us. Even its leaves and fruits were prickly. The cactus was a real nuisance.

"You cut its leaf, throw it on a rock, and there it will sprout and grow." That is what folks used to say. In some places, the cactus had spread so much that it had obliterated the sight of our thatched mud huts. The cactus thorns blew in the wind and if they blew over you, they made you itch unbearably.

Once the cactus had grown very tall over our hut. My father toiled for days, carefully removing every root, every trace of the cactus. He then cleared some land behind the house and tilled the ground to plant maize. He wanted to make a fence around the tilled land and so we went into the wood and collected an armful of babul twigs.

We were on our way home, carrying the load of twigs. The road was mucky. All of a sudden, a wild boar came charging at us. Some passersby saw this and began shouting. I was terrified and hid behind a tree, peeping, with my heart racing. My father heard the shouts and hastily dropped the bundle. Just then, the boar charged and the load went flying. The bundle hit Baba's face as he slid to the ground, and one big thorn punctured his lip. All the passersby began screaming and approached the boar as a big mob. The boar turned and went off into the trees. The people picked up Baba and carried him home. One of the Chambhars pulled out the thorn with the needle he used to sew shoes.

Even with our new fence and the tilled ground, the cactus continued to grow. In town after town, village after village, people struggled against this cactus. Then one day a European saheb brought some magic powder in a tiny box and sprinkled it on the cactus. In a day or so, the cactus shriveled up and dried. Everyone was grateful to this European saheb and his magic and praised God for sending him.

*　　*　　*

Our neighbor Tulsirambaba was a folk musician and a godman. He preached religion by singing devotional songs, wandering from one town to the next, reciting and singing hymns. He showed us pictures, brought back from the big cities, with his magic lantern, which he perched on a makeshift tripod. We had to stand facing the sun and look at the pictures one by one. He called it Babaji's cinema. We were thrilled to see the pictures in the box. For this treat, we were willing to run any number of errands for Tulsirambaba.

The pictures took us to a very different world. There were so many new sights from Mumbai—wide streets, high-rise buildings, trains, planes, and big steamer ships. We believed that these places must be the heaven that people described. If we did good deeds, we were constantly told, we would be rewarded by going to heaven after we died. I wanted to go to heaven but I did not want to die.

Once I accompanied Hari mama to a nearby town. On the way, the road passed through a tunnel. While we were there, a goods train came rumbling along. I was scared stiff and was as terrified as if it were a demon. Grabbing my uncle around his waist, I began screaming, "Hari mama, Hari mama, look, there is a mountain running toward us."

Hari mama said, "You muddlehead, that's a train. Don't be afraid." I stared and stared at the wheels of the train. They were moving like the legs of a centipede. When I came home, I bragged to all the boys about the marvel I had seen.

Little did I know that when I grew up, I was going to spend years working with the railways.

I thought about the first time that we left our village to go to Mumbai. That must have been in 1919. I was about twelve years old.

The whole village was abuzz with a scandal. Madhav, my cousin, was accused of having an illicit affair with a high-caste woman.

Madhav was a wrestler and was well respected in the community. The honor Madhav received as a wrestler had made him totally fearless, even of the upper-castes. He went around the village throwing his weight about.

The woman's brother, Ganpat, got wind of the alleged affair and was enraged. He immediately sought the support of the local rowdies. Bearing rods and canes, they caught hold of Madhav, surrounded him, and began thrashing him. But even as a group of six, they were no match for Madhav. All of them fled but Madhav managed to catch hold of Ganpat and beat him until he was bloody and unconscious.

Ganpat was in critical condition with a serious head injury. If he died Madhav would be tried for murder.

The entire Mahar community held a secret meeting in the dead of night, and decided that the only way to avert this calamity was to make Madhav disappear. After a long discussion, they decided that Madhav should run off to Mumbai, since that was known to be a survivor's haven.

Madhav absconded right away, hitching a ride to Mumbai. The next morning the family feigned surprise and raised an alarm, saying Madhav was missing. The calamity was averted but our whole family was devastated. Madhav had always been mean to me, and I was secretly happy when I realized he would no longer stay with us, but I hated it when all the boys of our community discussed different versions of the gossip and asked me which one was true.

A few weeks later, we received news that Madhav was having a difficult time in Mumbai. He had sent word, asking if my mother could come to cook for him and otherwise help out. Aaee decided to go to Mumbai right away. After that, our lives took a completely different turn.

We continued walking, lost in our thoughts, and I could tell that we had covered a good distance. I could not stop thinking about what awaited us in Mumbai. I did not want to tell Sonu about my worries, but as if she could sense what I was thinking, she started talking about the city.

"I came to Mumbai several times to visit my father before you brought me to stay with you," she said, "but I never really liked it."

"Then tell me, honestly . . . why did you marry me?" I asked her. "I have wanted to ask you for a long time now . . . you are so fair and delicate, so how come you agreed to marry a dark and rough bumpkin like me? And I was staying in Mumbai of all places."

Sonu just gave a coy smile. Looking at her, though, I could tell she was immensely pleased.

SONU

I was afraid of Mumbai, but I could not tell this to Damu.

"You still have not told me why you agreed to marry me," my man persisted.

What could I tell him?

"My Aba asked me to marry you and that is what I did," I replied nonchalantly.

I gave a burst of laughter when I remembered that I had not even seen him before my wedding and did not know if he was light-colored or dark, tall or short.

The first time when Aba told Aaee and me that I would have to go live in Mumbai, I did not believe him. I could not imagine living in Mumbai. Try as I might to feel happy, the thought dampened my spirits. Each time we came back to our village from Mumbai, Aaee went on and on about how she hated the city. I had never liked Mumbai, either.

"I wonder what treasure your father buried in Mumbai, Sonu. I will never understand," she always said, shaking her head in resignation.

My father, thinking about my marriage, had brought a beautiful piece of material to make me a skirt. I wondered what other presents I would get for my wedding. I began imagining how I would look in the green skirt, but Aaee came and whisked it away from me.

"Why?" she asked Aba sarcastically. "If you are going to get your daughter married, you should have got her a sari instead."

Aaee's anger was smoldering.

"So, she is your daughter and you think you can decide on your own who will marry her? Did I hear you say that you fixed an alliance? And in Mumbai of all godforsaken places?" Aaee's voice was quivering with emotion. "My daughter is not going to live in Mumbai."

"Why not?" my father asked

"Mumbai is dirty. It is crowded. There are hordes of people all around, but none that you can call your own. All the people there are after money. Are these people going to take their money with them when they die?" She ignored the disapproving look on Aba's face and continued.

"Tell me, is there a river like we have here? Arre, there is not even enough water to have a hair bath on the fourth day. And, tell me, is there fresh air like this mountain gives us? All you breathe is the dirty soot from those factories and textile mills. There are no open spaces anywhere. Only buildings and hutments . . . where will the children play?" she asked.

"Now be quiet and listen," Aba said. "There is money and that is all that matters. I don't want to sit worrying about whether my child is getting a good square meal or not. Fresh air! Do you think one can survive on air?"

"I don't want to talk anymore," Aaee said dejectedly. "You have made a decision. You don't care about asking me. You don't even care that Sonu is still so young."

My mother had tears in her eyes.

"Why are you in such a hurry to send her off? If she has become too much of a burden for you, I will feed her with the money I make by shelling pods."

Aba was furious. "Look, don't get me all riled up for nothing now. I have thought about everything. This is a golden opportunity and I will not allow your silly objections to cloud my thinking. You may want to clutch your daughter to your chest forever, for all I know!"

"But Sonu is still a child, she is not even ten years old," Aaee said.

"Open your eyes and look at her. In your eyes, she will always remain a child. But look how fast her body is filling up. We ought to marry her young . . . she is so pretty. Haven't you seen how people look at her now? You are her mother. You should be noticing these things and nagging me."

Aaee pondered this for a minute and snapped back, "You say there is money in Mumbai. What bride money are you getting for Sonu?"

"Look, who is talking about money now?"

"Isn't that natural? My daughter is so beautiful, she must get her due."

They were talking about me as if I was not around. I sat huddled in a corner. But something was happening to me. No one had ever told me before that I looked pretty. Aaee must have mentioned it at least ten times that day. She had never said that to me earlier, perhaps she had not even noticed it before.

I knew I was strong. I also knew that I was not like my friend Sakhu, who kept falling ill all the time. And Mother would never take me to the farm to work as she took my brother. She always said, "You sit at home and guard the fort. Who knows, someone may cast an evil eye on you."

Sometimes I was allowed to take lunch to the field. Mother patted and baked the bhakris in the morning before she left. I made up some chutney with raw mangoes or wild berries, or took some onions and garlic for them to eat with the bhakris. Mother made sure that my skirt was of full length and covered me well. Then, she would warn me to go straight home and talk to no one on the way back.

Aaee always washed and combed my hair and plaited it tightly. She got very cross if I dirtied my hair while playing. One day I went swimming in the river with my friends. Later, Aaee was passing by and caught me sitting under the trees with my hair disheveled and hanging loose to dry. She came charging at me and pulled me by the hair. "All you girls, don't you have anything better to do? Look at you with your hair let loose, sitting under this peepul tree. What are you trying to do, tempt the spirits?"

I was intrigued by this new revelation about my being pretty. But there was no mirror in our house to find out for myself.

The issue of my marriage continued to spiral into heated discussions. Aba flared up again when my mother mentioned money. He said that his daughter was not for sale to the highest bidder. What he was looking for was a man who would earn enough to keep his wife and children well fed and well clothed.

"I don't want the money for myself. What I want is a healthy person with proper skills to work in Mumbai and keep my daughter happy."

"That is true," Aaee agreed. "But to have all that, he ought to be a man and not an immature young boy."

"Yes, the one I have in mind is a man, and he is very clever," Aba said. "They say he has worked in many places with Gora sahebs and has learned a lot. He even speaks the language of the Gora sahebs!"

"Okay, enough . . . let it be. I have seen and heard a lot about these half-witted youth trying to imitate the lifestyle of those shameless Gora sahebs. I will not allow such a fellow to touch my Sonu. Yes, I am telling you . . . it is better to drown her in a well than to marry her off to somebody like that."

"Listen, I have asked around discreetly and everybody speaks well of him. Do you think I don't care about Sonu's future?"

"But tell me, have you seen him for yourself? Have you met him? Have you talked to him? How does he look?" Aaee's anxiety surfaced in every word.

"I have seen him but I have not met him. He was talking to some big bosses in our railway colony. Don't ask me too many questions now. He is of our caste, healthy, and earns well. That is it. His people will be coming here to discuss the wedding arrangements tomorrow."

"I want the wedding to be here, in our village," Aaee yelled. "I am not coming to your Mumbai for that. I want the couple to be married here in front of Mariaai, seeking her blessings. And I want the whole Mahar community to turn up for Sonu's wedding feast and to bless the couple. And I don't want that cantankerous old aunt of yours to interfere in this wedding. I want this . . ."

She went on and on. I was too young to think of what I wanted. All I knew was that I wanted a mirror to see how pretty I was.

Aaee did not sleep at all that night. I could hear her talking to Aba, who kept urging her to sleep. She woke me very early the next morning and did not head to the farm, as was her routine. Instead, she frantically rushed about the hut, in an attempt to arrange everything neatly.

Then she took a little chickpea flour, mixed it with goat's milk, and rubbed it on my face, arms, and legs. She bathed me and washed my hair. She combed my hair and plaited it tightly.

She had taken out one of her good saris that she kept in a small trunk. I protested when I realized that I was to wear a sari. Aaee silenced my protests with a thump on my back. She asked me to stand straight with my arms raised.

She turned me this way and that and asked me to stand with my legs apart. One part of the sari passed between my legs to be tucked into the waistband. The other free-flowing end was draped around my midriff and chest and then left to flow loosely down my left shoulder, nice and long.

It was a green-colored sari and had a broad yellow border to it. The sari was old and frayed in places, and Aaee kept warning me to be very careful with it. The loose flowing end on my shoulder, the padar, trailed behind me.

"Soney," Aaee called out my name, pronouncing it "Son-hey" for a special moment.

"When I was even younger than you are now, my mother draped this very sari on me when your Aba's people came to see me. I hope it brings you good luck like it brought me. Take it as your grandmother's blessing."

She waved her palms around my head and made crackling sounds with her knuckles and spat above my head, and began singing to ward off evil spirits lurking around:

Here comes the warning as you look at my Soney
Listen ye, a warning once and for all . . .
For the one who comes and the one who goes . . .
Whether it be the flowing streams
Or the gurgling brooks
The clinging creepers
Or the towering trees . . .
Anyone, anything up and down,
Over, under, wherever
Leave my Soney be hale and hearty
Watch out!
For your evil thoughts will come back to haunt you.

The sari was really too big for me, and I walked about awkwardly and almost drowned in it. Mother showed me how to walk demurely, and then how to sit carefully. She made me practice walking up and down, and then sitting down and getting up. I was instructed how to pay obeisance to the guests by bending and reaching out my palms as if to almost touch their feet, though I was never to actually touch their feet. She then tidied herself. She had cooked a special semolina dessert, and we all waited in readiness for the guests to come.

Two turbaned men arrived. I was told not to look at their faces directly. Even when they asked me something, I was to look at the floor and talk. Meeting their eyes would mean disrespect, so I did not know how either of them looked. My father washed their feet, a customary ritual, and they came in and sat on the mat that was spread out for them. My father began talking to them, exchanging notes about the family members and extended kin.

All along, I was sitting in a corner with my mother. When Aba asked me to come over and pay my respects to them, I began trembling. Mustering up courage, I gathered my sari around me, draped the loose end around my back and pulled it across in front, adding a second layer over my chest. I took short steps, did what I was told to do, and stood in front of the men.

They asked me my name, and asked me to walk up and down to make sure that I was not handicapped in any way. Then, to my horror, I was asked to turn around and they had a close look at my calves. I felt like cattle in the bazaar being inspected for defects. Thank God, they didn't touch me as they did the cattle.

They asked me to sit down in front of them. One of them asked me, "Can you pat the bhakri nice and round?" I merely nodded, looking down at the floor. This happened naturally, as I was feeling nervous and felt the blood throb at my temples.

Aaee told them that I did the cooking every day, since she had to go to the farm. That was that. They had tea and sweets and discussed a few things about the wedding arrangements. When it was time for them to go, one of them said to the other, "We did not ask her to thread a needle . . . who knows if her eyesight is good?"

"Arre, look at her . . . she is perfectly healthy. Didn't you see how supple and agile she looks?"

As soon as they had turned their backs, my mother impatiently asked my father, "Which one of them was the groom?"

"Are you out of your mind? He was not here. That was his uncle and his cousin."

"Why did he not come? I wanted to see how he looked."

"He was busy at his work and did not get time. Besides, why do you want to see him? I told you he is a fine young lad. What more do you want?"

Aaee kept grumbling under her breath. I hastily rushed to unwrap myself from the winding sari and be back in my skirt.

After a lot of back-and-forth and amid rounds of sulking and placating, the wedding was fixed. It was to take place in ten days. Aaee was excited beyond measure. She went around the neighborhood showing off her good fortune.

"Soney's man, they say he speaks the language of the Gora saheb!" she told everyone, her eyes widening proudly.

"My Soney was born with such good fortune. She will be rolling in wealth, I tell you . . . her man works with the train company!"

One day a fight broke out when one of the women said, "Who knows sitting here if Sonu's man is blind or deaf? He is in Mumbai . . . who has gone to see what he does there? For all you know, he might be a beggar there!"

Other people had to intervene and pull them apart as they tugged at each other's hair.

Just before the wedding, there was a frenzy of activity. Each of my cousins was assigned to different duties. The walls and the floor of our mud hut were given a fresh coat of cow-dung wash. Every afternoon, Aaee and a few other women gathered to grind grain and prepare for the wedding feast. They had a good time, singing folk songs and remembering stories from their weddings amid a lot of teasing.

How well a wedding was conducted was a matter of concern for the entire village, not just for the family whose daughter was to be married. Any lapse or neglect in tending to the groom's party put the honor of the village at stake. So, everyone, including the village headman, took an active interest in making sure everything was in order.

Some women made auspicious patterns on the walls and on the floor with rangoli, white-powdered limestone. Two tender banana saplings were planted on both sides of our front door to ward off evil and welcome the wedding guests.

Marigold flowers and mango leaves tied together adorned the front door. A few charpoys were placed under the shade of the banyan tree. Aaee and her friends hardly slept the night before the event after they had cooked the wedding meal.

There was raw papaya chutney, and usal, a spicy lentil curry. As they cooked the usal, the aroma permeated the whole house, mixing with the fragrance of the flowers. The most experienced of the women was responsible for making sweet boondi rice. There were two kinds of bhakris and steamed rice, banana pudding, and semolina sheera. And of course, there was paan, supari, and tobacco.

Amid singing and dancing, elderly women rubbed my body with turmeric paste and milk and then bathed me and washed my hair. Some of the women draped me in the new sari given by my in-laws. Strings of black beads were tied around my neck. I also had jingling green glass bangles on my arms, almost up to my elbows. I wore anklets with hundreds of tiny bells that tinkled every time I moved.

I reveled in all the attention. All my friends gathered around, casting admiring but envious glances at me. My skin glowed from the turmeric paste the women had applied. Each woman who came to see me applied a pinch of the auspicious vermilion on my forehead. Tiny particles of the powder gradually started slipping off my forehead and somehow found their way into my eyes. Tears flowed out of my eyes as the vermilion burned. Now whoever came to see me said, "Don't cry, Soney, you've been born a girl . . . you are born to leave your mother's house and set up your own nest. Look, all of us have gone through the same thing."

Then there was a loud noise of drums beating and cymbals crashing, announcing the arrival of the marriage party. Every-one—all the guests, the relatives, and our neighbors—rushed forward, crowding around to get a better view. Some women broke into song and began dancing. The verses were sung rather loudly in a singsong, high-pitched way so that they could be heard in spite of the drumbeats. Oh, the verses they sang!

Some of them showered abuse and curses on the bridegroom, since he was to marry their beloved girl and take her away. Some sang the praises of the bride and how talented and skillful she was, and how the groom was lucky to be marrying such a girl. Other songs warned the mother-in-law that if she dared to treat the bride badly, all kinds of curses would befall her. Finally, some songs addressed the father-in-law, pleading with him to treat the bride just as he would his own daughter:

> *Prince on horseback,*
> *Better hold on to your reins*
> *Do you think we love*
> *Our daughter in vain?*

> *All the groom wants is a silver ring*
> *A gold mine is our princess*
> *But he is no king!*

> *Why look for dowry, metal pot or pan*
> *When you have our daughter with a golden tan.*
> *Silly billy goat the foolish groom*
> *Trouble our daughter and*
> *We beat you with a broom.*

> *Dowdy the ungrateful groom*
> *Flaunts our golden chain*
> *If he has no thanks for us*
> *We look at him in disdain.*

The songs were full of abuse, but it was all taken in a spirit of good cheer. This was the only way to express sadness at the parting of a daughter.

After the wedding party had refreshed themselves and settled down, the marriage rites started. Finally, after a long time, I heard them calling out, "Who is the bride's uncle? Come on, hurry! Ask the bride's uncle to lead the bride out."

After the wedding feast that evening, we were taken in a procession to my husband's village. There was much singing and dancing amidst the beating of drums. Firecrackers went off along the way. I was afraid of the loud noises, and waited with bated breath for them to burst.

Three bullock carts trailed behind ours. The others were following us on foot. After a few more rites and rituals, my people went back to my village, bidding me a tearful farewell. I alone had to stay in the new place, with many strange people around me.

Marriages often mean disputes and even fights over protocol, gifts, or wedding arrangements. Any excuse is good enough to set the groom's party on the warpath. The bride's father would then have to plead and cajole, often with the promise of additional gifts. Sometimes, if the groom was sulking or if the groom's father was threatening to walk out, the bride's father would take off his headgear and place the turban at their feet and apologize, even when he was not actually in the wrong. Thank God, my wedding had gone off smoothly.

I had to stay with my new in-laws for only four days. My husband had to go back to Mumbai, as he did not have any more leave. His uncles and cousins teased him that he was spending only four days with his new bride. I saw him moving around the house and, at times, sitting next to me whenever some rituals were to be performed. The three nights that I stayed there, I slept next to my mother-in-law. She soothed my forehead and told me that I looked very pretty. Whenever I thought of Aaee and of our familiar hut back home, I started crying.

After the wedding rituals were over, I did not have to sit next to my husband or talk to him. And he never talked to me. On the fourth day, my husband and a few others left for Mumbai. My mother-in-law told me to get ready because my brother was coming to take me home. My joy knew no bounds at this news.

But the more I thought about it, the more I worried. Most of the girls who were married had to go and stay in their husband's house. But sometimes a girl was abandoned by her husband. Then she was sent back to her village to live with her parents. That was the biggest dishonor to the girl's family. Improper respect, not exchanging the promised dowry and gifts, were some of the reasons why a girl was sent back. I wondered what we had done that I was being sent back. Only later did I realize that I was yet to mature and attain puberty. Until that big day, I would have to stay with my parents.

I returned home relieved that I would no longer have to wear a sari. Aaee was waiting expectantly and wanted to know every little detail about what had happened in that house.

"Where did you sleep? How big is their hut? What did they serve for dinner? Were you made to wash the vessels?" She ferreted out endless details from me. She had a special feast of semolina pudding made for me. That was it. I was pampered just for that one day.

The next day life went back to its routine. It was all as if in a dream. All my jewelry and new clothes were put away for the big day when I would go to my husband's house. The only thing that had changed was that every once in a while, Aaee would nag me to wear a sari. Then she would tell me to be careful about draping the sari properly across my chest.

"Be very careful and don't let it slip. Take it around your waist and tuck it into the waistband when you are working."

Whenever there was a visitor, I was asked to touch his feet and pay obeisance. I also had to help Aaee a lot more in the kitchen. I was expected to become proficient in cooking and running the house. I was no longer sure that this was what I had dreamed of. I had only thought about the wedding and the presents.

Aaee's constant efforts were aimed at bringing me to perfection in all the housework. She kept commenting that if I was not good enough, my in-laws would be unhappy with my upbringing and would complain that my mother had not taught me anything at all.

"Don't do this and don't do that, don't sit this way, don't walk that way, don't eat fast and loud, and don't be noisy while working in the kitchen," was her perpetual refrain. I whined and threw tantrums at times.

But the slights and barbs continued.

"I am preparing you for things to come," she said, or, "I want to cure your hide to make you thick-skinned. Then, whatever they say to you, you will be able to face it."

She had tears in her eyes and drew me close, patting my back. "Poor lass, what can I do? We have the curse of being born female. I went through all the sufferings and now I have to see you go through it. That's why they say, never beget a daughter."

Mother's barbs and comments about my behavior and my in-laws' reactions, and her helpless face as she said these things, engraved themselves deeply in my mind. Even today, the slightest reference brings the whole period alive in my mind.

By and by, I began to do all the household chores, grind the grain every day, and make dinner. I still played with my friends, but I was not allowed to play with the boys in the neighborhood. If I was seen talking to a boy even a little longer than was perfunctory, whoever had seen me would scold me. It was as if everybody older than me in the village had authority over me.

"You are no longer a carefree girl," some would say.

"Till you go to your husband's house once and for all, you are the responsibility of our village and for that we have to watch you hawk-eyed."

Any visitor to my house praised my fate. I thought that I must be lucky to have married that man. I remembered that in the four days that I stayed with my husband's family, my fair color and good looks were brought up time and again. The more I thought about it, the more curious I became to know how I looked. I would ask, "Aaee, tell me, how do I look?"

"You look like me," she would say indulgently.

But I would persist. Then she would lose her patience and retort, "Look at you. Nowadays you seem interested only in your appearance. Learn to do the housework well, and when you go to your man, ask him all you will about your looks."

Yet I was very conscious of the changes in my body. I was extremely embarrassed to notice the distinctive maturing of my breasts. I had seen other women breast-feed their children, but I thought that they developed breasts only when they gave birth to a child.

The broadening of my thighs, the curve of my waist, and the glow on my arms and legs, the hair in my armpits and between my legs—all the changes seemed to happen overnight. I noticed these things, yet did not understand their meaning. I could not talk about what was happening to me. Mother was always busy, and I was afraid that she would rebuff me if I went to her.

I now felt shy in the company of boys and men, as I found their stares embarrassing. To make matters worse, whenever I talked to them, I would feel compelled to cover myself with my sari, or turn away shyly.

Finally, the time had come for me to go to Mumbai. It was no more a dreaded event. Aaee pampered me, and cooked all my favorite dishes. She sat by me and lovingly watched me relish the food. Usually, only the men were given this special treatment. Only they were served with bhakris fresh and sizzling from the skillet. But now, I was extended that honor.

"Eat, my dear, eat to your heart's content, and eat peacefully. Who knows what the future has in store for you? At your husband's house, you will have to please your mother-in-law to get good portions of food. Your grandmother would have had me dead if she had her way. It was your kind Aba who would serve himself more than he could eat, and pass me the leftovers from his plate."

I looked forward to meeting my mother-in-law. She had taken good care of me when I stayed with her for those few days. I could not imagine her not giving me enough food to eat. I had no anxieties. I was going to leave my mother but there was my husband's mother in Mumbai. So the thought of leaving my Aaee and my home didn't sadden me. Something new, something exciting, was in sight.

Soon after my father sent the message to my in-laws in Mumbai that I was ready, my husband and one of his cousins came to Taru Kherda. Aaee had woken me up very early and dressed me up in all the finery of my wedding day. She had made special food to send with me. They were supposed to come at noon, but we were ready early that morning. We waited long into the afternoon. Finally they arrived. Their train was delayed in the ghats. They came with gifts for me and I felt flattered.

Just before we set off, Aaee made my husband and me sit together as she applied vermilion to our foreheads to protect us from all evil. I was wearing a sari and she asked me to open out the padar. She put a fruit, an unshelled coconut, a few coins, and a sprinkling of rice grains in it. This was an auspicious symbol of fruition, and I was to carry all of it with me to my new house. She asked me to tie the padar into a knot around all the things, and tuck the end into my waistband. Then I had to pay obeisance to all the elders, including my husband.

"Always remember," she said with a stern voice when I was touching my husband's feet, "your husband is your god from today. He knows what is right and what is wrong. At all costs, you must obey him. Never, ever displease him. Do whatever he asks of you. Make him happy. He is older than you and knows the ways of the world."

I did not quite get what she was saying, but I nodded and promised her I would remember what she had told me.

She then chanted a blessing, her voice quivering with emotion: "May your hands always be blessed with happiness and abundance! May scarcity always desert you!"

Another piece of advice, given right on the doorstep, was that I should always obey my in-laws and look after them too, along with my husband.

"Remember what I have told you and you will always be happy."

She had tears in her eyes, but my husband was kind enough to assure her that he would look after me and keep me happy. She and my Aba were the ones who were tearful, but she kept telling me, "Don't cry, my little one . . . you are now going to your own house," as if she was trying to convince herself, more than me.

"One day you will have to send your daughter to her house in the same way. Then you will remember my words just as I am remembering my mother's and missing her now."

Barely twelve years old, I was still naive and knew nothing about the ways of the world. I followed my husband wherever he led me, to his village in a bullock cart and from there on a train to Mumbai. I had been on a train to Mumbai before, but we had always traveled in the ladies' compartment, and on the floor. We never had the money to actually buy a seat. This time I was traveling with two men and we were sitting in a general compartment.

My husband kept talking to his cousin about his railway company. I sat listening to them but could not understand anything. I amused myself by looking out the window at the passing scenery of hills and rivers, farms and trees.

All of a sudden, the train was enveloped in pitch-darkness and made wailing sounds. The sharp intake of my breath must have been loud because immediately my husband said, "It's only a tunnel. Don't be afraid."

"I am not afraid," I said. "I have been to Mumbai before and passed through a tunnel."

I did not want him to know that I was indeed scared. I was not afraid of the tunnel, but I was afraid of what lay on the other side.

The sun was about to set and evening shadows were falling. We had reached Mumbai at last, but before I could heave a sigh of relief, my husband told me that we had to walk a little to get home.

The little walk seemed to be never-ending. I walked on, clutching the folds of my sari in one hand and one of my trunks in the other. All I focused on was putting one foot in front of the other, and walking behind my husband, following his footsteps. Mother had told me that a chaste woman with good upbringing never walked alongside her husband. My husband walked on, fast-paced, effortlessly carrying our heavy luggage, and without paying any attention to me.

Tired and hungry, I felt tears forming in my eyes. They were not tears of exhaustion but of uncertainty. I did not know what to expect, or what would be expected of me. How I wished one of my friends from the village had come along with me.

We neared an old sprawling building and my husband said, "This is our chawl." As we neared it, I noticed that the building looked rickety and old with a number of boxlike rooms. There was a long balcony running across the entire length, with a few women looking out. Some windows opened out onto the balcony. The windows too had faces peeping out. Some men were returning home, carrying bags with vegetables or milk. Women stood in groups, chatting and watching over children who were running around and playing.

One of the kids, barely six or seven years old, saw us and came running, screaming excitedly.

"Damu kaka, Damu kaka," he said, and ran away shyly when he saw me. He raced ahead of us, screaming to everyone that we had arrived.

My husband told me that the boy was Raju, the son of our neighbor Lakshmi kaku. Amid the commotion, a lot of folks gathered around us with smiles and greetings. Some waved at us while others spoke a few words.

We walked past all these people. My mother-in-law and sister-in-law, Najuka, rushed out to see if we had indeed arrived. Raju stood in one corner, his face beaming with happiness.

My mother-in-law hurriedly approached us and stopped us at the door.

"Wait here!" she said sharply. "Don't enter."

I was baffled and wondered what lay ahead. But she soon returned with a pitcher of water and a piece of bhakri. She twirled it around us and washed our feet with the water. Then she flung the bread far away, muttering curses to befall those who cast an evil eye on us, and beckoned us to enter.

A little tin pail of rice was placed on the threshold. I was asked to kick it as hard as I could with my right foot before entering the house. I sent the rice flying, as far as possible, and in all corners of the room. This ritual symbolized the spread of wealth and prosperity that my good fortune would bring our family.

My husband heaved a sigh and asked for some tea. I remembered Aaee's instructions and signaled him to join me in paying our obeisance to his Aaee. My mother-in-law was full of praises for me. She lovingly patted my back and told me to call her Sasubai. I thought it was a good beginning for our life together.

That evening, I was at a loss, not knowing what to do. I felt Najuka's eyes follow me everywhere, observing my actions. Then a few women came to visit us.

"Let us see for ourselves the fair, moon-faced bride everyone is talking about," they said and burst out laughing. I sat in one corner with the padar of my sari drawn over my head. As five or six of them came and sat in front of me, laughing and joking, I cringed and shrank into myself, full of embarrassment. All of them were talking to me at the same time.

"Eh, tell us your name—" one of them said, and was interrupted by another.

"Why are you asking her for her name? Let us ask her to tell us her husband's name!" They all broke into peals of laughter.

I kept quiet, knowing full well that women were not supposed to utter the names of their husbands in public.

"Tell us, has your man held your hand yet?"

Sasubai came and sat among them and there was a hush.

"Why are you troubling that poor child? Look, how she is dying of embarrassment."

"No, we were just asking her if they have gone to worship Lord Khandoba yet," one of them said, and the others giggled.

"No, we are waiting for the auspicious day of Purnima, the full moon. We are all going next week. The Lord has been kind to us and given Damu as pretty a wife as I had prayed for, and now I have to fulfill my promise and offer a goat."

"Everyone says she is a pretty bride. Come on, show us your face . . . let us look at you." So saying, one of them came closer and raised my chin. Then slowly she raised the corner of the sari.

"Aga, don't be shy. It is only I, not your husband."

Again they started giggling and one of them said, "Maybe she is shy because she is thinking of the time when her husband looked at her!"

"My, my! Look at her. She is dazzling like the moonlight. Poor girl, how did you fall into our dark and ugly Damu's trap?"

Sasubai had waited to hear the praise showered on me. Her face gleamed with pride as if I was her prize catch, meant to be shown off. Later, however, she clutched a few mustard seeds and salt in her hands and performed the usual rite, to ward off evil spirits.

"Soney, what are you thinking? You are lost. Are you still thinking about why you married me?" My man teased me.

"I told you . . . my Aba got me married off . . ."

"But tell me, do you at least like it a little with us?" he asked.

My heart gave a tiny flutter as I realized what he was trying to ask me. He had caught me blushing and I did not need words to answer him.

"I like it a liiiitttle," I said mischievously, and then added, "but not a lot."

I remembered those first few months in Mumbai. Even Aba's house in Mumbai was better compared to my husband's cramped house.

The house I had entered was not at all like the home I was used to. My father's Port Trust tenement was small too, but it was airy. It had large windows that let in sunlight and gave a roomy appearance. It also had a large compound where we used to run around, playing hide-and-seek and catch.

My husband's house in Kurla was small and dingy. There was only one window, which opened onto the common balcony. Already three of them—his mother, Najuka, and he—were staying there.

There was hardly any room to move. In one corner of the house, there was the stove and all the pots and pans. In another corner was a small washing area separated by water pitchers, and a big drum brimming with water for washing up. There were community bathrooms and toilets outside, shared by all the residents.

The chawl was right on the road, and there was no place to play or sit outside in the open air. The rooms opened out onto a common balcony and anyone walking by could see right inside through the open doors and windows. It was truly like communal living—everyone went in and out of one another's houses and knew all the details of what was going on.

All the residents intervened in one another's family disputes with fervor. In my village too there was a spirit of community, but people did not walk in and out of one another's houses constantly.

The noise and din of the chawl was new to me. In the mornings, at home in my village, I was used to getting up to my mother's melodic voice singing couplets as she turned the wheel of her grinding stone. The next thing was to go wash up and come back to a meal of fresh bhakris and goat's milk.

In Mumbai, the morning chores started with a rush for water. Najuka asked me to follow her with two buckets. We went down the long balcony and came to the area where there were common toilets and running water.

All the women were pushing and shoving each other to get their buckets filled. I was reminded of the river at our village. The women there lined up plunging their pitchers, singing and teasing. They playfully targeted one of the women and splashed water on her. It was a time for bonding and releasing the strain of family tensions. At times, they all held hands to form a circle and sway, singing songs. These songs would target one of the women, and her name would be playfully linked with different men, finally to settle upon her husband.

In the city, getting water was an ordeal. Women pushed, shoved, fought, and even pulled one another's hair in their bid for water.

"This is the municipal tap for drinking water," said Najuka, as I looked on shocked. "The drinking water flows only at certain times. Usually it comes early in the morning and runs dry within an hour." I told her how we washed our clothes in the river and filled up the pitchers to carry them home, and how pleasant it was to gossip with the other girls in the village and pick berries and tamarinds to eat on the way.

"None of that will be found here," Najuka retorted with finality to her tone, indicating that there was no need for more discussion. "Come on. We have no time to waste. You are here, and now we must fill more water."

She walked on ahead, talking to herself, and I heard her mumbling, "You will use up all our stored water with your ways of the river . . ."

The taps would run dry by six in the morning, and everyone had to get enough water by then. Perhaps some bullies wanted to have more than they needed. This was Mumbai, and I was just beginning to learn the ways of city life. I wondered about my man and how he had felt when he came to Mumbai for the first time.

DAMU

The Mumbai of my dreams was woven with the pictures I had seen as a child on Tulsirambaba's magic lantern. It had tall buildings, wide roads with speeding cars, and trains that snaked along. Now here I was, in 1919, going to Mumbai as a twelve-year-old. What did I feel—fear, anxiety? I was worried about the future and its uncertainty.

"The reason I was happy to go to Mumbai, Sonu, was that I was actually going to travel by train. I could not contain my excitement. You know, the first time I had seen a train, I had screamed, 'The mountain is coming at us!'"

The grin on my face gave way to the memories of my village, creating a dull ache in my chest, and I felt my eyes moisten.

"Hmm, I'm listening, go on . . ." Sonu reminded me.

"The railway compartment was packed. I sat on the floor, holding on to a sack of vegetables from our farm. Najuka was asleep in my mother's lap. I tried to see the world that whirred past at a terrific speed, but from the floor, all I could see were the shoes of other travelers. I was dozing off when Pavala *atya* roused me by shaking my shoulder and said we had reached Mumbai. I jumped out onto the platform.

"Oh what crowds! It was a crazy melee.

"I had never seen so many people in my life. Some people looked like they were big sahebs, hurrying somewhere. Others looked as if they were about to drop under the tremendous burdens they carried. There were lots of trains standing in the station.

"Until that day, I had never seen a passenger train, and there I was in the middle of dozens of them.

"Did trains have friends too? I wondered. Did they talk to each other, sharing happiness or sorrow? Intrigued by this thought, I smiled.

"Outside the station, the hawkers were selling many kinds of food from their pushcarts. I stared longingly at them. There were fritters, roasted skewers of shining meat, and a variety of nuts. The vendors had their fares dished out in little paper plates, and they ferried the plates around, tempting the passersby, making sure that we caught the appetizing whiff. The vendors shouted constantly, hawking their wares in a singsong fashion that was not exactly coherent.

"'Come one, come all, my fares come from the paradise mall.'

"'Have fun, one anna, enjoy yourself, one anna, just one anna, don't you miss this—one anna.'

"I stared hungrily at them, the smells inviting, making me hungrier than ever. But I dared not open my mouth to ask for anything. That did not stop me, however, from lingering and looking longingly, hoping that my aunt would notice. But all that I got was a rap on my head, and a curt 'Do you want to get lost in all this crowd?'

"Not knowing where we were going to find my cousin Madhav, we followed Pavala atya blindly. Najuka and I both clung to our mother. Then, sensing that she herself was feeling lost and overwhelmed, I realized I was the only man in the family and felt the need to take care of her. I mumbled something like, 'Don't worry, Aaee, soon we will be home,' in an effort to reassure her. She responded with a smile and tousled my hair.

"We went to the railway quarters in Ghatkopar, a suburb of Mumbai. People living there seemed very poor. Everywhere there were small houses and huts, crowded and filthy. This was certainly not what I had expected of Mumbai. I was disappointed and longed for the clean air and rolling fields back home in Ozar. Pavala atya made us stand outside a small, dilapidated building to guard our belongings. 'Watch your belongings hawk-eyed,' she said. 'This is Mumbai . . . within a blink of your eyes your stuff will be stolen.' She then disappeared into one of the rooms, talked to someone, and beckoned us inside. She told us we could stay there for a few days and then she left.

"How Aaee tried to search for Madhav, but in vain. Nobody seemed to know his whereabouts. Mother was worried, since we had come all the way to Mumbai only because he had sent for us. Pavala atya had abruptly departed, and suddenly we were lost in the confines of that little room. I could read a million different feelings writ large on Aaee's face.

"We found out that close to twenty people lived in that small room. Most of them were railway workers who worked and slept in different shifts. Apparently, everyone had organized routines and they worked well. I remembered the immense crowds I had seen at the railway station. They had seemed like ants engaged in a flurry of activity, limbs moving incessantly. Come night in that little room, four or five couples slept in the same room with curtains and cloth partitions attached to a maze of crisscrossed strings held by nails on the walls, demarcating their private space. Aaee avoided looking anyone in the eye, and discreetly cooked a pile of bhakris on the small mud stove in one corner.

"While I was eating, an intense discussion erupted among some men about whether I was young enough to be allowed to sleep in the room along with the women. They decided that since I was a borderline case, I had to follow them for a nocturnal open-air snooze. I went with the men to the railway station, carrying my bedroll on my shoulder as they all did. I felt Aaee's anxious eyes follow me along the short walk with these unknown men.

"It was nearing midnight and a pall of quiet had descended on the station. One of the men told me that this was the local train station for travel within Mumbai. I stood confused, wondering where we were all going to sleep. Soon, I came upon a few human shapes bundled in odd postures all around. Looking at what the others were doing, I too secured a place for myself near a pillar and spread my bedroll of old sacks on the platform.

"Soon the entire platform was occupied with sleeping bodies, mainly men, but a few women and children as well. A fight broke out over sleeping places and I was afraid that I would be driven away from mine. I buried my face under Aaee's old sari that I was using as a coverlet. Through the frayed sari I took in everything that was going on, aghast at the life in Mumbai, so different from Ozar.

"It was exciting to be in Mumbai. I made friends with some of the boys who slept on the platform. Pandu and Marutya were brothers. Maru, as everyone called him, was blind. During the day, he sat on the railway platform, begging for money. If he managed to collect a booty, he would throw a sivarai coin or two my way.

"Aaee managed to find work mowing grass and pulling out weeds. She had worked in fields all her life, so she was good at it. In the village, she had earned two to three annas a day. In Mumbai, she was paid twelve to fourteen annas for the same work. Aaee could not believe her luck and thanked her gods profusely. Gradually, however, it dawned on her that the city that lured folks with good pay had its own ways of extracting its pound of flesh.

"In the beginning, I stayed home to take care of Najuka. I grew restless, and sometimes left her alone and went to play with the urchins at the railway station. Whenever Maru felt generous enough to pass me a coin, I always bought Najuka a candy or two. Najuka waited excitedly each day for me to return. Her face fell when I returned empty-handed, but she never moaned or grumbled.

"Pandu knew every part of Mumbai. Whenever he had a few coins, he took me around and showed me the sights. He loved playing elder brother to me. He reveled in the fact that he was mentor to an awestruck country bumpkin like me. As soon as Aaee left for work, I slipped out of the house, instructing Najuka to behave herself and not talk to strangers.

"My clothes were tattered. I had no shoes and I had long out-grown the slippers that my uncle had bought me. But nothing mattered to me, as I was happy. Pandu and I roamed barefoot through the wide roads and narrow, twisting lanes. Overhead, the sun was blazing hot and the tar road burned our feet, but we couldn't care less. I was thrilled to see so many new sights—tall, multi-storied buildings; wide streets full of cars, taxis, buses, and trains with wires on top to move them. Pandu told me these were called trams. The most amusing additions to the chaotic traffic were the horse-drawn buggies. They reminded me of bullock carts in Ozar.

"One day Pandu suggested, 'Let's go to Chowpatty.'

" 'What's that?' I asked him.

" 'There's a big sea there. Lots of water and lots of sand and you get yummy stuff to eat.'

"I was excited. I had never seen the sea before. I imagined it to be a big river like our Godavari River in Ozar. With the money we had saved, Aaee had bought me a vest and shorts. This was the second time I had new clothes. The only other new clothes I had owned were the ones my cousin Shankar had stitched for me. I couldn't wait to wear these. The whole night I was frightened that Pandu would desert me in the morning and refuse to take me. The next day, I washed myself under the outdoor water pipe and put on my new clothes, then went from one room to the other in the colony, showing them off to everyone.

"Pandu and I crossed the rails and climbed into a train without buying a ticket. The train was crowded with well-dressed people going to their offices, so no one checked on us and we weren't caught. When Pandu said, 'Jump!' I jumped as the train was slow-ing down at the station. We crawled under a barbed wire fence and out onto the road. We walked for a long time through wide streets and narrow lanes.

"Pandu said, 'I'm hungry. Let's eat something.'

"I looked around. There were no hawkers vending food on the streets. With a tolerant look, he beckoned me to follow him.

"Boldly, he entered a corner teashop. I was afraid to go in, but I followed him. We sat at a round marble-topped table. I sat on the edge of the chair, afraid they would throw us out. In our village, I could not have entered a teashop without being identified as a Mahar, and would surely have been driven out instantly.

"Pandu ordered a samosa and tea. I did not know what a samosa was, but I managed to confidently order the same from the waiter, who was a little boy much like us. The samosa arrived, golden brown and triangular in shape. It gave off a spicy smell and my mouth watered when I bit into the crisp flaky crust with a potato filling inside.

"I savored every last bit, mentally making a note that I should never let go of Pandu, as he was a gateway to the wonderful things in life. I had been initiated into city life, and now I rarely missed the village. As we paid and left, I thought I should look for a job in a teashop. That way, I could eat free samosas and get paid as well.

"We walked all the way to Chowpatty. There, I could not believe my eyes. A heaving mass of water stretched from one end of the sky to the other in a never-ending expanse. The sand was the shiny color of gold, and as I stepped on it, it felt coarse and grainy. Yet it was smooth and warm and slipped between my toes. Awkwardly, I began to walk around. It took me some time to move as briskly as Pandu.

"Pandu had already stripped and was watching me, amused at my inhibitions. Finally, I took off my clothes. I was scared of the sea but Pandu assured me that it was safe. Slowly, I entered the water, which was shockingly cold under the blazing sun.

"After every wave that crashed, there was a slight pull on my feet as the wave receded, and I had to brace myself by digging my feet into the sand. I soon overcame my fear and let the waves crash all over me. It was so much fun. On the way back, it was so hot that the tar road had softened. It created a shiny mirage. The road tickled my feet, and I laughed to myself, clapping my hands in wild abandon, then sat for a while in the shade of a tree.

"Pandu bought two betel-nut leaves, relished as an intoxicating delicacy. He called them paans and asked for 'extra' tobacco. He gave me one triangular fold of the green leaf and raised his head, saying, 'Hmm, line it against your cheek, and let the juices flow slowly.' Chewing happily on our paans, we walked, passing by tall buildings and sparkling clean roads.

"Slowly my mouth was filled with the red betel juice. It threatened to ooze out of my mouth and I gulped it down all at once. The strong juice burned its way down my throat, and as I gasped for air, it gave me a sudden kick. My head felt light and dizzy. Everything spun around me. I glanced at Pandu from the corner of my eyes. He had not noticed anything amiss, and was happily striding along, humming a song and enjoying his paan.

"We climbed a steep road that had a very large house with a garden. Pandu pointed to that house and said, 'The governor saheb lives there.' I knew he must be a very important person because the house was palatial. Pandu took me to the surrounding gardens, which contained many sculptures of lions and tigers. I could not swallow the paan anymore but was afraid to spit it out in those beautiful gardens, so I spat it into my new vest, then balled it up and stuck it under my arm.

"I was awestruck by the opulence, and I did not even realize that the spit had started leaking out of my vest. Pandu asked, 'What are you hiding in there? Let me see.' On a closer look, he started shouting, 'Oh my God, look at you . . . you are bleeding!' His face went ashen and he asked, 'Are you all right? Let me see.' I showed him the chewed-up betel leaves that had stained my vest red. He burst out into uncontrollable laughter. I joined him."

"Every day Pandu and I roamed the city, in pelting rain and scorching heat alike. One evening, when we returned home, hungry and tired, Aaee was waiting. She was very cross with me. 'You good-for-nothing lout! Do you think money grows on trees?' I had never felt so ashamed and irresponsible. I knew I had to look for work.

"Someone told us that there was a big project under way at a suburb called Thane, digging a tunnel for trains. I heard that they were paying six annas daily, which was good enough for me. The next day, along with seven or eight other guys, I went there. They hired a few of the others but told me that I was too young to do heavy work.

"I was curious to see how the work was done, and I persuaded Pandu to go inside the tunnel with me. The tunnel was already half a furlong deep. Inside, they had placed a huge mirror to catch the light from the sun. Workers were digging in that light.

"The tunnel smelled of burnt metal or tar or something similar. We felt suffocated. I imagined that something would go wrong and the tunnel would cave in, trapping us all. My imagination was carrying me away so vividly that I broke into a sweat. I began imagining that I could not breathe, and could not see a thing and lay under debris of mud. They were carrying out rescue operations but they did not find me . . . or they did but it was too late. I had already died of choking and suffocation in the mud.

"Suddenly one of the workers yelled at us, 'Get the hell out of this place. Do you think this is a tamasha that you have come to see?' This shook me out of my reverie and I clutched Pandu's arm and bolted out of the tunnel.

"I began going to the station, doing all sorts of odd jobs. Slowly, people started recognizing me and got to know me better. A man named Gangaram hired me to sell newspapers. I earned five annas the first day, and thus began a new phase in my life."

"That is where you met the Gora saheb, isn't it?" Sonu asked.

"Yes. Among the customers who regularly bought newspapers from me was a Gora saheb, named Nearle. Every day without fail, he would buy *The Chronicle*. If it was sold out, and I told him,

'No paper, saheb,' he would get most upset. One day in his broken Hindi, he managed to say, 'Keep one copy for me. I will pay you extra.' I began saving one copy for him. He became friendly with me. One day he said, 'Come with me.' Thinking that he might want me to run some errands, I followed him, but he took me to his house near Ghatkopar railway station, not very far from where I stayed. The bungalow was huge, with a big well-kept garden, and a small playground with a swing and a slide.

"I stood shyly in a corner. A beautiful Anglo-Indian woman whom I took to be the saheb's wife asked me to sit down. As was customary for us in our village, I sat on the floor. The saheb was surprised, and he gave me a hand to stand up and made me sit on the couch next to him. I was very uncomfortable and felt totally out of place. My lowly place was so deeply etched in my mind that when I was treated well, I could not believe it. I thought there was something wrong. After much thought, I reasoned that perhaps the saheb did not know that I was an untouchable.

"On a low table in front of us were plates full of fruits, pastries, and biscuits. The saheb dished out some papaya cubes in two bowls, one for himself and one for me. A girl was sitting in one corner. From the corner of my eyes, I kept looking at her. She was very fair, with golden hair and blue eyes, just like a doll. I had never seen such a pretty girl in all my life.

"I thought of Najuka, who was considered to be quite beautiful, with her shiny black eyes and long jet-black hair. But she was not as beautiful as this girl. The saheb said, 'This is my daughter, Robin. Whenever you have time, come here to play with her.'

"He called out to Robin and she came and perched herself on the saheb's lap. He kissed her pink cheeks and told her that he had found a friend for her. I thought of my father and of my Aaee . . . never had they allowed me to sit on their lap and never had they kissed my cheek.

"The saheb's daughter seemed very happy to meet me. She took my hand and led me to her room, which was full of toys. I was lost playing with her and suddenly remembered that I was supposed to go to the press offices. But I did not want to leave and lingered. Finally, when I was going, the saheb gave me two rupees as a gift. I was happy with the money, but more than that, I was happy that I had found a friend.

"At first I couldn't wait to meet Pandu and tell him all about the golden-haired girl. But then I decided to keep this a secret. It was too good to be true. If the others found out and told the saheb that I was an untouchable, then I would never be allowed inside their house and I would not be able to play with Missybaba. I felt confused as I returned home wondering when the saheb would ask me to play with her again.

"Every day, around four-thirty in the afternoon, after finishing my newspaper delivery work, I began going to the bungalow to play with Missybaba. We ran around in the garden, playing hide-and-seek and other games. The saheb and memsaheb sat in armchairs on the veranda, watching us play. Sometimes we played with skipping ropes, and the saheb came and swung the rope from one end, while I swung it from the other, and Missybaba would jump skillfully, skipping the swinging rope. Then it was my turn to jump the rope and, goaded by Missybaba's praise, I jumped higher and higher until I gasped for air. In no time, the saheb or Missybaba tired of swinging the rope.

"Missybaba and I grew very fond of each other. I took my evening meal with them and then returned home. If for some reason I had to leave early, Missybaba got upset and threw tantrums.

"They were very kind to me. I was happy there, but I paid less and less attention to the newspaper business. The saheb realized this. He began paying me eight rupees a month."

"One day the saheb took photos of us as we were playing. Without letting us know, he sent the photos to England. His old mother lived there, taking care of his two sons from his first wife. Soon Robin received a letter from her grandmother and brothers: 'The boy who is playing with you in the picture has no shoes. Be careful when you are playing with him. Don't step on his feet. If you do, you will hurt him.' Immediately after this letter, the saheb bought me a pair of shoes.

"It was only when I was given the shoes that I realized I had been without them for so long.

"One day the saheb called me and said that from the following week, I would have to accompany Missybaba to school. I nodded and went back to our game. The saheb and memsaheb talked about something. The next day, they bought me new clothes. The memsaheb showed me the clothes. I was so happy that I could not believe it. The opening day of school was still far away, but Missybaba started preparing me. She taught me the basics, beginning with A B C D . . .

"On the first day of school, I rose early and got ready in a hurry. I wore the new clothes and appeared before the memsaheb. She looked pleased at my appearance and gave me a tie. She tied it around my neck with her own hands. By that time, I had learned a few everyday phrases in English. I could neither read nor write my mother tongue, Marathi, but I had learned a little English because of Missybaba.

"The sun was shining upon us as we drove to school in the saheb's car. I sat in the front next to the driver. I thought this was a great honor. The school was near the Victoria Terminus railway station. I recognized the station and told the saheb that this is where the train from my village had brought me. The saheb smiled.

"The car pulled up outside the school but I did not want to get out. I was terrified that the school people would make an issue of the fact that I was an untouchable and then Missybaba would no longer play with me. I went inside the school hesitantly with Missybaba and stood quietly to one side.

"Another saheb took me by the hand and led me to a chair. I was grateful. I was overcome and felt my throat constrict . . . I felt awkward, unsure and confused, and I did not know what to expect, or how to conduct myself. I had never been to a real school in Ozar.

I believed that if I had gone to a real school, I would have sat in that chair as my right.

"For some incomprehensible reason, I was not enrolled in the school. However, that was the moment when I began to think for myself. It was strange knowing that I was the one who could decide what was right for me. I felt strong and powerful."

"The saheb's wife was Missybaba's stepmother. Sometimes, when she had an argument with the saheb, she would treat the little girl very badly while he was not at home. At times, she would grab her hair and beat Missybaba if she did not do as she was told.

"I hated it when she mistreated Missybaba. I wanted to shout, 'Beat me instead—leave Missybaba alone.' The memsaheb did not have any children of her own and craved a son. I always respected her and stepped in and helped whenever needed, so she treated me well.

"The saheb and memsaheb often quarreled. He would yell and throw things about the house during these fights. I would then take Missybaba to her room and entertain her, playing with toys and clowning around. Whenever the saheb drank, he acted strangely. He used to throw off his clothes and run to the fields stark naked.

"Once, late at night, they had a terrible fight and the saheb left the house in a fit of anger. They lived next to the railway lines. The memsaheb thought he had gone and thrown himself under a train. She began wailing loudly, 'The saheb has killed himself. Go and see if you can find him.' I reassured her that I would bring the saheb back in no time. The memsaheb stopped wailing for a minute as if surprised by what I said. She nodded, but as soon as my back was turned, she began sobbing loudly again.

"The railway tracks were not very far away. We could see them from the house. I took a lantern and started out, but what looked like a human body from a distance was actually a large paper fluttering in the breeze. On the way back, I heard groans from the wild grass. I ran in that direction. It was our saheb sprawled on the ground. He had only his pants on but they were soaking wet, for he had urinated in them. His whole body was soaked and stinking. I hoisted him onto my shoulders and with the help of two others carried him home and gently placed him on the bed. The memsaheb stood by and watched as I took off his shoes. The saheb began to stir and come to his senses. From that time, the memsaheb began treating me like her son. I was given a room in the house where I would occasionally spend the night.

"There were three or four papaya trees in their garden. Missybaba and I loved to eat papayas. We longed for the fruit to ripen. As soon as they turned yellow, I climbed the tree, picked the fruits, and placed them in Missybaba's room under an old blanket. The warmth made them golden and deliciously sweet. Then, we hid and ate them, just the two of us. Sometimes during the day, when Missybaba was in school, I stealthily ate the papayas by myself.

"Once I ate three papayas. They were so tempting that I could not stop eating them, one after the other. In a day or two, there were big bumpy boils all over my body.

"The memsaheb called out to me, 'Damuboy, come here.' Her voice was now very sharp and stern. 'Damuboy, do you hear me? I want you to come here at once.'

"I ran and stood before her. She looked at my face and asked, 'Damu, what's the matter with you?'

"I told her, 'I have got boils.'

"She said, 'Hmm. Looks like the papaya tree is growing inside your body. Tomorrow papayas will start growing on your head!'

"I was worried, imagining a tree sprouting from my head.

"'Don't worry,' she said, 'I will give you medicine. Don't eat anything tomorrow, understand? Go now.'

"I went to my room and lay on my bed. Soon, the memsaheb called me. She poured some brandy in a wineglass, added some cod liver oil, and then some more brandy. She gave it to me. I gulped it and a fiery burning sensation constricted my throat. My stomach was uneasy all night long. I could not sleep, and I went to the toilet again and again. I wondered whether it was better to have boils on my face than this misery."

"The saheb was addicted to both alcohol and betting on horses. He often sent me with a note to the horse races at Pune. I carried the money very carefully and handed it over to a bookie, Mr. Pearson, there, who was an expert. After the races, I collected a sealed envelope from Pearson and took the evening train back to Mumbai. Sometimes, Pearson took me to the station in his car.

"I reached Mumbai by about eleven at night, went directly to the saheb's bungalow, and turned in for the night. In the morning after I had handed over the envelope, the saheb gave me some money. My share of the money depended on how much he had won. When he earned huge amounts in the races, he was on top of the world, and tossed some money in the air for me as a gift.

"I regaled Missybaba with stories about my adventures. Before the onset of the monsoons, the winding railway tracks through the ghats would be full of little rivulets. The trees were a lush green and monkeys swung from them. One day, Missybaba wanted to come with me to the races. She was very persistent even when I refused. Just when she began screaming at me, the saheb walked in and intervened. Missybaba quietly walked away and I was left facing the saheb. I was desperately trying to think of something to say, when Ramji, the butler, called the saheb away to attend to a telephone call. I heaved a sigh of relief and went to look for Missybaba. Without saying anything, she gave me forty rupees to play the horses.

"By now, I had learned a lot about horses just by observing people and waiting around the racecourse the whole day. I had made friends with a few bookies and talking to them had taught me the rules of betting. I chose the horses on my own, relying on my judgment, and put Missybaba's money on them. I was pleasantly shocked when Silverstar, the horse that I had chosen, won the race and I got seven hundred rupees. I put the money in an envelope

122

and sealed it. I did not know how much money Pearson had made for the saheb. I had his envelope too. The saheb was waiting for me on the veranda that evening. I was so excited that I could not wait to meet Missybaba, but it was very late in the night. As I placed the envelope in his hand, the saheb noticed something unusual about me and kept on probing. I pleaded that I was just tired and went to my room.

"The next morning, the saheb gave me fifty rupees. I was over-joyed. But that was nothing compared with my joy when I ran to Missybaba and quietly slipped the envelope into her hand before I left to attend to my newspaper vending. She took it without counting the amount.

"That evening she called me to her room. She was radiant. I had never seen her looking so happy. With a beaming smile, she embraced me, and said, 'You lucky man,' and handed me a hundred-rupee note. I refused to take the money, but she stuffed it into my pocket and again gave me a hug before fleeing the room. I was elated but confused. Taking money from Missybaba had hurt me deeply. Yet her affection and warmth had touched me beyond comprehension. I went home that night in a stupor. It was the first time that a girl had hugged me as far as I could recollect. I kept reliving the incident, and each time I felt a fountain of emotions burst in my heart. I thought my heart would surely burst from holding so much happiness. The incident with Missybaba resulted in my total commitment toward her and her family. There was no question of refusing them anything."

"Once a saheb and memsaheb and their two sons were guests at my saheb's house. My saheb called me and said, 'Listen, Damu, go with this saheb and help him with whatever he wants done . . . You will go with him to Lonavala.'

"Obediently, I went with them. I did not think twice about leaving my newspaper business unattended.

"We first went to the other saheb's bungalow in Mumbai, on a hilltop, near the Temple of Mahalaxmi. There was a large lake next to it and several kinds of birds and peacocks in the garden.

"We were to leave the next morning for Lonavala. First, I helped the memsaheb pack her stuff. Then, I had to help their cook pack hampers for us. Next, the saheb asked me to wash and clean their car. He then checked it carefully. Behind the car, there was a pipe for smoke to escape. The saheb showed me how to attach a brass whistle to that pipe.

"We left early, around six in the morning. They constantly munched things from the hamper and kept offering me different things. I was not used to small snacks. All I was used to were two substantial meals a day. They gave me something like a fritter, and biting into it, I was reminded of the samosas that I had first tasted with Pandu on our day out to the Chowpatty beach. I missed those carefree days.

"Soon, we left Mumbai behind and were in the mountains. The saheb left the road and began skirting a mountain. He stopped the car a little distance from the mountain and fixed some nets on the windowpanes. The saheb and memsaheb took out guns and the three of us got down. He locked the doors and windows of the car. The saheb told his two sons, 'If you find an animal approaching the car, blow this whistle. We will come running. Don't be afraid.'

"We walked along the edge of the mountain, looking all around. In a valley, a tigress was suckling her cubs. The saheb saw her and raised his gun. The tigress roared with anger and leaped. Both the saheb and memsaheb fired their guns. The tigress crashed to the ground, and I rushed forward. The saheb yelled at me, 'Hey, boy! Wait, don't go near her . . . she may be still alive and attack you.' We did not go near her for quite some time.

"We waited, looking around, eating more goodies, and then approached her. She was cold and motionless. The two cubs, as tiny as kittens, played nearby. I tried to pick up the tigress but she was so heavy that she would not budge. I tried dragging her by the tail, and I stood slanting at an acute angle, yet she did not move. The three of us then somehow managed to drag the tigress to the shade of a tree and we returned to the car with the cubs. We had a leisurely lunch and the saheb told us stories, all about his hunting experiences. We played with the tiger cubs as if they were little kittens and it was a lot of fun. I kept wondering, as we were playing with the cubs, what if they suddenly turned into fully grown tigers?

"We roamed about on the mountaintop picking wild berries and munching them. The railway line was just below us. We could see trains go by. Many local folks of the Bhil tribe, their wives and children, had come there to pick wild berries. From a distance, they were watching this strange sight. A Gora saheb and memsaheb, and their children, were playing with tiger cubs. I remembered a local song that said that the Gora saheb was a magician. He could even drive a cart without the power of bullocks. Or so the song went.

"Just then, we heard the whistle of an approaching train. The tribal women and children came running to see it. The train was followed by a small trailer. The tribal women were very excited. 'See that train?' one of the women said. 'Now her baby is running after her.' I heard this and burst out laughing. The saheb asked me why I was laughing, and when I told him what they were saying, he laughed too.

"A little later the saheb asked the tribals to lift the tigress and haul her onto the top of the car. The saheb gave them some money and they left. After we had traveled a few miles farther, we saw a herd of deer. The saheb stopped the car and the two of them got out. They began shooting at the deer. Two of the deer died; one was a baby. We lifted them and tied them on top of the car. We returned home that evening, and the saheb was jubilant.

"In the saheb's house in Mumbai, I put a plastic tube in a bottle and fed the tiger cubs with milk. Anyone who came to visit thought they were kittens. They look the same now, I thought, but what a difference when they grow up.

"Every evening, I carried the cubs in my arms to the garden and played with them. Gradually, word spread that they were tiger cubs, and crowds would gather to watch us.

"I remembered Missybaba and wanted to carry a cub for her. I stayed with that saheb for a week. He did not want to let me go, but I missed Missybaba."

"One day, when the saheb and I were walking home along the railway tracks, he said to me, 'Don't walk along the line anymore. In a few days, there will be an electric train on this line. That train will suck you under it, and you could die. Never, never walk along the line.'

"I did not understand what he meant. How could the train pull me under it from a distance? Then the saheb said, 'When you sing bhajans, people who sit far away cannot hear you. In a few days, if people run in England, you will be able to hear their footsteps here. If they sing a bhajan in England, you will be able to hear it here.'

"How could that be? I could not believe what he said."

"One day, my saheb and his big saheb had an argument. They no longer got along with each other and they argued all the time. Missybaba told me that the family had been given a month's notice to return to England. I was very sad when I heard this. The memsaheb had stopped talking to anyone.

"The saheb did a lot of shopping. I accompanied him everywhere, carrying armloads of packages and keeping them in the car and going back for more. He even bought expensive cotton material to get a shirt stitched for me. Then the saheb took me with him to the tailor and ordered him to take my measurements. I could not believe that I was going to get new clothes. The saheb also bought me another pair of shoes. A few days later, the tailor delivered the stitched clothes, but they did not give them to me at that time. Every day I wondered if I had done something wrong.

"One day several guests came to the bungalow. The saheb had

bought lots of liquor bottles. Everyone got drunk. Even the memsaheb was drunk. Missybaba came with two glasses of colored liquid and said, 'This is wine . . . have some.' Everyone was eating, drinking, and dancing. Some people sat on the veranda, while others strolled through the garden embracing each other.

"Missybaba and I sat together, but we were unusually quiet. We had not spoken about it, but we both knew we would never meet after she went off to England.

"After some time, a photowallah came to the bungalow. He clicked several photos and took a group picture too. He also took one photo of Missybaba and me, hand in hand. I wore the new clothes that the saheb had bought for me the previous day. The saheb also fixed a tie around my neck. Later, the photowallah gave me a copy of that photo.

"About a month later, the saheb and Missybaba returned to England, but he was not able to take the memsaheb with him because she was half-Indian. He left her the house that they were staying in and asked me to stay as long as I wished, taking care of the memsaheb. Missybaba cried a lot.

"I fought hard to control my tears. But later that night, when I was alone, I pulled out the copy of our photo and let my tears flow unabashedly. I will never forget Missybaba or her father. I was their employee, but I never felt inferior, and they never treated me like a servant. With them I had forgotten that I was a Mahar, an untouchable. Nobody had ever mentioned it. It was a strange world, but I had sailed smoothly and come out of it an entirely different person. But now they were gone."

"Soney, you have still not told me why you married me. Look at you, delicate, fair-complexioned. You almost have the coloring of Missybaba. The first time I saw you during our wedding, that was what struck me."

"Tch, hmmpf . . ." Sonu fretted. I thought she would be pleased and here she was sulking.

SONU

That Missybaba again. I felt a knife twist in my stomach whenever he mentioned Missybaba. He'd get that faraway look in his eyes, reminiscent and nostalgic, and I would feel that I had lost him to his private world.

Even when I was new to Mumbai he never had time for me. All he talked about was Babasaheb and his movement, and at other times he told me about Robin—Missybaba.

Many times I got annoyed at him and fretted all day long. Sasubai would draw me aside and ask what was wrong with me. How could I tell her? I also thought about the times when he was kind to me, when he had that dreamy look on his face, when he told me that I made him very happy. I had to learn to make do with those memories.

I also had tricks of my own to distract him. I was amazed at my own ability to be coy—I sent him fleeting glances and looked away just when he seemed to have caught my eye. Then, I would sigh and arrange my hair or my sari, and sure enough, I would have succeeded in distracting him.

Then, he used that special soft tone to tell me I had big brown eyes and lashes that curled long. He praised my straight nose, and said that when we had a daughter, she would look just like me. I lapped up these compliments, and all would be well until he said that I had a fair complexion, almost like that Gora girl, and that was enough to reduce to ashes all the good things he had said.

He sometimes said we were a mismatched couple to look at—he was dark and rough, and no match for me. I didn't care so long as he appreciated my beauty. If he were handsome, I would have lost my privileged position in everyone's eyes, including those of Sasubai, who always appreciated my beauty.

In the beginning, his talk of the social movement didn't interest me much. More than what he said, I was often caught up in how he said it—the way his eyes sparkled, his expressions, his gestures. Whenever he was agitated, he paced up and down in that little room of our house like a tiger, raring to go but confined to a cage.

Sometimes he came home charged from a meeting or a talk, and that was it. Day and night, he went on, Babasaheb said this, and Babasaheb said that. He talked about how learned Babasaheb was, and how he was going to participate in Babasaheb's social movement.

He said, "Soney, when we have children, we will send them to school and teach them to read and write," and I would shyly turn away.

He talked endlessly about the people of our caste. When he was in these moods, he was so involved in his thoughts that he forgot that I was his wife. To him then, I was just someone who sat listening for hours on end to what he was saying.

I don't know how much my husband earned when we were in Mumbai, but every month when he got paid, he brought something home for us—tasty fritters or snacks, or hot and sweet jalebis. He handed over the remaining money to Sasubai.

By and by, I began to know him better as a person. At first, I had characterized him as a tall, dark mountain. Now I thought he was like the tender whole coconuts he sometimes bought—a tough hard shell on the outside, but sweet and tender inside.

As we were walking, I thought I saw a tall temple spire. Then, as we drew near, I could see a saffron-colored flag fluttering in the wind.

"Look, there is a temple. Let us stop and worship God," I requested hesitatingly.

"You go ahead. I will wait near this tree for you," he said curtly.

"But we have to worship as a couple," I protested. His hard, angry look silenced me.

I could imagine how Sasubai must have felt when, after our wedding, he had been reluctant to worship at the Khandoba Temple in Jejuri. As we walked on silently, I thought of our trip to Jejuri.

We reached Jejuri at about ten in the morning. Najuka excitedly tugged at my hand and began to show me around. On one side of the hillock I could see steps hewed out of the mountain that went right to the top, exposing the white stone of the mountain, forming a crisscross pattern. I craned my neck to look at the peak and could see the steps tapering off.

There were throngs of devotees walking the path, playing cymbals and beating drums. A few of them danced along, swaying, totally engrossed in their chanting.

"*Malhari Martand,*" some chanted, and the rest responded with "*Jai Malhari.*" Others would add to the rhythm by chanting, "*Yelkot, Yelkot, Jai Malhar.*" As the climb became steeper and more difficult, the devotees increased the beat to a fast-paced crescendo and everyone seemed to climb on effortlessly. I was amazed by Sasubai's stamina as she chanted the bhajans and marched to their beat.

The spire of the temple was soon visible. We could see a few priests, topless and adorned with beads, ashes smeared across their forehead and chest. They carried a brass pot called kamandalu in one hand with the sacred water, and vermilion paste in the other. They approached the passing devotees, urging them to make ritual offerings of different kinds.

Looking at my garb, the green sari and the green bangles up to my elbows, they could tell that I was a new bride. They approached Sasubai and badgered her to let them perform a ritual puja for only eleven rupees.

"Allow me to do the puja; the couple's union will soon be blessed with a male child. You will have a grandson to carry forth your family name," said one priest, who followed us for quite some distance. As we neared the temple, the same priest finally said, "You look very devout. For your sake, I will chant the mantras and do the puja for only five rupees."

Sasubai relented at this and asked my husband to give five rupees to the priest, who happily began chanting mantras in earnest. He made my husband and me walk together, and a few steps later, all of a sudden, asked Damu to carry me across the threshold.

I could not believe that he was actually asking my husband to do the very thing that Najuka had hinted. My husband, however, paid no attention and continued to walk ahead.

Sasubai called out sternly and wanted him to do what the priest had asked. Without a word, and before I even realized what was happening, he effortlessly picked me up. One of his hands was under my knees and the other supported my back.

I was shocked as he walked on nonchalantly, looking straight ahead as if it were the most natural thing. The priest guided him to take seven steps, chanting his mantras. He explained the importance of those seven steps, and the responsibility of married life.

We crossed the threshold of the temple and my husband was still carrying me. Najuka was laughing at us and Sasubai too seemed amused. I was so embarrassed that I pleaded with him to put me down. Fortunately, we were in the sanctum sanctorum, and the priest asked him to place me at the foot of the Lord. Another priest held a flaring lamp in a copper plate. He twirled the plate, feeding a few camphor pieces to the flame. With the drum beating steadily, the fire greedily consumed the offering.

The priest applied some vermilion to my forehead and sprinkled some rice confetti on us. He asked me to open out the free-flowing end of my sari and placed some fruits, grain, and a coconut in it. Sasubai asked us to make obeisance to Lord Khandoba. We bent down together and the priest chanted a blessing, "Long live your husband and may you be fertile forever."

Then we paid our respects to Sasubai, and she blessed us, saying, "May you bear eight hale and hearty sons and keep our clan growing."

She then told the priest that she had made a vow to offer a goat to the Lord. The next day was Purnima, an auspicious date. The goat would be slaughtered exactly at noon.

"You are very fortunate," said the priest, "to have a son who respects you so much and abides by all your wishes. You should see some of the young men. They don't believe in worship and offering penance."

"Aaee, I will not be able to stay for the sacrifice tomorrow," said my husband. "You stay if you want to."

He requested the priest to find accommodation for us in the ladies' dharmashala.

"I am leaving now. My bus is at five," he said.

"Arre, why don't you rest awhile now that you have come so far?" Sasubai asked. "Eat some bhakri and the potatoes your wife has cooked."

While we were eating, Sasubai started chatting with other families who had come there for a special festival that would last seven days, culminating in a feast.

She proudly said, "This is my new daughter-in-law. We are going to offer a goat tomorrow. The Lord has been kind to us."

The women asked Sasubai all the details: which village we belonged to, how many sons she had, were they all married, how many grandchildren, and where and how long we were staying.

"It brings good fortune to attend the Lord's festival. It begins tomorrow. You should stay for the week," said an elderly woman when she heard that we were going back the next day after the sacrifice.

Another woman agreed. "Only those with good fortune are drawn to Khandoba's festival. It is only the fortunate who can take part in the celebrations."

"It would be a shame to turn back on such an auspicious day," said still another. "See . . . people are pouring in from far-off places. You are already here and you are leaving."

Sasubai looked at my husband, who was growing more uneasy by the minute.

"Damu, what these people are saying is true. We have come so far, spending so much money . . . who knows whether I will be able to come here again?"

He was not happy but said that we could stay.

"Perhaps you should take Sonu back with you," Sasubai said. "Who will cook for you when we are not there? Seven days is a long time for you to look after yourself. Najuka will keep me company."

I was upset at the idea of living alone with this mountain of a man. I recalled how we were entwined in the night, and I decided that I would not go back.

My husband went to buy us tea, and I took that opportunity to plead with Sasubai to allow me to stay, but she was suddenly stern with me.

"Sonu, don't act like a child. Remember that he is your husband and your rightful place is with him. Didn't your mother teach you anything? Go with him and obey him at all times. If it ever comes to me that you troubled him, I will send you back to your village and get a new wife for Damu."

When my husband returned with tea, he saw the tears that I was trying to hide. He asked Sasubai what was wrong, and she said that I was missing my Aaee.

DAMU

I worried about getting a job once we reached Mumbai. The thought of doing the rounds in search of daily labor, the long walk home . . . all began to weigh on me.

Sonu echoed my worries. "What job will you do when we get back to Mumbai?"

"Something will come up, Sonu. Something always does."

After the Gora saheb left, I wandered about aimlessly. I had no job for quite some time. Then I went back to Gangaram and his newspaper business. He was happy to take me back, and I began working diligently and quickly learned more tricks of the trade.

I remember it was around 1921, and the national independence movement was in full swing. Tilak, who was called the Father of Indian Discontent, had died, and Mahatma Gandhi had emerged as a leader of the national movement.

Gandhi had launched the civil disobedience campaign and had called for a general strike throughout India. In response, students were leaving educational institutions in large numbers. Gandhi also called for a boycott of all imported goods. Some people in Mumbai lit huge bonfires and burned imported cloth worth millions of rupees in the presence of Gandhi.[9] The change and ferment was good for our newspaper business.

Normally, most newspapers were priced at a modest five paise. At times, though, people were so desperate that they were willing to pay four annas or sometimes even eight for a copy. They were so afraid of the police that often they bought a newspaper and hurried away without waiting for their change, and we ended up making a fair amount of money.

At about nine every night, I went to the newspaper office to hand in the money I had collected during the day. Gangaram rented a room near Dadar railway station in Mumbai. He paid me around ten rupees a week and I collected tips from customers as well. In a little while, I had managed to save some money and I would sit by the window in our office, which overlooked the station, watching the trains come and go, and weaving dreams about my future.

Once, in the newspaper office, I heard there was a housing project for lower-income people near the Charni Road station. I found out all the details and went to meet the officials.

"Join our housing society," they said. "Pay five hundred rupees as down payment and become a member."

I was excited because I had saved enough money. On my way home, I began dreaming once again of how proud my mother would be that her son had found a decent place for the family to live. I went home and chattered animatedly to Najuka and Aaee.

"We don't want it." Aaee brushed me off. "We don't belong here, and the people here don't belong to us. The land of our birth is Ozar. We don't want to stay here for long. I just want to return to Ozar."

I was dejected and did not eat anything that night or talk to anyone. Najuka kept trying to placate me. Finally, I lost my temper and raised my hand to strike her. Aaee intervened and pushed me away, saying, "The money that you earn has blinded you . . . if you think you have become too smart for us, go wherever you want, and do whatever you want." The next day I went and canceled my registration in the housing project.

The newspaper business was booming. Every night I went from one press to the other, settling accounts and asking after all the people I knew there. They offered me tea along with tidbits of information. The last place that I went was the office of the *Bombay Samachar* press. After settling accounts, I spread newspapers on the floor and lay down exhausted, covering myself with more newspapers. I was often so tired that before I knew it, I would start snoring. The next morning the hustle and bustle of the press would wake me up around four o'clock. After a quick wash at the municipal tap, I would again do the rounds of the press offices, collecting fresh papers for the day.

A couple of years went by. All of a sudden, Gangaram died. Without children of his own, he had begun to treat me like a son. I performed all the final rituals for Gangaram that his own son would have. Without him, I felt orphaned again. Soon the paper agency began to lose money, and it was no longer the place it used to be. The other boys tampered with the accounts and kept large chunks of money to themselves. I refused to join them and they saw this as a threat. Soon, I moved on.

Once again, I was on the street looking for work. Fortunately, I was hired by the Great Indian Peninsula Railway, but only as a daily wage laborer. This meant I had to wait outside the premises every morning. If any of their workers did not turn up, or if the railroad had extra work, I would be called in. Some days, I waited all day to be called, only to see a shift end. All the other workers left clutching the eleven annas that they were paid, but I returned home frustrated and hungry. I knew this had to stop.

Eventually, I found some work in Thane, where a new railway line was being laid. There I had to work with cement and concrete. We dug large ditches for the electricity poles, and then filled them with cement after holding the poles in place. The saheb entrusted four men and women to help me and arranged for a boat to ferry us across Kalyan Creek. I navigated the little boat both ways. My job was to get the work done and give a report to my bosses. I maintained cordial relations with the workers and sometimes pitched in to help them. The workers appreciated this and always cooperated.

The other side of the creek was dense with forest inhabited by wild animals. We were scared, as often there was not a soul around except us. Sometimes when we were in a group of four or five, we crossed the creek and picked sackfuls of berries or tamarind. I brought them home to distribute to the people in the chawl. After that job was finished, they sent me to another team of workers—the filewallahs.

Each work team here was called a file. We had to follow strict rules. Old worn-out logs of wood, called sleepers, had to be removed from under the railway tracks and replaced with new ones. It was hard and laborious work. The workers gathered at eight o'clock in the morning. Some sat down and ate their breakfast of bhakris, and some chatted and gossiped.

I ate the sizzling bhakris that Aaee made for me at home before I left in the morning. In this way I was able to start work as soon as I arrived. While the others were busy eating, I measured the appropriate distances and dug small holes on the marked places. The workers appreciated this, because it meant that they could start work right away. After they finished digging, they brought me the sleepers one at a time and placed them in the sockets dug for them. Then I fitted them to the rails with a big iron key. We then filled up the surrounding space with gravel. I finished my share of work before the others, and then helped anyone who was having trouble.

"You know, Sonu, I forgot to tell you about my sister. Once we were working in a remote area between Dombivli and Kalyan. The sky was overcast, and soon there was pelting rain. All day long, it rained heavily. There were no trees or any shelter. We were completely soaked and cold. Our bhakris had become lumps of wet dough. We were so hungry, but there was nothing to eat, and of course, the work had to be completed. Both Dombivli and Kalyan railway stations were far away. We had no place to go except some huts that were visible in the distance.

"I began walking in the direction of the huts and managed to reach them. Three women were talking in one of the huts. They looked at me suspiciously as I stood outside the door, shivering uncontrollably.

"'What do you want?' one of them asked.

"I was shivering so much that I couldn't answer. My teeth were chattering. They asked me to sit in the porch of the hut. I wrung the water from my clothes and felt a little warmth return. The woman brought me steaming hot tea in a glass. The tea, sweetened with jaggery, warmed my insides. I felt better.

"'Who are you? Why are you out in such heavy rain?'

"I explained the situation, and they felt sorry for us.

"'How many workers are with you?'

"'Ten,' I said.

"Quickly, they began making bhakris and cooking gram dal. Some other women handed me a copper pot with tea.

"'Take this tea to your workers till we finish cooking. When you come back, we will have some food ready.'

"They gave me a makeshift raincoat made of old sacks. I returned to my workers and gave them tea. They were very grateful. The rain had stopped but the sun had not come out.

"I took the copper vessel back to the women. They handed me ten hot bhakris and some spicy roasted gram dal. My workers ate gratefully. Once again, I took the vessels back and thanked them.

"A few days later we were paid for the work we had done. I said to the workers, 'Let us buy something for that kind woman.' We collected one rupee from each person, and bought a sari for seven-fifty, and cotton fabric for a blouse for twelve annas.

"We went back to that place. They were initially suspicious about us but one woman recognized me. Their men gathered, not knowing who we were, and angrily approached us.

"'Why have you come here?'

"'I have come to meet my sister,' I replied.

"One of our workers handed me the sari and I placed it in front of the woman who had given me the tea. She smiled shyly, and then the men warmed to us as well. They welcomed us, took us to another hut, and started the still. While we drank the fresh liquor, they slaughtered a chicken and the women roasted it for us. We ate with them, thanked them, and returned home happily. So that means you have one more sister-in-law, other than Najuka.

"That project was completed a few days later. Our file returned to the Kurla train shed. I was then given some odd jobs like unloading sacks of cement from the truck and taking them inside the warehouse. That work was backbreaking. But I was on good terms with the supervisor, and eventually I was given the job of carrying water in large buckets to construction sites, a small respite. It was here that I finally got a break.

"Once when I was carrying water at Kurla Station, I saw a crowd under the bridge. I thought someone had been crushed under a train. Curious, I pushed ahead among the crowd. I still could not figure out what was happening. I asked one of the men what had happened.

"'They are hiring workers here,' he replied. I forced my way in. There was a Gora saheb sitting at a table with a big register in front of him. No one had the courage to be the first one to go before the Gora saheb. They were afraid that at the slightest provocation, the Gora saheb would shoot them.

"I could speak a smattering of butlery English well and went straight ahead and did salaam to the saheb.

"'Who are you?' the saheb asked me in English.

"I understood what he said.

"'I am a man,' I said.

"He started laughing, and then asked, 'What do you want?'

"I replied, 'I want work.'

"'What work?'

"I said, 'I will do any work.'

"Immediately, he took me on. Many people barged into the office after me, but he recruited only three more and told the others to leave.

"The next day I had to be examined by a doctor. And on November 1, 1924, I became a regular worker of the Great Indian Peninsula Railway.'

I was hired with some other workers because the electric train was going to be launched. As an apprentice, I was required to do many things. I wiped up any oil spilled on the engines, put oil in the machines, and checked to see if any of the engine parts had become overheated. Earlier, I was a temporary worker and with great difficulty I made eighteen rupees a month. Now I had become permanent, and as a regular worker I received twenty rupees and eight annas. I worked with William saheb. He patiently explained my duties to me. I put my heart and soul into my work and learned much in just a few days. The saheb was very pleased with me.

Sometime around January 1925, the first electric train started in Mumbai. I remember one of the early incidents. On the harbor railway track, a power plant was being built next to the main track. A three-by-three-inch hole was dug about a furlong away from this power plant. The engineers had connected a wire to the overhead wire and put its other end in the hole, which had water in it. After some time, we saw the water begin to bubble and spurt out. The saheb then knew that electricity had arrived. The big sahebs were informed and everyone gathered around. A few minutes later, an electric train pulled in. The chief saheb first tied a thick garland of marigold flowers and mango leaves to the engine. Then amid a lot of clapping and cheering, he cut a red ribbon and all the officials clambered aboard the train. We did not get to do so, but we clapped our hands in joy.

Soon I was transferred to the main railway station, called Victoria Terminus. Everyone referred to it as VT. The Gora sahebs named this station after Queen Victoria. They had done away with the old Indian name, Bori Bunder. William saheb was also working there and he was very happy to see me. I worked under him for two years at Bori Bunder. He trusted me and used to leave me in charge while he went out.

When a train came into the station, I would ask the driver if there was any problem. I fixed whatever he asked me to, and cleaned any oil spills and carbon soot that had accumulated on the engine. I never let the work suffer. I was also friendly with all the drivers, so we chatted and joked and had a good time. Work was fun and my pay went up to twenty-seven rupees a month.

Once, a fire broke out in a local train. It came into the station, whistling furiously. That alerted me and I ran to it. Many of the passengers panicked and jumped onto the platform, hurting themselves.

The whole station was filled with smoke. We couldn't see anything. There was total chaos with passengers scrambling to get away from the train.

Some ten minutes later when some of the smoke had dispersed, I went to our office to look for the saheb, but he was nowhere to be seen. I put on the saheb's boiler suit and rushed back to fix the train.

I opened the armature cover with a twisted iron rod. A huge burst of smoke escaped and hit me in the face. I recoiled as my eyes started burning and watering. When the smoke cleared, I looked inside the armature. It was red-hot. I called the station sweepers and asked them to bring sand in metal buckets. I threw sand on the red-hot parts. A crowd had gathered. But I was so engrossed in my work that I did not notice the people around us.

I examined the armature. In some places, it had large bulbs of molten metal clinging to it. I scraped them off and then sanded it. I also checked the carbon brushes. One had become twisted and broken into bits inside. I thought, this is it—this is what has caused the fire. With a blower, I blew off the broken pieces, which began flying around. I screwed my eyes into tiny slits to prevent any splinters getting into my eyes. I took the other carbon brushes out and polished them with sandpaper. I made sure everything was clean and working well. Finally, I closed the armature with a sigh and looked up—shocked to see a huge crowd watching me.

The engine driver came forward and tried the engine. "Everything is working perfectly," he told me. I was happy.

One of the senior officers on the platform asked me, "Where is your saheb?"

I lied with a straight face. "Sir, there is some problem with a train, and he has gone to Bandra to fix it." The officer did not say anything. I was soaked in sweat and my face was blackened with soot. I went to a nearby bench on the platform and lay down.

I was thinking of my saheb. I was worried that he might come back and know nothing of what had happened or how I had covered for him. I was sure that the saheb was with a woman who lived in a chawl next to Sewri Station. He visited her every day. The saheb had told me, "If there is any problem, tell some engine driver to blow two whistles when the train enters Sewri Station. Then I will come back by the next train." I did exactly that. In a few minutes, my saheb came back. I told him all that had happened. He wrote up the report.

Next day, the big railway officer sent a note for my saheb. I had gone to platform number six to examine a train. When I came back to our office, my saheb told me that we had been summoned to the big saheb's office.

I stood outside the big saheb's cabin with my heart pounding. My saheb went in. Immediately, they called me in. I saluted the big saheb and stood there, willing my heart to stop palpitating. The two sahebs discussed something in rapid English and I could barely understand anything. The big saheb gave me ten rupees as baksheesh.

He said, "You are a good man," and shook hands with me. Once again, I saluted and returned to our office. William saheb stayed there. He came back later looking very pleased and, seeing me, he smiled.

"What happened, saheb?" I asked.

"The big saheb is very pleased with you. You may get the chance for a bigger job."

The next day, a man in a railway uniform came and gave my saheb a piece of paper. Again, we had to go to the big saheb's office.

The big saheb said, "From today, we have promoted you. Keep up the good work."

I got the post of electric motor mechanic. My pay was raised and I started receiving forty-two rupees.

Then I was transferred to the Kurla train shed. In my new job, I had to inspect every train that was stationed there overnight. I had to open every part of the engine, and replace any part that was broken or damaged. As soon as I took on this new job, I learned to operate the train, as I had to drive the inspected train to the station in the order it was scheduled to leave. There, I handed over charge to the driver who was waiting. Other workers who had worked with me in my previous department now looked at me with respect.

I remember Aaee saying, "Looks like our good days have finally arrived."

SONU

Two years into our marriage and all was going well. My husband had a good job in the railways, and my mother-in-law was also working there. I took care of the house and, for the first time since coming to Mumbai, I had time for socializing.

It must have been around 1928. It was sometime in August and Lord Ganapati's festival was in full swing. A tent erected in the space between the two chawls was decorated with garlands and streamers. Amid loud music and dancing, an earthen idol of Ganapati was brought in a procession and placed in the center. For ten days and nights, fervent devotees worshipped it with ritual prayers. Each household took turns and cooked the favorite sweets of Ganesha—as our Lord Ganapati is also known—as an offering to the god, usually sheera, modak, or ladoo. The dish was offered ritualistically while chanting prayers and beseeching the Lord to bless it. Then it was distributed to everyone. It was treated with great reverence and received in the right palm.

Every locality had an icon, and some placed Babasaheb's framed picture alongside. The devotees worshipped Babasaheb too, offering flowers with equal reverence.

Every night, there were programs like skits, plays, folk dances, or competitions. They even had a competition to see who could eat the most bananas in the least amount of time. I enjoyed these activities and looked forward to them. They reminded me of the community spirit of my village.

Sometimes when there were music programs—jalsas—my husband asked Sasubai if he could take Najuka and me with him. I loved the lilting music, and the full-bodied voices of the singers resonated in my ears long after we had returned.

Often, we had to walk long distances to attend these programs. I could never walk fast because of the flowing pleats of my sari. The roads bustled with cars, horse-drawn carriages, and carts, apart from the crowds, and I was easily flustered. I was scared to cross the road as the others did, sprinting across, dodging the traffic. My man often held my hand and pulled me along, much to my embarrassment.

My man often reminded us that the program was not merely about the lilting tunes; it was more important to understand what they were singing. He explained the different social themes of the songs, ranging from untouchability and the caste system, to education and principled living.

Another important part of the Ganapati festival, at least for my husband, was the lectures. Late at night, after dinner, people thronged to listen to the local wise men. They talked about Babasaheb and his thoughts and teachings. My husband dragged me along with him to these lectures.

"Soney, take more interest in these talks instead of the song and dance you like to see. They are about our community and about the uplifting of our people."

I thought, even in our village, we had lived among the Mahars and no one had ever questioned the age-old system. This was Mumbai, however, and people thought about bigger issues than merely filling their bellies.

The speakers talked about Babasaheb's protest in Mahad. They also talked about entry into Hindu temples. "We are labeled untouchables and not allowed entry into Hindu temples. After all, we too are human beings. Is it a sin to be born a Mahar? Babasaheb has made us aware that we are as human as any other people. We have to unite and agitate against discrimination."

The crowds listened attentively. Men and women, old and young, everyone who came shouted, "*Jai* Bhim" in unison at the end of each session. Then they sang bhajans, incorporating Babasaheb's exhortations.

On the tenth day of the Ganapati festival, the idol was taken in a procession, amid music and dance, to be immersed in the creek at Chunabhatti. Everyone would join in and, after the immersion, stand on the streets to watch the other processions. My man was among the volunteers who guided the procession from our locality.

Actually, we untouchables were not allowed to worship Ganapati, the god of the upper castes. Over the years, however, the Ganapati festival had become a social event. I was told it was a good way of reaching the masses and uniting them toward a cause. The upper castes were certainly not happy about this. The sanctity of their god was being polluted, they maintained.

I was quite happy with the way our life was going. I went along with my man wherever he took me. Sometimes, I got bored when he talked endlessly about Babasaheb's speeches. Of course, I dutifully followed him, but secretly I told myself, "It is enough to have that social ghost sitting on my husband's head . . . I am better off without it."

Before I knew it, though, all those speeches and my husband's talks had an effect on me. Then an incident occurred that totally changed my passive attitude.

During that year's festival, some high-caste organizations spread a malicious rumor that, under the pretext of worshipping Ganapati, we untouchables were going to symbolically hang the idol instead of immersing it. This had inflamed religious sentiments. Police vans were parked at every corner, and armed policemen rounded up suspicious-looking people.

Our procession contained about three thousand men and women and was among the largest. We were under police protection, and the police had decided to let us go first. The other small processions from different areas were held back behind ropes as we passed through.

Everything was going fine with people dancing and singing to the accompaniment of drums and cymbals, around the cart with the decorated idol. Women and passersby showered the idol with petals. It was great fun and we were all excited.

Suddenly, someone hurled a stone. This created a commotion and people began screaming abuse and trying to locate the miscreants. Some people threw stones back in the direction the stone had come from. Soon it became a fight. Stones were flying in all directions. The volunteers blew shrill whistles trying to quiet everyone and bring the situation under control, but things only got worse.

People started running for their lives. By then the culprits had mingled with the procession. They saw this as an opportunity to molest young girls. I saw a group of men misbehaving with girls under the pretext of controlling the crowds, and others throwing stones. They were not wearing armbands with Babasaheb's picture on them.

I became so enraged at their behavior that I snatched a baton from one of the volunteers. Emboldened by me, even Najuka snatched a baton and together we started hitting the miscreants. We hit them so hard that finally the police intervened. The police threatened that they would put us behind bars if we did not stop. I complained to them that they were not able to do their duty well, and therefore we had to step in. The police finally succeeded in taking control of the situation.

Eventually, our procession continued in a low-key manner and we immersed the idol. When we returned home, everyone fussed over us and called us brave women and garlanded us. It was a big day and my husband was very proud of me.

"I am so glad that you are not just a pretty face," he said.

Sasubai was also proud of me, and she was happy that Najuka was learning to be brave.

One of the old women from our chawl came up to me and

expressed her shock at my unfeminine behavior. But nothing could stop me. I was charged up by what had happened.

"How long do we take things lying down?" I blurted out. "We are not allowed to enter their temples. We can't drink from their wells. We are not allowed to worship Ganapati because we honor Babasaheb alongside. And now, we are not to have a procession to immerse our idol. We won't let them bully us in Mumbai. This is a big city, not a village."

Everyone was shocked at my outburst. That woman who had questioned my behavior quietly walked away.

My husband beamed from ear to ear.

We were living well. But the winds of fate turned. It was sometime around 1929. One day my husband came home dejected and told us that there was a strike in the Great Indian Peninsula Railway.

I wondered why he was so upset, and how the strike would affect us. I had so many questions. He was happy that I took an active interest in his work. And my curiosity was always rewarded with patient answers.

He explained that he was a member of the workers' union. The union had given a call to stop work unless they were given better wages. The union's demand was legitimate and unless the workers organized and threatened, nobody was going to increase their wages.

My man realized that the union could not have chosen a worse time to go on strike. He went to the union officials and tried to reason, respectfully at first. But it had come to blows when the officials questioned his integrity. He explained to the officials that Babasaheb was touring the country, making speeches exhorting workers not to support the strike. Babasaheb was saying there was a worldwide Great Depression, and a strike meant a lot of people would lose their jobs.

"Don't tell us what that self-serving Babasaheb is preaching," the officials told him. "It is all because of him that you low-caste people are losing track of your place in society and trying to mingle with everyone. If you are a member of our union, you have to honor the strike. This is not a time to back out."

My man begged the union to defer the strike for a few months, but the officials were unyielding.

"We gave you a patient hearing because you are a good man and you have worked very hard for our union. Come to your senses and stop listening to the nonsense spread by Babasaheb."

That was the last thing he wanted to hear. In a fit of temper, he gave up his union membership. Now he did not enjoy the protection of being a union member, and things got worse.

One day, he refused to eat any dinner. He even refused to have tea. That was when I suspected something was amiss. I had never known my man to refuse a good cup of tea. I sat by him quietly, waiting for him to open up.

"What can I tell you, Soney? I have let you down," he said feebly. "And I feel let down myself. So many years of hard work, the name I made for myself there with all my good work, everything has gone down the drain."

His face was ashen, and I struggled to understand what he was saying.

"The officials were very happy with my work. They promised to give me a raise . . . and I used to work with even more dedication . . . everything has blown away, Sonu, it has slipped right out of my hands. Many of us are now dismissed from our company. We have all lost our jobs."

He held his head in his hands and in that instant shrank within himself. I can never forget that moment; it is etched in my mind forever.

It was while he was in this dire situation that my man gave in to emotional pressure from his mother and agreed to accept the Yeskar duty in his village.

At first I could not understand why he was not willing to conform to tradition. I could not fathom his anger, or his frustration. I thought that the duties were only a matter of months.

I now knew that things were not as simple as they appeared.

When we reached the outskirts of Nashik, we had been walking continuously for almost four hours. He bought us tea at a small roadside shop where truck drivers gathered. He inquired whether anyone could take us to Mumbai. Unfortunately, they said they had just returned from there.

We sat on the pavement, sipping tea. He had not eaten anything for almost two days. I offered him a bhakri. His face lit up and without a word he polished off all the bhakris, one after another.

"You are very clever, I must say," he said in a soft tone, a playful smile on his face.

He took a deep breath and, looking at the wide expanse of the sky, said, "At last I can breathe freely. I am a human being again. The master of my will."

The tea boy told us of a dharmashala where we could stay, an hour away. Fortified by the tea and his kind words, I was ready to walk on again.

It was midmorning by the time we set out, after catching a few winks of sleep. He told me to wait for him by a tree, and asked around, looking for ways to go to Mumbai. Instead, he came back excited and told me that Babasaheb's posters were everywhere. Someone told him that Babasaheb was to come to Nashik to launch a peaceful agitation—satyagraha—to gain entry into the Kala Ram Temple.

My man looked completely taken in by this idea. Nowhere could I see in him signs of the despair of the previous night.

"We will stay in Nashik and look for work," he said.

"Are we not going to Mumbai?" I asked him.

"We will participate in this movement. Why should Mahars be prevented from entering the temple?" He then added, "Not that I believe in idol worship, or in God for that matter. However, we are also human, and no one can stop us from going where others are allowed. It is a question of our rights, and we are going to fight for them."

III

—⁓⁓⁓—

THE STRUGGLE

DAMU

Nashik had become the hub of activity, with energized groups of Mahars attending meetings, having parleys, and making plans. Everywhere, there were posters with Babasaheb's picture on one side and that of a temple on the other. The message in the center was stark and clear: God belongs to everyone. All Hindus must be allowed into the temple.

Things could not have been more fortuitous for us. I was still in shock at my defiance of village tradition, inspired by Babasaheb, and here was this movement unfolding right before my eyes. Hordes of Mahars from far-off places had gathered, and all of them wore badges on their left shoulder.

We began mingling with the crowds, but I was keen to join them and do something. I could not contain my excitement and went to a volunteer guiding the crowds.

"*Jai* Bhim, hail Babasaheb!" I greeted him loudly and explained that we had neither the badges nor the two annas to buy them, but we were Babasaheb's dedicated followers.

"Never mind," he said. "Come with me." He took us to a small makeshift office in a tent and gave us two badges after entering our names in a register. Proudly, I pinned the badges on Sonu and myself, excited to belong to the social force taking shape right there.

There were many women in the crowd, some with a child in their arms and some with a whole brood of children.

A few volunteers moved among the crowds explaining what was happening.

"We are launching a satyagraha and civil disobedience until they allow us untouchables to enter the Hindu temples. We are equally human and, moreover, we are Hindus. We must be given entry into temples."

Our sentiments would explode in a united cry of "*Jai* Bhim."

I marveled at the choice of venue. Just like the Mahad agitation, Babasaheb had carefully chosen the Kala Ram Temple to launch this agitation.

In the evening, as we sat talking with some activists, I told them about the Chavdar tank march in Mahad.

"You mean you have seen Babasaheb in person?" one of them asked.

I was suddenly elevated in their eyes, and they wanted to know more about the movement in Mumbai. I needed no persuasion, and our talk lasted well into the night while I recited as much of Babasaheb's speeches as I could recall.

They, in turn, told me that preparation had been going on for months, and Babasaheb was guiding them from Mumbai. He would come to Nashik on Ram Navami Day. A committee of local activists was formed to confer with the trustees of the temple, but that had not been of much use, since the trustees refused to even speak to the committee.

The activists threatened to launch an agitation if the trustees did not respond within a week. A call was already issued to untouchables all over the state of Maharashtra to come to Nashik and assert their right to worship Lord Ram in the Kala Ram Temple.[10]

On the day of the agitation, there were people everywhere, greeting each other with "*Jai* Bhim." Around twenty thousand had assembled there. Truly, with such a big force, who would dare treat us as subhuman? I wondered. I was beginning to understand why Babasaheb exhorted all untouchables to unite. So many had flocked to Nashik in response to Babasaheb's call, and our movement had gained momentum.

The meeting began under Babasaheb's stewardship. Local leaders spoke first and outlined the plan. Then as Babasaheb rose to speak, the great mass of people cheered wildly. He explained the purpose of the struggle and recounted his efforts toward peaceful negotiations. "We will not die if we aren't allowed into the temple, nor are we going to be immortalized by gaining entry. We are fighting for equal rights as human beings, and we are not going to accept anything less," he said to thunderous applause.

After the meeting began the great march, the largest I had ever seen. Babasaheb was leading. The band followed him, playing martial tunes, reminding us of the Mahar community's association with the British army. Then came the volunteers. Next in line were about five hundred women. This was a revolution in itself, as it was the first time that Dalit women were participating in a mass movement. They were followed by thousands of orderly protesters, walking with discipline and determination.[11]

When our procession reached the temple, the gates were closed and barricaded. A contingent of armed police, led by a British police superintendent named Reynolds, was guarding the main entrance.

Babasaheb spoke to the police superintendent and then directed the procession to the Godavari River, where another rally was held. Babasaheb announced a peaceful protest in front of the temple gates, beginning the next day. All of us formally enlisted ourselves as volunteers and returned to our tents.

The peaceful agitation began the next day. We joined the crowds at the temple's main gate. There were four gates, with the east gate being the main entrance. The atmosphere was tense. There were hundreds of armed police at each gate, while others watched the protesters like hawks. Reynolds had set up office in a tent, pitched right in front of the temple, and had camped there expecting the agitators to strike in the dead of night.

With thousands of protesters taking turns and forming a human barricade, the temple was sealed and nobody allowed to enter.

The rumor going around was that hundreds of high-caste people were hiding in houses nearby, armed with sticks and batons, ready to attack if we tried to forcibly enter the temple, but we merely squatted at the main entrance, singing. Babasaheb's strict instructions were to maintain a peaceful agitation.

The next day, local leaders called a public meeting and informed us that the upper castes had held an assembly to find a way out of the impasse. It was reported that some liberal Hindu trustees sympathized with the untouchables' demands. However, the orthodox were unwilling to relent. Some had even pelted the liberals with stones and shoes. A few diehards declared that even Lord Ram himself could not make them open the temple to untouchables. Not surprisingly, the meeting ended in confusion.

We were even more determined after this and our sit-in continued amid tension but, thankfully, without any untoward incident.

Two days later, the impasse continued. In the afternoon, an old Brahmin, passing by the temple, saw us squatting at the entrance, singing under the scorching sun. He was so overwhelmed by our determination that he opened his little purse in front of us and gave away all his money. He mocked the upper castes, saying, "Even the stone walls of the temple would melt in the face of your determination to worship the Lord, but not the hearts of the orthodox!"[12]

A few people among the protesters started giving speeches, asking people to renounce Hinduism and join other religions.

"If Hindus do not treat us as equals, what is the point in subscribing to the Hindu religion?"

At that time, Nashik was ablaze with a sensational story. A Brahmin who sympathized with the untouchables had been badly beaten by highborn bullies. He had maintained that untouchability was a stigma on Hinduism and fought to abolish it.

In desperation, he renounced Hinduism and adopted Islam.

He even changed his name from Ganesh Abaji Kulkarni to Khan Mohammed. One day he entered a restaurant and sat in the area reserved for Muslims but was beaten by the highborn hotel owner and thrown out.

A few leaders argued that a change of religion was not the solution. Babasaheb also maintained that renouncing Hinduism would not change anything. The only way to transform things was to reform Hinduism from within.

The agitation continued for the sixth day. In one public meeting on the seventh day, it was announced that Mahatma Gandhi had defied the salt laws imposed by the British in a nearby town called Dandi. Gandhi had also announced a nationwide civil disobedience movement against British rule on behalf of the Indian National Congress.

Meanwhile, a few leaders of the Indian National Congress who had initially supported the abolition of untouchability and the temple entry movement started pressuring Babasaheb to withdraw the agitation. Babasaheb refused to call it off. "They can no longer deny us our basic human rights, and the benefits of civilization and culture," our leader said. "We must continue our movement till we succeed in claiming our birthright.'"

The next day, the regional commissioner, an Indian, came to review the situation, accompanied by the district collector and an armed policeman. To their surprise, we did not stand up to greet them as was expected of us. We just kept singing and chanting slogans, ignoring their presence.

Soon Babasaheb arrived to address our rally and everyone cheered enthusiastically. The officials turned red in anger.

The temple trustees took up their case with the authorities. They claimed that the temple was private property and, therefore, they had the ultimate authority on right of entry. The rumor mill, however, said they were unable to provide documentary evidence of private ownership.

On the other hand, we had evidence that the temple received an annual grant of one thousand rupees from the government and, therefore, was public property. The deadlock continued. Then the commissioner recommended that any gathering in the temple's vicinity be declared unlawful. After much debate, the government rejected this and ordered the commissioner's transfer. The agitation continued.

All this time we were staying in the temporary accommodations erected for the thousands of volunteers. We cooked food and shared it among ourselves. It was an exhilarating experience for both Sonu and myself, to be part of a great social struggle.

At the end of March, Ram Navami, Lord Ram's birth anniversary, was drawing close. The trustees opened the temple almost a month after it was sealed. We were waiting for this, and sprang into action. We formed a human barricade at the entrance, insisting that worship ought to be allowed on a first-come, first-served basis. The gates were hurriedly closed again.

Thousands courted arrest for crossing picket lines and acting as barricades. With baton blows raining upon us, we were packed into police vans, myself included. The local jails were overflowing with protesters. We were driven outside the city and dumped there, with no food, water, or shelter. We remained unfazed. We marched right back, singing and chanting, and within four to five hours were back at the temple. This strategy continued for quite some time. The police did not have enough vans to cart all of us away, and finally they gave up.

The next day, the priests played a foul trick. The head priest's house had a passage and a separate entrance, leading straight to the temple's inner sanctum. The priests quietly began allowing the high castes to enter the temple through the priest's house.

We wanted to block the way to the priest's house, but our leaders maintained that the priest's house was private property and we could not lawfully do so. Babasaheb's instructions had been to launch a peaceful *and* lawful protest.

Nonetheless, Babasaheb took up this matter with the British government. He warned them that such devious acts by the priests were highly provocative.

April 7 was Ram Navami Day, and the priests came up with yet another idea to get around the protesters. Serpentine queues of devotees formed in front of the temple for a glimpse of Lord Ram. Groups of priests flanked every entrance, and they asked the devotees which caste they belonged to before allowing them in. Only high-castes were allowed to go inside.

The high-caste people were angered that they were being asked for their caste before being allowed in.

"Don't you know who we are?"

"You suspect us to be untouchables? And you want us to prove our caste?" they thundered.

"No . . . no, we have no doubt, you are all highborn, but please don't mind our questions. We are helpless, there are Mahars everywhere," the priests explained apologetically. Whatever they did, the priests could not distinguish between people of different castes. When we found this out, some of us started posing as high-castes, and hundreds of untouchables thus entered the temple.

Inside, before offering worship, priests customarily asked people for the family or clan name. To the priests' dismay, many began declaring Mahar names. The priests raised an alarm and demanded police intervention. The police started beating up any untouchable found in the temple. In that stampede, an untouchable girl was shoved by a priest, and to everyone's amazement, she gave him a resounding slap.

Two days after Ram Navami, tradition called for a procession of Lord Ram's chariot through Nashik. Although the untouchables were not admitted to the temple, they were allowed to pull the chariot. In light of the current disturbance, a compromise was reached—the high castes would pull the chariot up to the temple's eastern gate, and from there it would be carried by the untouchables.

But tensions were still running high. The priests became objects of ridicule, since the untouchables had entered the temple right under their noses. The high-castes were angry that the temple had been polluted. They were determined to take revenge.

The priests announced a time for the procession and then quietly gathered much earlier. The highborn hastily led the chariot, cheered on by the priests, and went well past the eastern gate. We were caught unawares, but we quickly got into action and collectively forced the chariot to a halt midway.

The chariot was sidetracked as fights ensued. The police beat us back with sticks, pushing us into alleys. Their batons flew freely and they spared no one, not even women and children. In that frenzy, Sonu escaped unhurt, whereas I received a blow on my right leg. Others cowered with their hands covering their heads as advised by the more experienced among the volunteers. There was rioting and a few agitators set some shops on fire. The fire spread rapidly, damaging a lot of property, bicycles, and cars.

Many protesters, including Babasaheb, were injured. Most of us who were hurt were Mahars, unable to escape the stampede. We were furious and wanted revenge, but Babasaheb addressed us, injured though he was, and calmed us.

All gatherings near the temple were now forbidden and would warrant arrest. The matter went to court, and there was a lull, pending a decision. Babasaheb left for Mumbai to meet the home minister, and the agitation was temporarily suspended.

There was nothing to be done in Nashik now, and all the protesters started returning to their villages.

"What are we going to do? Even if we go to Mumbai, what will we do there?" Sonu asked worriedly.

All my uncertainties came back. I had no idea what awaited us in Mumbai, and I didn't know how to face my mother. But still I was at peace. I had participated in Babasaheb's movement and redeemed the promise that I had made to myself to stand up against injustice.

I was happy that Sonu had stayed with me throughout, shoulder to shoulder. We would fight to give our children a better life than we had had, so they could live with dignity as human beings. Together, we would free ourselves from our shackled existence.

SONU

We returned home to Mumbai. The situation was no better than when we had left. If anything, it was worse. There were long queues outside shops selling subsidized grain. Corruption was rampant, and the subsidized food was resold at higher prices on the black market. There were no jobs and people did not even have money to pay rent.

It was a terribly depressing time. Sasubai was suffering from various ailments. We did not have enough money for meals, so buying medicine or taking her to a doctor was out of the question. I would keep nagging my man to go back to the village. There we would not have to pay rent, we could claim our share of grain, and we could find jobs. Besides, the clean village air would do Sasubai good, I reasoned.

"Have you gone out of your mind?" he yelled at me. "Soney, no matter how much I teach you, you will always be a nitwit."

Once again, my man started doing the rounds to find work. Sometimes he found a job, sometimes he did not. Whenever he worked, he came home exhausted and handed his wages over to Sasubai. When he did not find work, he came home beaten in mind and worn in body.

Once he got lucky and was hired at a construction site. Since he was not a regular, he was made to work longer than the usual eight hours. On top of that, he got only half the wages, while the contractor pocketed the other half. One day, my man approached the contractor to talk about this. But what had been intended as a peaceful dialogue turned into a row, and the next day, my man was out of work again. That did not bother him.

"I have been true to myself and to my beliefs," he declared proudly.

Sasubai was very angry. "At least we managed bhakris for both meals with whatever you were getting."

"I would rather starve than sell my soul for a few annas."

I was secretly happy that he had lost that job. It hurt me to see him come home with blisters and calluses on his hands. I would soothe them by gently rubbing them with coconut oil.

He started looking for work in textile mills but had no luck. Most of the mills had closed due to lockouts and strikes.

Sometimes Laxman, a man who had worked with him on odd jobs, visited us. Then they sat sipping tea and exchanging news — where to find work, and where it was futile to go searching. My man related to Laxman what he had to go through, and only then would I know what he had suffered.

Once I saw Laxman in the bazaar and invited him home for a cup of tea. My man was very dejected that day. I sat in the kitchen listening to them.

"Laxman, I am fed up walking two to three hours every day from Kurla to Pydhunie, and waiting for hours for the seth to assign me some work. Today, against my will, I pleaded for some work and had to return without a single anna. Things were not so bad last year," my man reminisced.

"This same seth was so impressed with me that once he even gave me double the money. Another time, he entrusted me with a road-laying job at Sion and asked me to find workers. He was willing to pay fourteen annas to the men and eleven to the women.

"I gathered a few people and set each one to dig twenty-five-foot-long pits. The work was going very slowly and they were not able to dig even fifteen feet, as the ground was very hard. The gravel and pebbles flew with every blow and hit the workers. Many were getting hurt and I could tell they were very unhappy.

"I knew this would not do. Suddenly I had an idea. I told the women to bring in buckets of water and dump it on the ground to soften it. That way the pebbles would not fly when they started digging.

"I also bought eight annas' worth of liquor for the older men, a few bottles of toddy for the younger ones, and for the women I bought sweet jalebis for four annas. So for a rupee, I not only made them happy but also got more work done. Instead of twenty-five feet, they dug nearly thirty-five.

"The work was done much faster than the seth expected. The boss was very happy with me and asked me where I lived. He told me then that if I reported before nine in the morning, he would give me two annas extra, over and above the one rupee. But I can no longer find that man."

Laxman smiled.

"Damu, you are really clever. Why don't you think up some idea so we could get some money?"

I gave them tea and hastened to the kitchen, when Laxman said, "Sonubai, your husband is a very smart man. Just bear with the bad times now. I am sure he has some plan.

"Remember, Damu? When we first met on Gujarati seth's job, he wanted us to tear down a huge wall. A few workers were struggling with another wall. We began hammering at the wall with iron rods and hammers. But it did not even budge.

"It was already noon, and we were tired and hungry. The seth arrived and was infuriated to see us sitting in a corner. Before he could say anything, I showed him our blistered hands and asked for one anna so we could have some tea."

My man smiled at the memory.

"The seth grumbled but sent us some tea. We sat sipping it

while Damu was lost in thought. Then he snapped his fingers and shouted, 'Idya! It struck me that we only have to make three to four big holes in the wall.'

"I still did not understand what he was getting at. Then he put the rod into the hole. At his chant of '*Jai* Bhim,' with both of us holding either end of the rod, we shook and rattled the wall. We did this a few times and sure enough, the wall began to crumble. The rest was easy."

My man's face was beaming. "We got extra baksheesh and bought train tickets to return home. Those were the days, Laxman, those were the days. What can I tell you? Times are really bad. My ideas are useless now," he said dejectedly.

"But what about your watch repair skills?" Laxman asked.

"That man I was working with pretended to be a saint. He wore a saffron garb and talked to me about prayers and scriptures. We were doing really well. He paid me four annas for every watch that I repaired. I trusted him.

"I thought, how could such a god-fearing man cheat me? I gradually realized that he was not giving me even half of what was due to me. One day I repaired around fifteen watches and he paid me only two rupees.

"When I spoke to him about it, he began shouting, saying that if I wanted to continue working for him, I had to accept his terms.

"I stopped working with him. I will starve but never work for such a scoundrel. I will never cheat, but I will never keep quiet when I know someone is cheating me."

It all began with an upset stomach, loose bowels, and a stomachache. His stomach was on fire, and he would double up in pain after eating.

We gave him all kinds of herbs and medicines; we sent for some potions from a country doctor. I went to many fakirs and sorcerers. I tried out all their remedies. All to no avail. A few of them gave me black threads with charms and beads and said that my husband should wear them around his neck.

I shook my head in despair. I could move mountains but would never be able to persuade him to do such a thing.

I patiently listened to all his yelling, even abuse, without a word.

"I am the woman you have married. You cannot die and leave me alone," I told him.

Then I used a softer tone and asked, "Remember, it takes both rain and sunshine to make a rainbow. Who told me that?"

That made his eyes sparkle.

"We will have children, and we must send them to school to read and write as Babasaheb says. I will not allow you to die now."

I tried hard to be calm, but I broke down.

"I am willing to do whatever it takes to save you. I have fasted for days, without a sip of water. Can't you help me?" I appealed. "Can't you help me save you? Can't you wear this one small thing?"

He kept looking at me for a long time. My heart was fluttering and my face felt hot. My throat went dry as I wondered if his quiet demeanor was the calm before the storm.

But nothing happened. Grudgingly, he stood before me and extended his arm. In submission, he said, "Here, do whatever makes you happy."

Laxman brought him home one day during this period. He had felt suffocated and had begun sweating profusely at the construction site. He had continued working for fear that the contractor would consider him unfit and dismiss him. But he was unable to work for long, and fainted.

"Sonubai," Laxman said in hushed tones, "take him to the doctor immediately. . . . Something is terribly wrong."

We rushed him to the municipal hospital. The doctor said his condition was serious and admitted him immediately. He had ulcers and there were blisters in his intestines.

They continuously checked his pulse and poked needles into him. There were long, thick tubes coming out of his arms. He was always groggy and did not speak much. After eleven days, he came home.

The doctor put him on a diet of buttermilk. My tall, dark mountain was reduced to skin and bones. But every day he went with Laxman, in search of work. He felt guilty about the hospital and medical expenses. He tried all kinds of jobs, from painting and masonry to carpentry and furniture polishing. He soon became a jack-of-all-trades.

For two months he would carry a bottle of thin rice gruel and buttermilk for lunch, and he drank endless cups of tea. If he ate anything else, he suffered heartburn and an upset stomach.

One day we heard that there was a matchbox factory in Kurla, close to where we lived. As soon as I heard this, I asked Najuka to go with me. Najuka was married, but her husband had no job. She often stayed with us. My man was not at home, and Sasubai was too old and ailing to object. Najuka was afraid. She knew my husband would be enraged to know that we had gone looking for work.

I was in no mood to listen.

"I am going, with or without you," I said.

She relented, and we went searching for the place together. We saw a burly contractor talking to a few women. I told him we were sisters and needed a job. We could start working right then, if he wanted.

He let out a bellowing laugh and said, "What about the work? Do you know what it is? And will you be able to sustain it?"

"Saheb, we need this job. We are hardworking. We are prepared to learn. Please do not turn us away."

We were both hired and told to start the next day. We had to dip little sticks in a red mudlike paste and put them away for drying. Later, we had to fill boxes with the dried matchsticks. Then we had to apply some of the red paste to the side of the boxes where the matches could be struck.

The room where we worked was crowded and cramped. The red paste made our eyes smart. Most of us would be sniffling, with runny noses, and it was extremely unpleasant. Our hands blistered from constant contact with the paste.

There was no ventilation, and we sweated in the heat. By the end of our shift, we rushed into the open air, gasping. Though there was not much money in it, we had managed to find work.

Sasubai was kind to us. She had retired long ago and said she didn't mind the housework. I knew it was hard on her, fetching water, washing, and cooking, but in spite of her poor health, she kept food ready for us when we returned home. After a quick wash, we ate together, sharing the happenings of the day.

My man was unhappy that Najuka and I had to work. Sasubai had managed to brush off his protests, and he kept quiet only out of respect for her, though she would taunt him by saying he was gallivanting all day while the women worked hard.

"But you are alive. What kind of a son have I borne, who is ill all the time and gobbles up what the women earn? God is kind, at least I have a hardworking daughter and daughter-in-law. They are my precious tigresses."

Sasubai would turn on me when nothing she said provoked her son.

"You are the one responsible for his laziness. If you had pushed him harder, he would have gone and found some work, but you want to protect him. Look at you facing the brunt of it." Then she would start wailing, and pat my back and smooth my hair.

I liked it when she praised me; but by now, I knew my man well. He was not lazy. I knew how hard he tried, and that he starved the whole day. He looked like a skeleton. He was honest, and though his stubbornness landed him in trouble sometimes, he never compromised on values.

"Aga, Soney, look at you. You've withered to the bone, your

hands are blistered and your eyes dull. Look what we have done to you. If your parents saw you now, how would we face them?" I knew how hard he was trying and how much he was suffering.

One day, Laxman came by when my man was not home. I made him a cup of tea. I could sense that he was restless. Finally, after a long time, he said that I was like a sister to him. For my sake, he was breaking his promise to my man. He made me promise that I would take good care of my man.

I did not understand what he was getting at.

"Sonubai, how shall I tell you?" he said. "This happened about a month ago and Damu made me swear that I would tell no one. And I have not forgiven myself for leaving Damu and taking off, but I could not help it, Sonubai, I could not help it," he said, shaking his head.

"Sonubai, it is only because you are destined to keep the kumkum on your forehead," he said brokenly, "that Damu is still alive."

I shrieked in horror.

"Don't worry, he is fine now. Nothing will happen to him. It was the fourth day that we had walked three hours to get to Pydhunie to look for work. The previous few days, there had been nothing. Yet, each day, we walked long distances in hope.

"Damu had become so weak that every few minutes he would sit on the pavement out of breath. We longed to have a cup of tea to fortify ourselves. But we had no money for tea, or even a train ticket. I was very worried.

"I told Damu that we would travel without a ticket. There are many poor people who steal rides, so why shouldn't we? It is not as if we had the money, I reasoned with him, but he got angry, and amid bouts of coughing, scolded me.

"He told me that I had not learned anything from Babasaheb's teaching.

"But I was insistent. The seth had promised us some work that day and we had to reach there in time, otherwise there were hordes of people waiting to take our place.

"Soon a crowd had gathered around us. Damu was coughing and gasping, and hurling abuse at me, while I stood with my head bowed. Tell me, Sonubai, how could I retaliate against a friend who was so sick? I knew that part of his anger was at his own helplessness. I pleaded, begged, and finally raised my hand against Damu.

"It was unbearable to watch him. It was impossible for him to walk that distance under the blazing sun on an empty stomach. He shouted that he never wanted to see me again.

"Someone in the crowd booed me and said I was not man enough. Damu yelled that I was not a man. I stormed off and decided to go find work by myself.

"After about an hour of walking, I cooled off. Worried, I walked back in search of Damu. I prayed that I would find him sitting where I had left him, but I could not find him. Finally, I decided to come to you, and I found him sitting on that bench near the Hanuman Temple, looking lost but strangely calm.

"After a long silence, he told me that after I left, his entire life had flashed in front of him. He kept hearing the taunts of his mother. The thought of walking long distances for the fourth day in a row, and not finding any work, was so scary that he decided to end his life."

I listened, tears rolling down my face. He had not said a word to me. How could I not have realized something was amiss? I gestured for Laxman to go on.

"Damu told me that he had walked aimlessly till he reached the creek bridge between Kurla and Sion. He stood looking at the water and decided to jump into the creek. There was no point in living. He was a total failure. He could not face his mother or you.

"He climbed the electric tower at the end of the bridge so he could jump to his death from its top. He felt weak and giddy. The glare of the sun reflected off the water and made his eyes smart. Gasping for breath halfway up, he stopped to see if he had reached high enough to jump.

"He blinked to clear his eyes, but he kept seeing a man in saffron robes at the bottom of the tower, waving out to him.

"He rubbed his eyes, thinking it was an illusion, but he now heard the holy man.

"'Son,' the man called out in a gentle and loving tone, 'come down, don't do this. You are meant for bigger things. Come down and think calmly. Your desperation is temporary. It will soon pass, come down.'

"Damu was stupefied. In a daze, he climbed down. He ran around, trying to find the saffron-robed man. There was nobody there. The road was deserted.

"In a daze, Damu walked home. As he neared the house, the thought of facing his mother and the endless arguments and fights made him sit by the Hanuman Temple, pondering.

"He kept wondering if he had really seen a holy man, or if it was just an illusion . . . the voice of his conscience."

I had lost my words.

One day, my man woke up agitated. He said he had not slept the whole night.

"Why do you worry so much?" I tried to console him. "You will soon find a job. God will hear my pleas. Look, you need sleep to regain your health."

"I am not worried, I am hungry," he bellowed. "I could not sleep because I was thinking of spicy mutton mince."

I looked at him, bewildered.

"I know I am going to die whether I eat or not. I have been dreaming of eating some real food. Go: make me some spicy mince and a bhakri. If I have to die, at least let me die happily."

I was upset but could not refuse to please him, though I had no idea how I would find money for the meat.

All he had asked for was some mince. I could not disappoint him. I thought of the eleven rupees saved up for the rent. Mince would cost three rupees. There were ten more days before the rent was due.

I went to the butcher and asked for very finely ground, tender mince. I cooked it with very mild spices. Then I baked thin soft bhakris. I was happy to see him eat heartily after such a long time. That night, he slept well.

The next day, surprisingly, he woke up feeling fine and with a sparkle in his eyes. He decided to look for work. He found a few hours of construction work. His malady seemed to wane with work and good food. We were happy. It seemed to me as if my prayers were finally answered.

DAMU

Several months had passed since our return to Mumbai from the Kala Ram Temple agitation. I looked desperately for work. Wherever I went, I heard only one thing: it is the Great Depression. Aaee nagged me about finding work, but I could not explain to her something that I did not understand. All I could do was keep trying, but Aaee became more bitter by the day. She suggested several times that I should go to Tau Master and seek his help. Reluctantly, I gave in.

It was a Sunday morning in March 1931. Tau Master's face lit up when he saw me.

"Arre, Damu, come on in. Where have you been hiding, young man? And why do you look so weak?"

I murmured something but could not say what was on my mind.

"I heard what a great job Sonu and you did, participating in the Kala Ram Temple agitation. I must say, you made me proud of you."

"What is happening nowadays, Tau Master?" I asked, to keep the conversation going. That was all it took to get him started.

"Damu, which world do you live in? Don't you know that Babasaheb has just returned from England? He pleaded our case before the King Emperor! We have earned this right. See what Babasaheb's movement has won for us!" I looked at him uncomprehendingly.

"The British government convened a historic Round Table Conference in November 1930. Babasaheb was one of the two delegates to represent India's Dalits. Damu, you must keep yourself informed. Don't you read the newspapers? I know you have some difficulty reading, but you must try. Here, look at this. This is a new Marathi fortnightly started by Babasaheb, called *Janata*— The People."[13]

Tau Master showed me issues of the paper, which had details of Babasaheb's social movements, his speeches, and other Dalit issues.

"You must at least make it a point to read *Janata*," Tau Master said while seeing me off. I nodded.

I wanted to tell him, yes, I would like to read the paper. I wanted to read all about Babasaheb. I wanted to dedicate my life to Babasaheb's social movement. But my mind screamed, "First tell me, how do I make both ends meet for my family?" At this thought, I felt ashamed of myself. When Babasaheb was doing so much for Dalits, how could I think only of my family? If Babasaheb was doing so much to improve the lot of all Dalits, the least I could do was uplift at least one family—my own. I vowed to give my children the best possible education and raise them with the spirit of public service. Yes, that would be my mission, but now I desperately needed a job to sustain my family. I must keep trying.

I began doing the rounds yet again. Along with the responsibility of feeding my family, I had to tolerate my mother's bitterness; it was not easy to maintain my sanity. There was darkness all around, and yet I still dreamed of the future.

My mind kept going back to the social movement. I read *Janata* with the help of some people at the teashop. I attended public meetings, between my job searches. I was often torn between family responsibilities and the call of the social movement. But on one occasion in December 1931, nothing could stop me from participating in a black flag demonstration against Mahatma Gandhi.

On that cold December night, hundreds of Dalits assembled at the Mole Station—the marine terminal in Mumbai. They were eagerly awaiting Gandhi's return by ship from London after the Second Round Table Conference. People were saying that Gandhi had taken an uncharitable stand against the Dalits, and that he had strongly opposed Babasaheb Ambedkar. Earlier, at the First Round Table Conference, when Babasaheb was leaving for London, Gandhi's followers had protested with black flags, and this was going to be our return gift to Gandhi![14]

As the night wore on, we waited shivering. Hundreds of Congress activists were also waiting eagerly to welcome Gandhi. It was six in the morning when the ship docked and Gandhi emerged. That was the first time I saw him. With his simple homespun apparel, kind face, and humility of gesture, Gandhi looked like a loving father figure. Even seeing him from a distance I found my anger dissolving. Just then, the Dalit demonstrators began shouting slogans. The cheers from Gandhi's followers were drowned by our slogans. Gandhi remained calm. The battle of slogans soon turned physical. Stones, sticks, and bottles started flying. The police had difficulty controlling the mob, and several people were injured. I thought it was ironic that the arrival of the apostle of nonviolence should have caused so much violence.

As months passed, the differences between Babasaheb and Gandhi became sharper. There was talk of a truce in the Poona Pact of September 1932. I could not understand these developments clearly. I longed to talk to Tau Master. However, I had hardly any time. Then, one day, the opportunity came unexpectedly.

It was, I think, November 1932. A young man from Ozar suddenly turned up at our house. A slim, tall fellow with sharp features, wearing thick glasses, and with a scholarly look, he said he was a distant relative. He had passed matriculation and was hoping to enter a college in Mumbai. He wanted to stay with us for a few days until he could make other arrangements. His name was Rama but he insisted on being called by his Western initials—RD.

Considering our financial difficulties, the arrival of Rama was as welcome as a thirteenth month in a drought year. But Aaee was happy, since this reestablished our contact with the village. She even borrowed money so she could cook at least once a day and ensure that word of our difficulties did not reach Ozar.

While RD stayed with us, the responsibility of getting him used to the city fell on me. The following week, RD was to appear for a job interview and we had to get him ready.

We could make RD a perfect up-to-date gentleman with only a shirt, trousers, tie, and shoes. I knew a little about Western attire since I had worked with a Gora saheb. I took him to a few stores, scared that they would drive us out, but things went well when I explained that we needed clothes for an interview. RD didn't know how to knot a tie. I asked the shopkeeper to show us. RD still didn't get it, but I managed.

He had never worn shoes in his life, and to my amusement, he could not even balance himself, let alone walk in them. So the next morning, I gave RD a dress rehearsal. With Laxman on one side and me on the other, we made RD walk in his new shoes and clothes. We walked the entire tram route from Dadar to Byculla, a distance of five miles. We must have been a sight: RD shy and awkward, flanked by the two of us in our yellowed clothes, nudging him along. The strange looks only made RD more uncomfortable, but finally he got used to the shoes.

It was a big day for all of us when RD finally landed a decent job. Aaee made me take RD to see Tau Master, who was delighted to meet him. The conversation soon gravitated toward Babasaheb's movement, to Gandhi and his disputes with Babasaheb.

"But Tau Master, why don't these great leaders sort out their differences in private?"

Tau Master smiled and said, "They did try, but failed."

He continued, "At Gandhi's request, Babasaheb called on him last year. I gather it did not go well.[15] Do you know Gandhi thought that Babasaheb was not a Dalit? He thought Babasaheb was a benevolent Brahmin who took a deep interest in Dalits."[16]

"No, really?"

"Their approach to the problems of Dalits is fundamentally different. Take for example the expression 'Harijan.' Gandhi has coined this expression for Dalits, the 'people of God.' I think that is Gandhi's way of emphasizing the need for sympathy in dealing with Dalits. Babasaheb resents this because he thinks it is patronizing. Babasaheb says, 'We want our human rights, not sympathy.'"

"And what was the outcome of the Round Table Conference I hear about?"

"A lot of bitterness. Babasaheb responded to Gandhi by calling him 'petty-minded,' and said his behavior was 'unbecoming of a Mahatma.' He said that far from being a friend of the Dalits, Gandhi was not even being an honest foe."[17]

"Is that why they criticize Babasaheb?" I asked.

Before Tau Master could answer, RD butted in. "They condemn Babasaheb's behavior. But why shouldn't he speak like that? Haven't we waited for ages for their change of heart? If political slavery of a hundred and fifty years can justify extreme protests against the British government, surely Dalits are justified in lashing out."

I looked at RD with new respect. Tau Master smiled and said, "These are tactical matters, best left to our leaders."

"But is there a truce finally?" I asked. "They keep talking about the Poona Pact."

"In August the British granted separate seats for Dalits in provincial assemblies."

"Ha, Babasaheb was victorious," I said with a smile.

Tau Master continued. "But Gandhi went back on his word and declared he would fast unto death if separate electorates for Dalits were not abolished."

"Well, that's emotional blackmail!" RD exclaimed.

Tau Master smiled and said, "Young man, you don't understand. Mahatmas don't blackmail. They only exert moral pressure. A furious campaign was launched against Babasaheb. He was called a monster, a traitor, and a hireling. Babasaheb was in a dilemma. On the one hand, there was the life of a great man, and on the other, he had to safeguard Dalit interests. The Poona Pact was the compromise they worked out."

We were so engrossed that we had lost track of time. Tau Master's wife brought us back to earth. "Are you going to have politics for lunch as well?" We laughed, and RD and I got up to leave. Turning to Tau Master, his wife asked, "Did you at least ask Damu whether he has a regular job yet? He looks so haggard."

Tau Master looked at me questioningly. Sheepishly, I admitted I didn't.

"Why didn't you tell me, young man?" he asked. Then he thought for a moment and said, "Let me see, I will speak to someone in United Mills tomorrow. Go and meet the superintendent there after two or three days. Tell him that I have sent you. He may have something for you."

I hastened out, afraid they might see the tears in my eyes.

SONU

One of the local leaders in Babasaheb's movement was an influential man. He was able to get my man a job in the United Mills in Parel. My man was so excited to get a steady full-time job after years of searching.

He had to work eight-hour shifts, with a minimum expected output. Anything above this got him extra pay. He would be up and about before the sun and was at the mill long before his shift began. He would observe experienced workers and talk to them. He was determined to be proficient and began learning in earnest. Within a few months, he had managed to match the most experienced workers, but he was not satisfied. He wanted to be better than everyone.

Some days, my man came home and excitedly told us how he had produced much more than his quota. He was obsessed with being the best. There were also days when he came home frustrated and withdrawn. These times, he sat and sulked because he had not achieved his goal for the day.

Sasubai and I would tease him, but he would tell us about a sign in his mill—"Work Is Worship." He would say, "I believe in it."

Again the next morning he would be up at dawn, and off to the mill before any of us had even woken up.

My man was soon promoted. Skill rather than speed was of importance here. In this new job, the machines moved at high speed and the operator had to concentrate on the levers. My man was paid two rupees extra for this job. It held more excitement and challenge.

He was so proud of his work that one day he took me along. He showed me how he pushed and pulled the different levers and knobs that set the machines going.

I asked all kinds of questions.

"What if you pull this lever first? What does that knob do? What if you halt the process in between?"

He started laughing.

"Silly woman, the cloth will come out damaged."

I sat in a corner and watched him work. I tried to catch his eye, but he was engrossed in what he was doing. Whenever he had a moment, however, he looked at me and smiled. I thought I could sit there for hours just watching him, caressing him with my eyes, my heart overflowing with love.

Toward the end of his shift, he took me to another room. There was a long queue, and we went and stood in line. Slowly, the line inched forward. My man took his salary after signing a form.

"Here, Soney, let me give you my salary today," he said with a smile. I took it but gave it back to him, afraid to carry so much money.

We walked out of the mill to see a few men beating up a man. The man was shouting, "My wife and children will starve. At least leave me some money . . . I will pay you next month." He was screaming between blows.

The moneylenders were dressed peculiarly. They wore colorful turbans, loose, flowing trousers, and knee-length tunics. Their kohl-lined eyes were smudged black and gave them a ferocious look.

My man explained that most workers owed money to these men, the Pathans.

"On payday, the Pathans wait outside to intercept the workers.

They charge very high interest rates, often cheating uneducated people. Some workers hide or slip away unnoticed. A few head straight to the bars and gambling dens."

"What are these women doing here?" I asked.

"These are the wives. They come here to make sure that their husbands do not squander the money."

Listening to these stories, I felt blessed because my man's only hobbies were social service and attending speeches. He handed over his entire salary to Sasubai every month. I was glad that he had given me the money that day.

It was a long walk home, but for once my man slowed his pace for me. I was surprised by the unfamiliar surroundings. But he refused to tell me where we were going. He pointed out different places to me, but I was all mixed up.

"Where are we going? I want to go home. I am tired," was my refrain.

Soon I could see an endless expanse of water. We were at the seashore. For a moment, I thought of the river in my village. The sea crashed with huge waves and looked scary. It had none of the serenity of our river.

We walked barefoot on the silver sand that tickled our feet. It took me a while to find my balance, walking on the slippery sands. He walked right to the edge, close to the crashing waves, and insisted that I join him.

The more I told him I was afraid, the deeper he went into the sea. I was close to tears. Finally, he took pity on me and joined me.

We walked along the shore, munching peanuts. In our village, we always ate peanuts with jaggery. In Mumbai, they ate them salted. I was thirsty, and my man teased me incessantly.

"There is so much water in the sea," he said with a mischievous smile. "Drink as much as you want."

Then he bought us tender coconuts. We watched awestruck as the skinny Malabar boy swiftly struck the coconut shells with a long sharp knife. Two or three skillful blows and the coconut was open, without spilling a single drop of water. With equal ease, he scooped out the soft white coconut flesh.

We sipped the sweet water, gazing at the setting sun, the gentle breeze playing in my hair.

It was getting dark and we had a long walk ahead of us. I walked beside my man hoping that he would rest, but he marched on, lost in thought. Though I was tired, I refused to complain. Soon we could smell something sweet being fried.

"Hmm, those must be fresh, hot jalebis. Who can resist such heavenly sweets?" my man said, turning to me.

We stopped at one of the vendors. The golden yellow jalebis were fried and then dipped into an urn of syrup. We stood savoring the sweets. My man picked up the last piece and surprised me by putting it in my mouth. Hastily, I looked around to see if anyone had seen that intimate gesture.

It was almost eight years since we had been married, yet I had not been able to conceive. Sasubai wanted a grandchild. Her cousins, friends, and relatives pestered her. She told them that because I had to work so hard, my body had become weak and I could not conceive. Nobody believed her. They narrated their own examples.

"Look at us," they said. "We too work very hard, but we produce healthy children by the year!"

Some argued, "Why, even you worked all your life, so where did your children come from?"

"You are a farmer's daughter, you should know." They said, "You have seen how women work hard on the farm and yet have no problem having babies."

"Women in Mumbai work hard and they have children too."

"What are you suggesting?" Sasubai growled at them.

Once, a few women, Sasubai's friends, came to see our new quarters.

"Rahee Bai," they said, "where are the kids? We brought some sweets for the kids."

"How many years has your son been married?"

"About eight," Sasubai muttered.

"Eight years? I remember as though it were yesterday, that you told us what a beautiful, fair daughter-in-law you had got."

"Why? Is there something wrong with her?" one of them asked.

"Of course, it is clear that she cannot make babies,' someone else replied.

"You were very proud of your fair daughter-in-law. Arre, even a dark ugly one would have produced many grandchildren by now and made you happy in your old age."

"We are so sorry for you, Rahee Bai, this is very sad . . . You have no heir to carry on your name. What can you do? You just have to accept it."

I was making tea and they dared to say all these insulting things, knowing very well that I could hear them.

The next one to speak had a sharper tongue. "Why accept it? Your son is young, he can marry again."

"Yes, I agree," said someone else. "He should bring a second wife."

A third interjected, "You must have an heir to carry on your name. Otherwise, how can you die in peace?"

"What can I say? Who listens to me in this house?' Sasubai said, wiping her eyes with the end of her sari. Then she looked at me and said, "I have been thinking about getting him another wife. I love Sonu like a daughter, but I want to see my grandchildren before I die."

I could not take it anymore. I cried quietly, hiding my face between my knees.

"No need to make such a fuss," they taunted. "You cannot have it all. God has made you good-looking but he has not intended you to have children. That is all."

A neighbor who had heard the conversation joined in. "Soney, there is no need to cry. Look at it this way, the other woman can have children, and you can look after them."

"Maybe you women can talk to my son and put some sense into him. Perhaps he will listen to you," said Sasubai.

Two of the older women approached my man, who had been sitting in a corner of the room silently listening to all this talk. They told him how much they cared for his mother. They explained the importance of having an heir in order to die in peace.

"You are still so young. Get another wife. You will produce a child in no time."

"Think of how happy you will make your mother."

My man was taking it all in quietly. I could see how his ears reddened in anger. His face wore a severe expression. He saw me sitting in a corner, crying, and suddenly sprang up. He stood like a mountain, towering over everyone.

"Aaee," he said sharply. "I do not want to see these women in this house again. Do you understand?" He glared at Sasubai.

"I am not going to marry again, and that is that. We do not have such a large estate that we need to worry about having heirs. It doesn't matter if we do not have children."

He said to Sasubai, "If you are so eager to shower love and affection on grandchildren, gather all the urchins in our locality and love them as your own."

Sasubai was shocked into silence.

"If all you want is an heir, we will adopt one. We will have nothing to do with these women." He turned to the women. "Do not provoke my mother again. I do not mean to be rude. But this is my final warning."

Then he warned Sasubai, "Even if someone dies in their house, we will not go to offer condolences, and tell them that if someone dies here, they need not come to us. Nobody is going to tell me what I should do."

He began pacing the floor. Suddenly, he stopped in front of me and said, "And I don't want to see you crying again over this. I will never marry another woman."

Then he gently whispered, "Come on . . . at least smile now."

One day, it was past dinnertime, and there was no sign of my man. I was beginning to get worried.

"Why are you worried?" Sasubai tried to pacify me.

"Maybe he has gone to hear some speech."

I felt something was amiss. I stood at the door, my eyes scanning the road. Some men in the neighborhood often returned home late after drinking or gambling. In all the years of our marriage, I had never known my man to do that.

A few hours later, I saw him walking home accompanied by two men. I was relieved but worried about the unfamiliar men with him. As he came closer, I could see his arm in a sling, and his palm and thumb bandaged. I rushed forward, trying hard to control my tears.

His shirt was bloody and stained. The bandage too had spots of blood. I called out to Sasubai.

"What have you done, Damu, to make Soney scream like a madwoman?" she called out.

One of the men said, "Bai, he has lost his thumb. It was trapped in one of the machines. We took him to the hospital."

"Did the doctors make it all right?" I asked in a hushed voice. Nobody replied, and I began to get hysterical.

"Sonu, calm down. I have lost my thumb," my man said.

One of the men said apologetically, "The severed thumb was badly mangled under the machine, and the doctors were not able to do anything. They have put a few stitches on the wound and given him some medication."

The next morning, my man was ready to go to work at his usual time. Sasubai tried hard to dissuade him, but it only made him more determined. He was back before noon, raging with fever and anger.

"They have no work for me. They said it is dangerous to work without a thumb. I was one of their best workers. They gave me fifty rupees as compensation and dismissed me."

He was in shock, and so were we. None of us could believe how much our lives had changed in one day. The bad times had set their sights on us again.

DAMU

Losing my thumb was another big blow. I was frustrated earlier, doing odd jobs, making a rupee or two, but I had no words to describe what I felt now—turned away from one job after another when they saw my bandaged hand. I was at a complete loss, and even when I knew that I should probably stay at home and let my thumb heal, I continued doing the rounds looking for jobs—mostly so I could avoid being at home and facing my mother and Sonu.

To make matters worse, I had bitterly scolded Sonu when she told me of her various plans to bring home some money. That was more than I could bear: my wife going out to make money. That only made the realization hit me harder, that yet again I had failed her.

Sonu had my mother's unstinting support. While Sonu was out, she did whatever little housework her ailing health would permit. Unfazed by my tantrums, Sonu was up early in the morning to go to the wholesale market and buy fruits and vegetables to vend locally. In the mornings, she meticulously arranged her wares under a tree near the textile mill.

Sonu had a great knack for talking. She befriended many workers, who treated her as a sister. She asked after their families' well-being and offered bits of advice. I asked my friend Laxman to look out for her and he marveled at how Sonu conducted her business. She managed to bring in about eight to ten rupees every day. But

I never acknowledged her contribution. I felt that Sonu should earn enough only to take care of herself. I was determined to fend for myself, and made sure that I found some odd job even if it paid very little.

Once, I walked aimlessly for more than three hours. I came upon two boys with a handful of posters and a bucket of glue. They were going around sticking the posters on every wall. I could tell that the boys could not read the posters because some of them were stuck upside down. The boys burst out laughing when I told them what they were doing.

Intently, I tried to read what the posters said. I managed to read Babasaheb's name. After that, I walked with them, making sure all the posters were put on properly. It turned out that they were working for Tau Master's group, organizing Babasaheb's upcoming speech. I walked straight to Tau Master's home. As always, he was happy to see me. But when he saw my bandaged hand, he worried that I would not be able to do much work. I assured him that my hand did not bother me and that I wanted to do something, anything, to kill my boredom, and make a little money on the side.

Tau Master looked thoughtful for a while. Then he scribbled a note and asked me to visit his neighbor Upshum Guruji. Tau Master assured me that Guruji would have some work for me. I was hesitant to leave and tried persuading Tau Master to let me work for him. Sternly, he drove me out and asked me to report to him later.

Upshum Guruji's house was packed with people—activists discussing plans and assigning work. I found out that Guruji was Babasaheb's devoted activist and a local leader of the Dalit movement. I managed to approach him after waiting for several hours. Not a word emerged from my mouth, awed as I was by Guruji's persona; quietly, I proffered Tau Master's note to him.

"So you want some work. Hmm . . . you were in Nashik and Mahad too . . . looks like you have been involved in a few protests. Can you talk well?" he asked me.

I was thrilled and in a sudden bout of inspiration, I poured out all that I knew about what Babasaheb was doing. I became self-conscious when I realized that the activists were all looking at me. That put a stop to my blabbering and softly I said, "Yes, I can talk. I am willing to do any work that you give me."

He asked me to report the next morning. I would be paid three rupees for every day that I worked. At first I did odd chores such as getting posters printed, putting them up, or going from shop to shop collecting subscriptions, or publicizing Guruji's speeches. After about a month, I became Guruji's assistant and went everywhere with him. Now I earned four rupees a day, and, more important, got a lot of respect from the other activists.

Being an assistant required me to polish my reading skills. I was ashamed when Guruji caught me struggling to read out the news to him.

"Damu, you cannot read well," he said. "What will you teach your children? You have to set an example for them. From tomorrow, I want you to read the paper and then come and tell me the news."

That was all the prodding I needed. From then on, I spent every spare moment poring over the newspaper, my index finger following each line. I remembered the story Tau Master had told us about Mahatma Phule, and how he had faced society's wrath to educate Savitri, his wife.

"Sonu, do you know that Savitri started a school for women, teaching them to read and write? People threw stones at her and abused her when she walked to the school. But she went on teaching undeterred."

That managed to spark Sonu's interest, and soon she was learning too. I bought her a slate and chalk, and every night after dinner, I insisted that she practice writing the alphabet. Initially, my mother just shot us a few obnoxious looks. But after a few days, she could take it no more.

"Is Sonu going to be a barrister?" she asked contemptuously.

"No, but if she learns to read and write, she can make sure that our children become no less than a barrister," I replied.

"Then teach your children. Why her?"

"That we will, for sure. But I want Sonu to learn, so that we can raise our children better."

"You keep talking about your children, but where are they?"

Sonu burst into tears, and I was speechless.

By 1935, the national freedom struggle had cooled down considerably.[18] Over the years, I began understanding the political situation—initially, thanks to Tau Master, and later, because I had started reading the newspapers to follow Babasaheb's activities.

Our Dalit movement had lost momentum. Babasaheb had accepted a job as the head of Government Law College in Mumbai, and there was some talk of him being made a judge in the Mumbai High Court or a minister in the new government. Babasaheb had managed to spark national interest in our movement, and had succeeded in awakening the Dalit masses and uniting them. But we had reached an impasse. We had a few agitations and occasional public meetings, but there was none of the early fervor. Both major protests—the one at the Chavdar tank in Mahad, and at the Kala Ram Temple in Nashik—were, unfortunately, the subjects of litigation. Babasaheb was fighting the suits and the cases were dragging on.

I heard a lot of political gossip working with Upshum Guruji. The latest news created a furor in our community. While returning from Mahad to Mumbai from one of the court hearings, Babasaheb's car broke down on the way. It was raining but no one in that village would offer food or shelter to an untouchable. After spending the night under a tree, wet and hungry, Babasaheb was so agitated that on his return to Mumbai he shut himself in a room.

More stormy news. A local daily carried the news that Babasaheb was going to declare that Dalits should change their religion, renouncing Hinduism. I rushed to Upshum Guruji's house, to find him in a heated discussion with a group of men.

"Damu, I am glad you are here," he said.

"What is this I hear about conversion? Are we all going to change our religion?" I came straight to the point.

"It is true that Babasaheb has been contemplating renouncing the Hindu faith."

"But why?" asked someone. "All along Babasaheb has been telling us that the only way to reform the Hindu religion is by fighting it from within."

Everyone was agitated, asking questions. Someone said, "At the time of the First Round Table Conference, Babasaheb had demanded that we untouchables should be treated as a break-away group of Hindus."

"What does he have in mind now? Why doesn't he clearly state what he wants us to do?"

Guruji looked unflustered by the barrage of questions and sat slicing his betel nuts. Sometimes his coolness irritated me, but I knew that such calm could only come from wisdom. After chewing on a nut for a while, he finally began speaking in a firm but even voice.

"This has been going on for quite some time now. For the last decade, Babasaheb has tried to create a legitimate place for Dalits in Hindu society, and the upper castes have not budged. And now out of sheer frustration, he is seriously contemplating a change of religion. He is convinced that we Dalits cannot attain our full potential while crushed under the Hindu system. What is required is a new religion that will welcome us and restore our pride."

"What religion does he want us to adopt then? Islam? Christianity?" I asked, my heart racing with the thought of doing something revolutionary.

"Not so fast, young man. We all know that Babasaheb will not make a hasty decision. He will do what is best for all of us and he will do it when the time is right." For a while, everyone was quiet.

"Babasaheb has organized a conference in Yeola, a small town near Nashik, in October to review the situation in light of the Government of India Act, and its implications for our ten-year struggle against discrimination."

Then, raising his voice, Guruji said, "I would like all of you to volunteer. There is a lot of work to be done—organizing such a huge conference is a big challenge, my friends. Let's get on with it."

It was exciting to be made an officially recognized volunteer. I knew everything that was happening at the political level in great detail, and also learned a lot by watching Guruji in action. I was among the hundreds of activists making the arrangements for the more than ten thousand people expected to show up. This time Sonu did not join me. My mother forbade her from participating. We had to organize the printing and distribution of leaflets and posters announcing the conference. There was an acute shortage of funds. The conference was hardly a week away and a few of us left for Yeola to work out the details. We were exhausted yet giddy and working at a feverish pace. We would often discuss what Babasaheb was likely to announce.

Finally, the day arrived, and with it thousands of participants in Yeola. Amid loud cheering, Babasaheb thanked all of us for the unity we were demonstrating in our struggle. He spoke of our suffering under the hegemony of the upper castes.

Babasaheb described how our struggle over the past decade to secure basic rights and equal status within Hindu society had failed. Babasaheb asked us whether it would not be better to give up Hinduism, and embrace another faith that would unreservedly give us equal status.

There was an audible hush, and after a moment he announced: "Unfortunately, I was born a Hindu untouchable—there was nothing I could do to prevent it. However, it is well within my power to refuse to live under ignoble and humiliating conditions. I solemnly assure you that I will not die a Hindu."[19]

He then announced a change of strategy in our struggle. He

exhorted us to stop wasting our energy on fruitless endeavors, such as fighting for entry into Hindu temples, and redirect our efforts toward securing respect, independence, and equality with others through education.[20]

Babasaheb's speech sent shock waves throughout the country. Some called it a bluff and a political stunt. Others, who knew the strength of Babasaheb's character, could not doubt his determination. Some called him a messiah; others felt it was a suicidal step.

All eyes were on Gandhi for his reaction, which was not long in coming: "Religion is not like a house or a clock which can be changed at will. It is an integral part of one's own self, rather than of the body. I am convinced that a change of faith will not serve the cause which they have at heart." Gandhi also predicted that the millions of illiterate and unsophisticated Dalits would not renounce their faith,[21] for they were concerned with day-to-day survival rather than Babasaheb's "attention-seeking stunts." Gandhi's pronouncements did not convince other religious minorities such as the Muslims, Christians, and Sikhs. They saw this as a great opportunity to convert Dalits and gain strength for their own faiths. Babasaheb's house was flooded with letters and telegrams. Whereas most of them waxed eloquent about the reasons their religion was superior, some offered tangible rewards. A few letters, sent by Hindu fanatics, were reportedly written in blood.

Our social movement had taken on a new and exciting dimension. There was no turning back.

Following the Yeola conference, there were a number of other conferences—in Nashik, in Pune, and then a major one in Mumbai in 1936. Hundreds of activists like me had thrown themselves into the organization of these conferences. We discussed every small detail and often debated the merits of adopting a new religion.

But Babasaheb was always sure that Dalits would gain their freedom. "What will India gain by independence? Just as independence is necessary for India, change of religion is necessary for

Dalits. Hinduism made us untouchables, and giving up Hinduism is the only way to bring *touchability* to our lives. The underlying motive in both movements is the desire for freedom."[22]

Babasaheb's words resonated throughout the country. He said that religion is for man, and not man for religion. A religion that does not recognize untouchables as human beings, treats them worse than animals, or refuses to give them water from public wells, is not worthy of being called a religion.

Babasaheb exhorted us to seek refuge in logic and reason. That was the essence of his message, and it had a deep impact on me. I thought a lot about converting. While I had full faith in the path laid out for us by Babasaheb, I knew that it was not going to be easy to convince my wife and mother, both deeply entrenched in the Hindu way of life.

Over the years, Babasaheb had assumed the role of a father figure for millions of Dalits. We felt that he belonged to us. We worried that his health was failing. After the death of his wife, Ramabai, in 1935, he was extremely lonely, and he had no one to look after him. After repeated bouts of ill health, he was advised to seek a change of climate. Toward the end of 1936, he finally managed to find time to go to Europe.

For a while, there was no news from Babasaheb, and things quieted down. In 1937, a leading weekly broke the news that Babasaheb had married an Englishwoman in London and was returning to India with her.[23] Naturally, this caused an uproar among Dalits. Nobody knew whether it was just a rumor. Many people were uncomfortable with the idea, but no one was prepared to criticize Babasaheb.

Sonu brought us the gossip doing the rounds at the water pumps: "For Babasaheb, all Dalit women are like sisters, daughters, or mothers. He couldn't marry any of them and therefore he had to marry a foreigner!"

On the day that Babasaheb arrived, hundreds of Dalits gathered to greet him and his wife. A group of women were ready with the traditional welcome of garlands and lamps. Sonu and I were among the crowd jostling to get a better view. We could see Babasaheb wearing his distinctive felt hat, walking down the ramp from the ship. We struggled to see his companion but, alas, he had landed alone. Babasaheb had not married a white woman after all.

The first general election was scheduled for February 1937. After returning from Europe, Babasaheb founded a new political party called the Independent Labour Party. It drew up a comprehensive program addressing the grievances of landless laborers, farmers, and workers. Upshum Guruji was elected one of the secretaries of the party. I had become Guruji's right-hand man and, naturally, I was catapulted into election activity.

None of us had any experience working on a campaign. All we knew was that we were committed to Babasaheb and willing to work hard. I worked virtually around the clock—distributing leaflets, arranging meetings in surrounding towns, doing door-to-door publicity, and organizing demonstrations. The work was backbreaking, but several of our candidates won, and Babasaheb was elected with a huge majority.

In March 1937, more good news followed. The Bombay High Court settled the protracted Mahad case, allowing Dalits to use water from the Chavdar tank. There was jubilation all around.

Throughout the election process and even before, my role was limited to that of an activist at the grassroots level. The work was gratifying but I had no steady income. Volunteering had become my primary job, and I used my spare time to do some odd jobs here and there. After the elections, however, there wasn't much work for activists.

There was growing tension at home and I dreaded returning without any money, having to pacify my mother and assure her that I would do better the next day. I began staying at Guruji's house sometimes, sleeping on the veranda. But soon after, I got a regular job with the Mumbai Port Trust Railways.

I could not believe my good fortune. I still remember the day. It was May 1937. After much prying and badgering, Sonu finally admitted it was due to the efforts of my ailing mother, who had bribed an official to get me in. I was outraged, but under pressure from Sonu kept quiet about the secret.

With the new job, I had not only a steady income but also a small apartment in the official quarters. We were excited to move out of our dilapidated chawl in Kurla to a much better place in Wadala.

SONU

Mumbai Port Trust had allotted my man living quarters. We moved from our one room in Kurla to a three-room tenement in Wadala. Najuka lived close by with her husband, who also worked for the Mumbai Port Trust. I looked forward to our new life.

But it was not easy to leave Kurla. We carried with us years of memories. As I turned back for one last look, I remembered how I had kicked over the rice pail on the threshold, scared and shy. The thought of our first night together was enough to send my heart racing. The day Najuka first showed me the water pumps, the day the water pot slipped from my hand and crashed into pieces. The day my man lost his job. It was endless, but on the whole, this house had been good to us. I wondered whether the new quarters would bring us luck.

The spacious rooms and the homey atmosphere in the quarters quickly won us over. There was camaraderie among the families living there, many of them Dalits. All the children played together, under the watchful eyes of one neighbor or another. We had soon settled into a routine and began enjoying life in Wadala.

"Sonu, looks like there is good news on the way," elderly Lakshmi kaku said to me with a gleam in her eye. She had noticed me throwing up in the mornings. I missed a heartbeat, afraid to think what it could be . . . or not be.

For two weeks, I had been anxious. Each morning I expected my monthly curse. I had not even noticed that there was no sign of it. Then I began feeling queasy in the mornings. I made tea for everyone and before I had even sipped some, the smell of the brew would send me running to throw up.

"The way it looks, you are definitely having morning sickness. Let me take a look at you," Lakshmi kaku said kindly.

She came to our house when my husband was out. She asked me to lie down and felt my stomach all over. Then before I knew what she intended to do, she lifted my blouse and peered at my nipples. I felt embarrassed, but she assured me that she knew what she was doing. She told me I was six weeks pregnant. I could not believe it. I kept asking her if she was sure.

"But how can it be possible? If it did not happen for twelve years, how could it happen now? Are you sure, Lakshmi kaku? Everyone has told me that there is some problem with me."

"Aga Soney, don't question the will of God. Be happy with the gift sent by Him and rejoice. I have seen three daughters-in-law get pregnant and have babies faster than we could care for them. Don't worry, just arrange to send word to your Sasubai."

I ran from one room to the other, looking out of every window. I wanted to shout with joy, shout out my good news to the blue skies, the chirping birds, and cool green trees. I wanted to tell every passerby and stranger.

I could not stop smiling. I rushed to the mirror and peered at myself for a long time. I thought I saw a faint glow on my face. It was such good news. I waited eagerly by the window, waiting for my man to return.

I played around with what I would tell him. How I would tell him. What would he say? Each time the thought that I was going to be a mother hit me, I felt as if Lakshmi kaku was telling me the good news for the first time.

I saw my man approaching home and I rushed toward him, but

then embarrassed, turned back. I went into the kitchen to make him some tea, my heart thumping crazily.

"Someone looks very happy today," he teased me. I looked up at him, but no words came out.

I gave him tea, wanting to tell him, but I was too shy to break the good news. I kept trying to hint in different ways.

"We are going to have additional expenses now," I said, then added, "Soon we are going to lose a peaceful night's sleep."

"Yes, Ganapati festival is in the offing and we will have to buy new clothes, and they will play loud music till late in the night!"

I shook my head in consternation. This man who is so intelligent, how can he be so dense?

"We are going to have additional responsibilities now," I said. But still he did not understand what I was saying. In the end I forced myself to be brave.

"I was saying . . ."

I hesitated as my man looked at me expectantly.

"How about sending word to Sasubai to come to Mumbai as soon as possible?"

"Why? What's wrong? Let her stay in Nashik awhile. She has only just left."

Again, I fell silent. Finally, I thought of another hint.

"Nowadays, I crave to eat village berries, raw tamarind, and fresh mango pickle. Sasubai can get them from the village."

He suddenly looked at me sharply.

"You are . . . I am . . . I mean we . . ." he faltered.

I nodded, shyly averting my eyes. He was so overjoyed that he lifted me off the floor and spun me around the room. Then suddenly he stopped. Very gently, he put me down.

"What was I doing? Are you . . . is the . . . the baby all right?"

I was red with embarrassment. He rushed off to find somebody who was going to Nashik, to deliver the message personally.

He was still so excited when he returned that he pulled me away from the stove and made me sit next to him.

"I will cook today. You need to rest in your condition. Oh, when will Aaee come? I don't even know what needs to be done." He began pacing. "We must see a doctor at once to make sure," he said as if he had hit upon a great idea.

"But," I said, "doctors are men, and how will a man know these things?"

"My silly love," he said, pinching my nose, "now you need to grow up. Even women can be doctors, and we will find you one."

"But why do we need a doctor? Can't you trust me? I told you that Lakshmi kaku has examined me. She said I am six weeks in the family way."

"It is always better. It has happened a long time after our marriage and we need to make sure that everything is fine."

Every day he would fuss over me so much that it became embarrassing. A few neighbors even chided him that I was only pregnant, not incapacitated or sick. But he would not listen.

"Till Aaee comes back, I have to take care of Sonu. If anything happens to her, I will never forgive myself and, besides, Aaee will kill me."

In no time, Sasubai arrived with bags full of berries and everything else. She had abandoned her precious onion crop, ruined by her sister-in-law, who left the hose running one night. When she heard our news, she said, "Oh well! The onion crop is not as important as the baby and Sonubai."

Sasubai started fussing over me. She gave me lots to eat, but I couldn't eat at all. I was throwing up everything.

"Why are you forcing me to eat when I throw up all the time?"

My mother-in-law put her hand on my tummy and said, "The baby needs food to grow. You must eat for the two of you."

"Why does he make me throw it up then?"

She smiled when she noticed that I was referring to the baby as "he."

"He is getting stronger with the food you eat, but as he grows, he needs more room in your tummy so he makes you throw up the food. You will soon be all right."

My man insisted on taking me to a woman doctor, who gave me some medicine and instructed me to eat and sleep well. She also had me continue doing regular work, which Sasubai had forbidden.

After about three months, when I was feeling better, Sasubai went back to the village to look after the fields.

She assured me that I looked perfect and nothing would happen to me.

The days dragged. I was about six months pregnant and became tired easily.

I also enjoyed the sensation of the baby in my tummy—my own flesh and blood, moving and kicking. I felt at peace now that we were going to have an heir, even if we did not have much to leave him.

When I lay down beside my man after a hard day's work, and let him feel the movements in my stomach, I felt as if I owned the world. He would notice how my body was changing—my pelvis, my breasts, my waist, even my nose as I breathed and, of course, my stomach. I was proud and shy. We would often play the game of "Is it a boy or a girl?"

I wondered whether my mother-in-law would be disappointed if it was a girl. I wondered what names she and Najuka had chosen. As the aunt, Najuka would have the honor of naming the baby, but what about us? It was our baby and we should have the right to name it.

I was already getting possessive of the baby. My man kept telling me that irrespective of whether it was a boy or girl, we should just be happy to have a healthy baby.

I thought about the long years that I had waited for a child. It was about twelve years since we married. When I had first come to stay with my man, I was too young and had never thought of babies. They all treated me like a little girl back then. For me, marriage meant being with my man and in-laws, obeying them, and working hard for them.

I had learned a lot from my man. I had also learned a lot about Babasaheb, who said both men and women need to be educated, but I could never imagine myself going to school and learning to read and write. In the twelve years that I could not conceive, my man would keep encouraging me to go to school and do social service like Savitri, but I always knew that was not for me.

The thought that I would never have a baby of my own troubled me. Looking for a remedy to have a child, I had gone from one neighbor to another, and to their friends and relatives. I had done everything they had suggested. I fasted for two or three days at a stretch. I went without a sip of water on those days. I went to all the temples, took vows, and made offerings. I also went to the church in Mahim and offered a wax baby, which had cost me a lot of money.

I consulted sadhus, pirs, fakirs, and other holy men. I sent offerings to Mariaai and various village deities. I went to witch doctors. I worshipped the banyan tree, which has many branches and roots and is fruitful all year.

Earlier, I did all the housework in addition to working in the matchbox factory. That would leave me exhausted. Besides, I worried that they would get my man another wife. The fasting and penances were taking a toll on my health.

During my first pregnancy, I was always in and out of the doctor's clinic. Sasubai grumbled. She did not like the modern ways.

When the time came, everyone fussed over me. My contractions were feeble and they were worried. Everyone tried to keep my spirits up and did not let me sense that there was anything amiss. My water had broken and the baby was becoming dry. The nurses said they could see the baby's head, but it refused to come out. They were trying to decide whether an operation was in order, when I screamed my guts out and with one sharp, painful contraction, the baby was out.

They said they had to spank it to make it cry. "It's a boy! Congratulations, it's a boy!" they announced to Sasubai and my man.

My baby was born on July 13, 1938.

Sasubai was eager to hold the baby, but the doctor said he was too weak, weighing only three and a half pounds. The nurses asked my man to bring two bundles of cotton wool and instructed us to keep the baby cocooned in it. The doctor warned us to be extra careful.

That gave Sasubai the chance she was looking for. From that moment on, she was the only one to handle the baby. She would bathe him, change him, and wash his diapers. The only time I had the baby was for feeding. Luckily, the baby was so tiny that he could not drink much at a time, and had to be fed often.

Sasubai performed all the religious rites and fed the baby traditional herbal potions. The doctor had warned us not to do so, but she paid no heed. She was the authority and nobody could question her, as no one else knew anything about raising babies.

Najuka was invited for the naming ceremony, and although she was honored as the aunt, Sasubai had already chosen the name Janardan. She dressed the baby in the new clothes that she had stitched. She also put strings of black beads around his neck, wrists, and ankles to ward off evil spirits. As if that was not enough, she applied black dots of kohl on his forehead, cheeks, and chin.

Everyone gathered to look at him, and praised him. They were cooing and cuddling, when he started bawling with hunger. His whole face was smudged black and he looked like a little monkey. I laughed. "Look, my little chimp now looks exactly like his father, dark as a mountain wall!"

SONU

Years had passed since I was blessed with our first child. The excitement of a new baby in our family had long worn out. After the first one, I had more babies, more than we were able to cope with. I had six of them: four sons—Janu, Sudha, Dina and Chhotu; and two daughters—Leela and Trusha. Every three years I had a child, and we raised them without much ado. All of them, except Chhotu, who was still a toddler, were old enough to go to school.

My man's declaration that we would convert to Buddhism had set off a raging fight at home. It was understood that he would make all the decisions, and I would follow them unquestioningly. But this was different. It was he who had taught me to think and reason, and that is what I was going to do.

"Today you are saying you don't like Hinduism so you want to change. It is religion that you want to change, not clothes!"

"Sonu, what's wrong with you? You will do as I say," he thundered.

"It's always you, you, and you, Damodar Runjaji Jadhav. What about me? I am the insignificant Sonu, always nodding her head to whatever you say and walking behind you like your shadow?"

"I am going to get converted and so will my children."

"Your children? Your children?" I yelled.

"And so will you."

"There is no reason for all of us to get converted," I insisted.

"You will do as I say," he said with finality.

"I am doing just as you have said . . . did you not teach me to think for myself? That is what I am doing. You said that one should not be like mere cattle . . . nodding one's head . . ."

My man was shocked. He looked at me with his eyebrows raised. I stood in front of him with my hands on my hips, and glared right back. It was as if I were possessed.

"I want my children to grow up and have a dignified life," he declared. "I want them to be respected, and I am sending them to school just as Babasaheb has said. But if they remain Hindus, they will always be treated as inferior. They will never have a respectable place in society. I will see to it that my children don't suffer like we have."

"*Your* children?" I shrieked. "They are more my children than yours."

I could not control the quiver in my voice, but I would not give up. "The world may praise you for following Babasaheb's teachings and sending the children to school, but does that make them your children? Who do you think bore the kids? I am the one who carried them in my womb for nine months. I am the one who went through the excruciating labor pains."

My man looked bewildered, wondering if I was the same Sonu who trembled with fear when his temper flared up. Over the years, he had become used to the Sonu he had married—docile and shy, the Sonu who would hesitate to raise her downcast eyes and look him in the eye. But he had taught me to think for myself, and now I had found the nerve to voice my thoughts. I was gesticulating frantically, my voice rising.

Najuka, who was visiting us, was shocked. "Eh, Sonu," she said, "what's wrong with you? Don't you have any respect for my brother? If I had yelled at my husband like that, he would have socked me in the eye by now."

"Najuka, don't take his side just because he is your blood. You tell me. Is it not I who bore and raised the kids, bathed their mud-caked bodies, and washed their bums? And he says they are his children! Who got up at five o'clock in the morning to pat fresh bhakris for them? I labored when he snored under his blanket. Who stayed up nights through the children's teething and all their illnesses? He thinks he sent them to school, and that is why he is so great. Hah! Yes, he is right I am no one . . . I don't count."

I raged on. All that I had kept dammed up came pouring out. My man sat quietly, baffled, on the mat in a corner, our argument set aside, as Najuka and I talked on.

"I was not even ten when I married him. You were a little girl then, Najuka. . . . Let me see . . . now I have been married to him for more than thirty monsoons. It has been a long journey, and my journey all along was in the form of a shadow . . . walking behind him, following in his footsteps unquestioningly—whether I liked it or not. Who cared what I felt?

"Over the years, he taught me to think and question. He encouraged me to debate and argue with him—for the sake of arguing, and because it amused him to see me defy him. Now his amusement is over, it's back to reality, and to what Jadhav wishes."

I blushed at what I had said. Never had I referred to him by his family name, as the outsiders did out of respect. Najuka burst out laughing and tried to make light of my feelings. But there was no stopping the storm of my thoughts.

"I have come of age, Najuka, finally I have found my tongue. Over the years, I learned to think for myself, but until now I had never gathered the nerve to speak against him. One severe disapproving look from him and I would swallow the words on the tip of my tongue. It's not that I mean disrespect toward your brother— and you have seen me, since the time I came to this house years and years ago." I broke into a sob and cried on Najuka's shoulder. At a loss for words, my man left us alone.

An incredible lightness descended on me. I felt wonderful after letting go of all that I had held in on a tight leash. The lines had been drawn and I had created an identity by making myself heard. Not that it changed reality; my life was still tied to my man.

Najuka tried hard to console me but in the end, even she had tears in her eyes. She remembered a ditty that her mother used to sing:

> We, *the women, who rule the house*
> *But ours is not to question why . . .*
> *Ours is but to do and die and*
> *Husband never to defy.*

I had lived all my life in accordance with what my man wanted for us. But I could not do it unquestioningly anymore.

The next day, my man came home with the newspaper. This had become a ritual: surrounded by a group from our locality, he soaked up every word of the editorial and animatedly delivered it to his eager listeners.

I knew he had some difficulty reading, and I wondered how much he actually read from the paper and how much was hearsay. He was never short of news and seemed to know everything. Whether it was with Tau Master or with his friends, the only thing he talked about was the latest developments in the movement.

Well, it was natural for the men to talk about politics—what Babasaheb proclaimed, how Gandhi opposed it, and whose meetings drew larger crowds. We women gossiped at the hand pumps about who had cooked what, who had borne yet another daughter, how much money was paid as dowry in weddings, or who had bought what for the approaching festival. My man would frown at me, disapproval written all over his face when he caught me gossiping.

"Aga Soney, what do you get by yapping about mundane things? Grow out of your mule mentality. Look at what is happening in the country and think about what you can do for our Dalit cause. Come read something useful." Then he would get excited and make me sit next to him to practice my reading.

Though he had patiently tried to teach me to read whatever little he knew in our early days together, I was still not able to read by myself. I was always busy, doing housework, looking after the children, or earning a bit of money with a few odd jobs. I could sense Sasubai's resentment. "Damu, if you make a scholar out of your wife, you will need another wife to do the daily chores." But he just ignored her and left me to get caught in the crossfire.

It was an unwritten rule in our house that my man's word was law. Often, my eyes drooped with fatigue when I sat down for his reading lesson, but I did not complain, as it was the only time in the day when I got a chance to sit quietly in one place. He would begin reading out, in his broken way, from a book written by Babasaheb for Dalits or a book on some social worker and expect me to repeat every sentence after him. But after a while, he would get carried away and continue reading aloud by himself. Then, I would peacefully doze through the sessions. Nothing was lost, however. I knew the stories well, for he repeated them often when his friends came to visit, each time with renewed fervor. For want of an audience, he would repeat them to Najuka or to his mother, unmindful that they were not particularly interested.

Listening to Babasaheb's teachings in this manner gradually had an effect on Najuka and me. We were taken in by Babasaheb's thoughts on cleanliness and grooming. The first step toward gaining acceptance from others, and being proud of who you are, a Dalit, is to maintain good hygiene and neat and clean grooming, Babasaheb had said. We began to bathe daily and dress neatly with freshly washed clothes and tie our hair into a neat bun. We kept our house immaculately clean, with all the brass pots and pans polished and shining.

We sensed a change in the way we carried ourselves. We proudly proclaimed ourselves Dalits. Earlier, when I participated in the social movement, it was solely because my man was involved in it and I had to follow him. Gradually, I began believing in it. I could also see the results of what Babasaheb was doing for our community. Drawn into the melee during the Ganapati procession, I had taken part in almost every street protest and in the temple entry march as well.

I had become a committed participant, but there were still occasions when what my man suggested did not sit well with me. Although I was no longer the coy, scared bride afraid to argue with him, nothing really changed, since he always won. After I became assertive, he at least heard me out; that was my only satisfaction, for in the end, I had to accept his ways.

As my man stood peering into the newspaper, he who usually revered the editorial criticized it because it condemned Babasaheb's call to the Dalits to renounce Hinduism. According to my husband, whatever Babasaheb said had to be followed, no questions asked. My man was angry. His voice rose and his eyes grew fiery.

"What do these people want? They want us to meekly follow Hinduism, a religion that does not allow Hindus to enter temples? Why should we favor the religion that preaches untouchability and discrimination? Who has given the Brahmin class the authority to decide our fate? We are the masters of our destiny and have to reclaim our rightful place in society. We shall renounce Hinduism. Hail Babasaheb, the great one, who is our visionary, our savior!" This speech came rushing out all in one breath.

There was a hush among those gathered around him. No doubt we were of low caste and were not allowed to enter a Hindu temple, but we were still Hindus, although we suffered discrimination wherever we went. But I had reasoned out everything based on what I had always heard: the way things are is how God has ordained them; if we are being ill-treated, it is because of bad deeds in our past lifetime.

I had told myself, if this is our destiny, we have to accept it and live with it, seeking solace in worshipping our gods—Mariaai, Khandoba, and Vithoba at Pandharpur. Only they could save us from calamities. I remember how I prayed with deep devotion and then made sure to fulfill all the vows I had made when I wanted to conceive a child. All through my childhood, I had seen my mother's deep faith in God. After I was married, my mother-in-law had handed over to me brass idols of the family gods. I still remember what she had said: "Soney, take care of these idols and they will always take care of you." Accordingly, I had never failed to worship the idols every single day. I prayed to them when any problem worried me. I beseeched them when my man had no job. I implored them to make my man well when he was in hospital. I washed them with my tears when my children suffered ill health.

My prayers were always answered. My gods had never let me down. Now what was this new obsession possessing my man? It was one thing to worship Babasaheb, but it was quite another to blindly follow whatever he said. Had my man not taught me to think and to question? And here he was, carried away. I shook my head in disgust.

"Eh, Soney, what's wrong with you? Why, you look as if someone close to you has died . . ."

"Yes, you are out to kill my faith." I was surprised at the venom in my voice.

"No. What we are doing is rekindling our faith in ourselves as humans. We are giving up the religion where we are unwanted."

"We were born Hindus and all our forefathers have been Hindus unquestioningly. Now just because you say that you are giving it up does not mean we stop being Hindus. You can say what you want, but you can do nothing to obliterate our past."

My man gave a loud burst of laughter. "Wah, Soney! Look at you talk."

My eyes welled up. "Ridicule my thoughts, I do not care. That is the way I think and feel. You always thought that I could not think, but you are wrong. Everybody is capable of thinking, just as he is capable of eating, drinking, living, feeling happy or sad. Earlier, I was young and afraid of you and I did not know how to tell others what I was thinking."

"All that attention I gave you has gone to your head. Look at you snapping back at me!"

I could not sleep for a long time that night. I would not meekly accept whatever he had decided for us. Yes, we had to fight for our rights and reclaim our dignity, as Babasaheb said, but tampering with God and religion? That would be taking things too far. Deep down, I feared that I would have to follow my husband. I sent up a silent prayer to Mariaai, seeking strength to do the right thing. I only ended up remembering my mother's words when my man had come to take me to Mumbai: "Soney, your man is like your god. Obey him always, unquestioningly. Accept him wholly, whatever he does. He is all that you now have. You will be separated from him only by death."

Renouncing Hinduism would be like dying a spiritual death. We had neighbors who were Muslims and Christians, and I had met people who were Parsees and Jews. They were good people. They all went to different temples and worshipped differently, but that was how they were from their childhood, and so were their parents and grandparents. We liked them and respected them, but that did not mean we had to give up our own religion and follow them!

If God wanted us to be of some other religion, he would have given us birth in that religion. Just because I went to a church or a durgah occasionally did not mean that I was unhappy with our Hindu gods. I never questioned God's will or our Hindu religion, and I would certainly not do anything against it. Goddess Mariaai was like our mother. I broke out into a sob as her image floated in front of my eyes. We also worshipped Vithoba at Pandharpur. He is dark-complexioned, just like our people, and he has a lovely smiling face—kind, assuring, and benevolent. I started humming my favorite abhanga: "I offer you some grains of rice, my Lord, and when I have none, I offer you flowers, or just a single petal. I offer you only some water and if I have none, I just bow down and utter your name with my heart and soul and I am happy." Vithoba asks for nothing but love and devotion. Now, we were being asked to give up all our beloved gods and start worshipping Buddha.

Perhaps I could persuade my man that we could worship Buddha along with our Hindu gods. Just as I was falling asleep, I made a firm resolve that I would not follow him blindly this time. Tomorrow, I would tell him that I was not going to give up my faith.

The next morning, busy as I was cooking, feeding the children, and sending them to school, I had forgotten all about this issue. But in the afternoon, when I went to fetch water, all the women there were heatedly talking about the same thing: none of them were prepared to give up Hinduism, but they did not dare voice their opinion to their men. I quietly listened to them but was enraged when in the end they decided that they would follow their husbands.

It was a terrible time for me. I suffered from headaches and felt listless. I went about my work mechanically. All I wanted was to have a good cry. I wanted to fall at Mariaai's feet and ask her for some sign of Her will.

My silence did not go unnoticed. For the first time in our marriage, I heard my man raise his voice to me in front of our children.

"Soney, I am still alive. Stop going around as if you are mourning the death of your husband. Your tears are not going to affect me. My decision is final."

Later in the evening, he pulled me close to him and explained that we could not worship both the Hindu gods and the Buddha. Some Hindus had begun worshipping Buddha, claiming he was an incarnation of a Hindu deity—Vishnu. Babasaheb said that this was an attempt to absorb Buddhism into Hinduism. Some Hindu leaders referred to India as Hindustan. They said that everyone born in Hindustan is a Hindu. Babasaheb called our country Bharat and not Hindustan. I did not want anything to do with this quarrel. I did not care if Hindus wanted to pray to Buddha. All I wanted was to raise our children well and worship our gods, but in my heart I knew that I was waging a losing battle.

One day my man came home and told me that the mullahs had approached Babasaheb to adopt their religion for the sake of Dalits. In return, the Muslims wanted Dalit support in their demand for the country to be split into two: for Hindus and for Muslims. My man said that he was sure that Babasaheb would never agree to that. He loved our country dearly and had devoted his life to its betterment. Babasaheb wanted freedom for our country from the British and freedom for Dalits from discrimination.

The Christian missionaries were also keen on converting us Dalits. Some were even offering money to every family who would agree to convert. Babasaheb was outraged. He announced that we did not seek anybody's charity: the Dalits wanted to work hard and earn their bread with dignity.

As my man told me these stories, I imagined that if we were forced to convert to Christianity, I would have to wear a short frock and high shoes, and go to church. Or, if we converted to Sikhism, my man would grow his hair long and tie it under a turban. He would wear a steel bangle on his wrist. One day my man brought home a picture of Buddha. Our neighbors gathered around. The picture passed from hand to hand and a few of them joined hands in obeisance, while some others said he looked like a saint and not a god. I looked at the picture and saw a serene smiling face with one hand raised in benediction. It looked reassuring and I said that I would not mind worshipping him provided they did not make me throw away our traditional gods. Why couldn't they allow Buddha to be placed in our temples along with other deities?

I kept the picture next to the brass and clay idols that my

mother had given me. I said that we would pray and make offerings to him along with our gods.

"Soney, I have explained to you . . . that will not be possible," my man shouted. "When we take up this new religion, you will have to put away all those Hindu gods."

I felt terrible. "Does that mean we can no longer go to the temples? What about our village deity, Mariaai, our fairs and festivals? What about Sasubai? What about my children, will they never celebrate Diwali and Holi?" I burst into tears.

Here was my man, happy to convert. For him, Babasaheb was always right: he had done the thinking for all of us, and had opted for conversion only after being convinced that Buddhism was good for us. He repeated Babasaheb's argument: "Buddhism has no priestly class and certainly nobody is considered untouchable. All men and all women are equal, and they are treated as such. There are no rituals or rites, or strict disciplines to follow. You only follow your heart and your devotion."

Then he would say, in the hope of convincing me, "This is wonderful, Soney, what more do you want? Remember how you were pushed away and handled roughly near the Kala Ram Temple at Nashik? None of that will happen now."

Every day my man told us something new. I did not always understand him, and if I questioned him a lot, he lost his composure and said that I did not even try to understand what he was saying. Maybe he was right; I did not want to understand these things.

One day my man came home all excited. Babasaheb had finally fixed the date for the conversion. The initiation ceremony was to be held at Nagpur. There was to be a huge gathering of Dalits, and the Buddhist priests were to chant mantras and convert Babasaheb to Buddhism. He, in turn, would initiate all the Dalits desirous of following him.

I asked my man why it was Nagpur and not Mumbai. He said

that Nagpur was an auspicious place because Nagarjuna, a famous Buddhist monk and scientist, had lived there.

Babasaheb went around making speeches and people thronged to his meetings. They had unanimously accepted the new religion that he had chosen. Babasaheb was going to do a mass initiation. People were going to embrace Buddhism and, as was required, they had decided to do away with the idols that had occupied the prayer niches in their homes only a short while ago.

It pained me that they could just abandon the gods who had ensured their well-being for so many years. I had heard that when calamity struck and people could not look after their gods, they would leave the idols at the local temples, in the care of the priests. At least they made sure that someone cared for the gods and did not just throw them away.

The more I thought about it, the more I was convinced that I had to hide our gods somewhere, where nobody would ever find them. I would keep worshipping them secretly and bring them out after this madness had passed. I was sure that many other women had planned the same thing. None of us could discuss this openly or even breathe a word about it for fear of being branded traitors. I thought my heart would burst. Sometimes I tried to talk to Najuka, but she was so scared that she told me to shut up.

My man had already decided that we were all going to Nagpur to watch Babasaheb be converted. He was already talking excitedly about the ceremony and went around from house to house in our neighborhood, urging people not to miss it.

"Imagine!" he said. "We will witness the ceremony, and then Babasaheb himself will initiate us."

Why go to Nagpur? Surely, the same thing could be done in Mumbai. But he would not listen. He ordered us all to begin preparing to go to Nagpur. Everyone would go—the big family that we were now—boys and girls, and Najuka and I. It was a long journey of more than eighteen hours and it would be terribly expensive to buy tickets for all of us. There was also a rush at the booking office and everyone was saying that it was impossible to reserve tickets, but my man managed to get them through his contacts. The next thing was to buy new clothes—white saris for women and white shirts for men.

Najuka and I started cooking enough food to last for four or five days. I packed some rice and lentils that we could cook in Nagpur. I rolled our mats and packed some sheets. Nagpur was known to be cold at night, and we would probably be sleeping in the open. My man was trying to convince as many people as possible to come to Nagpur with us.

We were ready at last. Given my reluctance to go through the ritual of conversion, it was difficult to get everything done. My man kept up his animated chatter about how good things were going to be. Thoroughly convinced himself, he was making desperate efforts to convince me. The children were excited too, if only because of the train journey. The trains were terribly crowded. People sat in the corridors and even in the passage leading to the toilets. We sat huddled in one corner, but gradually our family split. The boys found their own places, and my man got busy exchanging news with different groups of people. We were so crowded in that train that there was enough warmth to ward off the cold winds from outside. Surprisingly, there were no fights or arguments over seats. We shared our food with the people next to us, and when sleepy, we rested on each other's shoulders, and the young ones sat on the knees of those who had seats.

We sang songs and hailed Babasaheb. We chatted about how the ceremony would unfold. We were all from different parts of Mumbai, but all of us spoke the same language and knew most of the songs and abhangas. There was a great spirit of togetherness, and we felt like proud soldiers going to the battlefield. After seeing the huge numbers in which our community had turned out for the conversion, whatever doubts I had seemed to wane.

The next morning, we reached Nagpur. I could not believe my

eyes. Hundreds of thousands of people had already arrived. I had never seen so many people on the streets, walking, or riding bicycles, or hanging from trucks and buses. They were all moving toward the canopies erected for the ceremony, so we just followed the crowds. The volunteers of the Samata Sainik Dal—the Youth Brigade—were directing people to other tents where they could pass the night. As we approached, we could see that there was no room anywhere. People were sitting by the roadside, and some had lit fires with the twigs they had collected. A few others were making bhakris for breakfast.

My man decided to find someone whom he knew in Nagpur to see if we could stay with them. We went from house to house but there was no room. The houses were jammed with people, some sleeping on verandas and in courtyards. We walked all around the parks nearby but had no luck. We were tired and dejected when a man hailed us. It was Narayan, who used to be a newspaper vendor with my man when they were young. He took us home and gave us a place on the terrace of his house to sleep. That was fine with us. It meant that the next morning we would be able to freshen up and dress neatly in the white garb for the ceremony. I helped his wife cook bhakris, and in no time we were stretched out on our mats under the sky. The next day we could not thank him enough for his hospitality.

Narayan was one of the volunteers, and he assured us that it would be an occasion to remember. No one, including Babasaheb, had expected that the turnout would be so high. The town was full, yet each train that came in brought hordes of eager Dalits. We marveled at how well the volunteers were coping. I remembered the stampede at Nashik when Babasaheb was leading the temple agitation. My man said that Babasaheb's meetings were always crowded, but people did not dare do anything that Babasaheb would consider shameful. I dozed off, but my man and Narayan kept talking late into the night and perhaps did not sleep at all. We got up very early, even before dawn, and quickly went through our morning ablutions and dressed in our crisp new clothes. After a quick breakfast of tea and bhakris we were off. It was a short walk toward the Diksha Bhoomi, where the conversion would take place, but it was so crowded that we just inched forward.

It was only about six in the morning. The streets were swept clean and there was an atmosphere of purity and holiness. The volunteers were guiding people to form queues to go inside the marquee. We managed to get good seats and soon it looked like an undulating sea of white. The volunteers would blow their whistles from time to time, silencing everyone.

It was October 14, 1956, and the festival of Dussehra, which celebrates the victory of good over evil with the burning of a cracker-filled effigy of the demon-king Ravana. A day on which we ritualistically exchange leaves of the shami tree, symbolizing prosperity and amity. A day when men are supposed to worship their weapons and symbolically cross the country's borders as if to defend it from outside invasions.

Here we are today, I thought, about to cross a different kind of border. We were going to leave the boundaries of Hinduism and, led by Babasaheb, enter the new religion of equality, compassion, and understanding.

I still had doubts about Buddhism and what it would do for us. Seeing so many people gathered for that cause reassured me. I was filled with hope. I was waiting for Babasaheb to appear on the stage and take the first determined and courageous step toward our claim for dignity.

The podium, set in the middle of a replica of the Sanchi Temple at Sarnath, was lined with white sheets. Members of the Youth Brigade gave us a running commentary. Huge flags with multicolored stripes fluttered on the stage. Buntings and banners were everywhere. A large bronze idol of Buddha, with two tigers crouching on either side, was on the table. A bowl of burning incense was placed before it. At the stroke of nine, four monks, heads shaved, saffron-clad, entered, holding staffs and bowls in their hands. It was a most impressive sight.

After a few minutes, Babasaheb entered, with his secretary on one side and his wife, Maisaheb, whom he had married in 1948, on the other. Babasaheb was wearing a white silk dhoti and a white silk jacket, and Maisaheb was wearing a white sari like us. One of the volunteers supported Babasaheb's tall gaunt figure. Though he looked radiant, you could see by his emaciated frame that he had been ill.

We all got up to cheer joyfully. The shouts of "*Jai* Bhim" and "Victory to Babasaheb" were heard everywhere, and for a moment I thought all the shouting would blow the tent away. A woman with a melodious voice sang a song in praise of Babasaheb. We joined in the chorus. Then we stood up for a minute of silence in honor of Babasaheb's departed father.

Soon the initiation began and a few men from the press rushed forward with their cameras. One of the old monks and his assistants started chanting in Pali, and Babasaheb and Maisaheb bowed before them. The Pali mantras were soon repeated in Marathi:

Buddham Saranam Gachhami,
Dammam Saranam Gachhami,
Sangham Saranam Gachhami.

This was followed by reciting the five tenets of Buddhism, called Panchsheel. It was a promise to walk on the path of righteousness: not to kill, not to steal, not to drink, not to speak lies, and not to indulge in wrongful sex. Babasaheb and Maisaheb bowed down thrice, their hands joined in prayer, and made offerings of white lotus flowers to Buddha's icon.

Their conversion was formally confirmed, and the crowd cheered as loudly as they could, hailing Babasaheb and Lord Buddha. Many people rushed to the stage and garlanded Babasaheb. Then, a saffron-robed monk presented Maisaheb with an icon of

Buddha. Babasaheb started his speech. He said that he was reborn as a Buddhist and no longer belonged to the oppressive Hindu religion. He vowed to follow the path laid down by the Buddha.

Babasaheb announced that he would no longer observe the death anniversary of his parents according to Hindu tradition. He would follow the main principles of Buddhism—knowledge, correct behavior, and love for fellow beings. I shivered with the intensity of the moment. Tears wet my cheeks and I could feel the radiance that Babasaheb emanated. I will never forget the moment when Babasaheb asked us all to stand up—men, women, and children—who had come from all corners of the country. We stood up proudly. Babasaheb was our leader and our savior who would lead us into a better life, where there was no caste and we would all be equal.

Babasaheb asked us to repeat after him the three pledges. He repeated them once again, in his clear resonant voice, but broke down, choked with emotion. His eyes streamed and it looked like he was speaking with all his being. He really looked reborn, and rebirth is never easy. A child coming out of the womb always cries with his first breath, and there is the sorrow of leaving the mother. It is also a moment of happiness, and the tears are a mixture of joy and sorrow. It was truly a great experience to listen to Babasaheb. I felt as if he were talking to me personally and felt a wave of emotion wash over me.

When Babasaheb first came on the stage, he looked frail and unwell, but as the ceremony progressed, he seemed to grow in strength. He talked to us as if he were taking all the responsibility for us, glad to have brought us so far. Now he expected us to be strong and follow him confidently. After the speech, we hailed Babasaheb and Maisaheb. Then a few people sang songs and the ceremony was over. People started leaving but we were reluctant to go. Slowly, we came out, and there were a lot of makeshift stalls selling food. A few had Buddhist scriptures and Buddha idols in brass and clay. We bought a few pictures of Buddha, and a big poster of Babasaheb. We walked around looking at the paintings of the Buddhist temples. I was entranced by a brass statue of the Buddha. The face was serene and his lips were parted in a smile.

The journey back was long. The trains were still crowded, but the mood was celebratory.

The serenity of the whole ceremony was still in my heart and I hoped that it would never go away. We were truly blessed to have him show us the way to emancipation. All my earlier anxiety and doubts seemed to disappear at the ceremony. I was proud and held on to the Buddha idol on our journey back.

We reached home and I got busy with cooking and unpacking. The others had their bath and sat down for a meal. Quietly, I went to the holy niche where I had kept my gods. It was empty. I silently asked for their forgiveness. I had hidden them, stitching them up in the lowermost mattress of my bed, and there they would remain.

I placed my Buddha statue on the mantel and showered it with a few petals, lit a butter lamp, and burned incense. I returned to our meal, praying that my man would not ask me what I had done with our Hindu gods. He was occupied with hanging Babasaheb's poster on the wall. The children were getting impatient and attacked the meal with their usual gusto as if nothing had changed.

DAMU

December 6, 1956

A bleak morning had dawned. The news spread like a flash. Everyone was talking about it in hushed tones. Everyone had heard it and yet did not want to believe it. "No, it could not have happened. How can Babasaheb be no more?" Sonu shrieked, as she caught hold of my shirt and shook me. "Tell me it's not true," she wailed. What could I say? I was in shock.

The newspapers had been giving daily updates about Babasaheb's condition: that he was ailing with incurable diabetes and had difficulty in walking. He was under medical supervision. After his first wife died, he had found it difficult to take care of himself, what with the work schedule he maintained. Eventually, he had married Maisaheb—a trained medical doctor. We felt he was in safe hands. Nobody had expected things to take such a turn. The last time I had seen Babasaheb was in Nagpur at the conversion. He had looked frail and thin, and required Maisaheb's support to walk to the stage.

In spite of his failing health, Babasaheb continued working for more than ten hours a day. He toured the country, giving speeches and motivating people . He worked on books, papers, and letters— all he wanted to do was work.

He had traveled all across the country, and everywhere hundreds of Dalits flocked to listen to him. All this touring, however, had taken a toll on Babasaheb's health. Babasaheb was in Delhi when death claimed him. The previous day, he had seemed listless and talked for hours to his secretary, Rattu. He inquired about the health of his old gardener in Mumbai and asked Rattu to send him some money. He also made Rattu promise that he would look after his dog. It was as though he had a premonition that the end was near.

The whole country grieved for Babasaheb. Although a controversial figure for the upper castes, he was respected for his knowledge. He had labored hard to draft the Constitution, and was known as the Father of the Indian Constitution.

All the newspapers were full of reports of his death. I heard even foreign papers, such as *The New York Times*, published obituaries. There was extensive reportage, editorials, letters, and articles on him. There were pictures of his childhood, his wedding, his speeches, as well as his corpse. In the pictures of his last speech in Delhi, he looked happy. He had planned a conversion ceremony in Mumbai, and the next day a meeting with Jain monks. How could he have left us?

All of us crowded around, reading all the editions of the newspapers as they came off the presses. What would happen to us now that he was gone? The radio repeated all the details, commenting on the events of the last few days. We crowded together to listen, consoling one another, and it was not easy to stay dry-eyed.

A serpentine queue of ministers, politicians, and followers gathered to pay their last respects. Prime Minister Jawaharlal Nehru was among the first to console Maisaheb. It was decided that Babasaheb's body would be flown to Mumbai. In Delhi, the procession took five hours to reach the airport as people crowded to have a last look.

As soon as we heard that the plane had taken off from Delhi, we rushed to the airport. We waited through the early hours of dawn. The crowd was so unmanageable that finally the police and the military were deployed. As word spread that the flight had arrived, loud cries and slogans rent the air. The body was placed on a decorated float. After a long time, Maisaheb, Rattu, and a few officials got off the plane and followed the cortege in an open car. They looked haggard, mourning their loss, and Rattu was beside himself with grief and helplessness. Maisaheb kept saying that she could not face any of us, who had trusted her to look after our beloved leader. She wailed that death had stolen this precious gem from under her nose. We felt orphaned without Babasaheb.

The roads leading to Babasaheb's house, Rajgriha, in Mumbai were overflowing. People from all over Maharashtra had rushed to Mumbai. They came by train, truck, bike, boat, or whatever means of transportation they could find. They all hoped to be his pallbearers. They looked lost, wordless, eager to catch a glimpse of his body. In Mumbai, everyone had to walk, since the roads were so full of people that there was not an inch free for any vehicle to pass. Volunteers were directing the crowds. It was announced that the cortege would move in a procession through major parts of the city.

It is customary not to cook food if there is a death in the family. On such occasions, other families bring food to the bereaved family. Since all Dalits felt as if there had been a death in their own family, all of us went without food or water that day. We had walked and waited for hours to get a glimpse of him. We could not turn back without seeing him and showering a few petals. We wanted to see him one last time, and yet, in seeing him, we would be forced to admit his death.

Eventually, the two-mile-long procession arrived at Rajgriha, with Babasaheb's body covered with flowers and wreaths. The smell of jasmine and lilies pervaded the atmosphere. Near the head of the body stood a statuette of Lord Buddha. Garlands and flowers had to be constantly cleared to enable people to catch a glimpse of him. Tearful monks chanted Buddhist prayers. People perched on treetops and on the balconies of buildings. Everyone was craning to get a better glimpse, but it was too crowded.

As the procession moved forward again, I choked and let out a mournful cry. The tall, strong man that we had always known Babasaheb to be, with shoulders broad enough to bear the woes of his people, lay quiet and unmoving. The one who had lived for us—and in doing so had overworked himself—had now died for us.

The collective sighs of mourners became an immense moan, and just as the truck moved, all of us rushed forward expecting that any moment Babasaheb would stand up to address us. We had our hands joined in prayer, and we could hear some people weeping and crying out, "We need you. . . . Why have you left us? . . . Talk to us!" The truck moved on and all was quiet. We had a thousand things to ask him and tell him, but he was beyond all hearing, all happiness or sorrow.

A great swell of people continued to walk behind the cortege chanting slogans, and the air filled with their cries: "Babasaheb *amar rahe*"—May Babasaheb remain immortal. He had passed away but his memory would never die. After about seven hours, the procession reached the cremation ground. Hundreds of policemen, along with top-ranking army officials, guided the procession, helping to maintain order. A radio broadcast later estimated that more than half a million people had attended the funeral.

Just before his pyre was lit at the crematorium, more than a hundred thousand people took the oath of embracing Buddhism to honor their dead father's last wish. His son, Yeshawant, lit the pyre amid loud Buddhist chants.

I returned home, heavyhearted and desolate. It took us a long time to get back to normal life. There was national mourning for ten days and flags flew at half-mast all over the country. His memory would always be with us and his words would ring in our ears. He left an indelible mark on history.

The Maharashtra government declared that Babasaheb's birthday would henceforth be a state holiday. The land in Nagpur where the first conversion had taken place was donated to the

Buddhist Society. A beautiful dome was erected on the Chaitya Bhoomi where Babasaheb was cremated and where Dalits could pay their respects. A huge life-size statue now stands near the secretariat in Mumbai.

Sonu and I take solace in the fact that we are faithfully following Babasaheb's wishes. We are fortunate to have come into contact with him. Circumstances brought us to Mumbai, and that city brought Babasaheb into our lives. He changed our lives and those of millions forever.

As devout followers of Babasaheb, Sonu and I strove to educate our family. Babasaheb had inculcated in us the belief that education was the solution to all our ills. As I stood with my eyes closed to pay my respects to Babasaheb, I vowed that giving my children the highest possible education would be the mission of my life. They would fulfill Babasaheb's dream, my dream.

IV

THE SECOND GENERATION

CHHOTU:
LOOKING BACK

December 22, 1997

An unusual crowd had gathered at Mumbai International Airport that evening. I was among them, yes, but I felt strangely detached. I felt as though it were all happening to someone else.

The airport buzzed with activity. Amid a sea of loved ones gathered to say good-bye, people were shaking my hand, congratulating me, wishing me good luck. I was on my way to Washington, D.C., to join the International Monetary Fund. I turned from group to group, a smile glued to my face, going through the motions of small talk.

Above all there rose the wailing of a woman trying to break away from the two men holding her back.

"Let go. Call Dhurva. Arre, at least let me be with my son for a few minutes. He's going beyond the seven seas. I'm an old woman dying, with one foot in the grave." She was old but also very determined, and with a jerk, she broke free and came to me.

"Bai," I called out, rushing to my mother, and bent to touch her feet, seeking her blessings. As was her wont, she harshly yelled at me: "I will never understand your reasons for leaving all that you worked so hard for. What are you searching for now across the seven seas that you couldn't find here? You have two square meals and more than you can ever put in your belly. What more do you want?" she pleaded.

"You have been like this ever since you were a child, always searching," she went on. "Never happy with what you had. Look at me. I am not going to live forever, you know, and what use will be your tears tomorrow? You will not be here to shed tears on my dead body."

She started howling now. "Your old man died and left me. Now you are leaving me, Dhurva."

As I groped for words, I too began to wonder why I was leaving my people behind. Why was I taking off for a country which, though promising for my career, lacked the warmth of my own flesh and blood? As I searched for words to convince my mother to let me go, I could find none; every word that came to my mind seemed hollow.

As I was holding my mother, the memory of my father surfaced. It had been eight years since his death. Bai had kept his memory alive within her, in the only way that she knew—by cursing him for leaving her alone. As for me, he was always there, never voicing his approval. I didn't need words. His twinkling eyes said it all. I could move mountains for that look.

I remembered the time I started getting good grades in school. Visitors would ask me, "What do you want to be when you grow up?" Normally, I would give them some bored answer. But once, my eldest brother, Janu, asked me the same question. In all honesty, I replied, "I want to be a writer." He pulled a face and murmured, "You are really hopeless! You are going to be a penniless beggar. Have you seen any writer making a good living?" Driven to tears, I stood on the veranda. I felt a hand on my shoulder but refused to look, thinking my brother had come to pacify me, but it was my father who had pulled me close.

"Look here, son," he said. "Folks will tell you, be a doctor, be an engineer, or be a barrister . . . but you must never listen to anybody.

Be what you think is the right thing to be. Even I will not tell you to be this or that," he continued in the soft tone he always used when he said something important.

"All I have to say to you is this: reach the top in whatever you do. You want to be a thief? No problem, but then, be so good at it that the world will salute you. The world should look at you and say, 'Oh, what a thief! What a crafty mind!'" I could not hide a smile, and even Dada broke into a toothless grin. "Never be content with less, you get me?" he said, his eyes gleaming.

Gradually, I grasped the homespun philosophy of my father. It found a permanent place in the recesses of my mind and became the driving force behind my ambition.

I remembered an incident following my return from America, a doctorate in hand. I spent hours studying. My mother, who had raised six children in acute poverty, prodded me endlessly to sit back and relax. After all, she said, I had plenty to eat and drink, so what was I worried about, and why was I working so hard? One day she nagged mercilessly and my father shouted an obscenity at her, later explaining that getting an academic degree is like getting a driver's license. You get a license, and you keep on driving. You don't just sit on it!

One of my brothers reminded me that my flight would be boarding soon. I was gripped by fear, wondering if this would be the last time I saw my mother. I closed my eyes, shutting out the world as I felt her drawing me close to her with the frailty of a child. I had an inexplicable urge to sob. I felt her soothing hand on my back as I fought a losing battle with tears. As rapidly as she had pulled me to her, she pushed me away, sensing that her Dhurva was being carried away by torrential feelings.

I became conscious of my people waiting to say a few parting words. My brothers were there; so were my sisters-in-law with the third generation of Jadhavs in various age groups. Then there were my two sisters with their families. Several relatives and family friends were also there. All of them were sad at the separation, and looking at them, even my wife, Vasundhara, had tears in her eyes, though she was going to join me shortly in Washington with our two children.

Dressed in their frayed and yellowed traditional garb, some of my relatives looked sorely out of place in the grossly overdecorated airport lounge. When I stepped on the plane, I would be the English-speaking professional from the Reserve Bank of India, but now I was simply Dhurva, the earthy guy-next-door mouthing sentences generously punctuated with slang, in Marathi, my native language.

My flight was announced. Another round of handshakes, hugs, and parting words, and I disentangled myself from the crowd and started toward the security check. As I walked away, I carried with me the image of my mother and her trembling half-raised palm, bidding good-bye.

There is no better place or time to be philosophical than when you are airborne. Suspended between heaven and earth, introspection becomes inevitable. The plane may be traveling at supersonic speed but the mind travels faster than light—seemingly without a sense of direction, but almost always with a definite purpose.

I thought of the friends and acquaintances who had come to see me off. All of them had referred to my lowly caste. An old man from my village had called me "Damu Mahar's son." Others made their point in a more subtle manner. Some others, the highborn, had praised me for making it big *despite* coming from a lowly caste.

The most ironic was my high-caste schoolteacher's remark made while bidding me farewell. This teacher used to publicly refer to me as the "government's son-in-law" because my tuition had been waived. Once when I had outperformed all the others in Sanskrit—supposedly the divine language, and an exclusive preserve of the high castes for centuries—he had said that he was beginning to lose faith in the education system.

For the millionth time I asked myself why they couldn't judge me on where I stood. Why did they always have to judge me on where I came from?

The words of Kabir, a fifteenth-century saint-poet, often ring in my mind:

I stood knocking at the doorsteps of heaven as I died...
"Who are you...?" I was asked.
"My entire existence on earth could not tell me who I
    was...
And that is what I have come to ask you..."
Who am I?

The bottom line always stood out: I was a mere Mahar, a Dalit, belonging to the lowest stratum of society. It was as if I had a tragic flaw inherited through birth. No matter what I did, where I went, or what success I achieved, I would always be looked upon as an untouchable, albeit one who had achieved success.

Yes, I do come from the Mahar caste. Yes, my father was a barely literate, lowly employee doing menial jobs to earn a meal for the family. Yes, my forefathers were untouchables. Yes, my forefathers were required to wear clay pots around their necks to keep their spit from polluting the ground, and brooms were tied to their rumps to obliterate their footprints as they walked. Yes, as village servants, my forefathers were mercilessly forced to run, foaming at the mouth under the scorching sun, to herald the carriages of government officials.

So what? Have I not reclaimed my dignity through my achievements? Why should the caste into which I was born count now?

I am often asked, "Now that you have reached a high position, do you ever face unpleasant experiences because of your caste?"

It is an unfortunate truth of our society that whatever heights a man might scale, his caste is never cast off; it remains an inseparable part of his identity. His caste always remains a cause for scorn or contempt. Only the *type* of humiliation changes.

When I was living in a Mumbai suburb, a well-educated neighbor stopped me to say, "That south Indian gentleman is all praise for you these days."

"Any special reason? I don't even know him well," I replied.

"Apparently, you gave him a lift in your car one day. He said we, the highborn, seem to have become uncivilized. But look at Jadhav, though he is a Dalit, he is so civilized!"

I had been on my way to drop my daughter, Apoorva, at school when I saw the gentleman walking with his granddaughter, whose uniform indicated that she went to the same school as Apoorva. I did not think twice about offering them a lift. It was common courtesy.

Another time one of my colleagues was telling me about a holy man. "You must meet him once. Swamiji is so wise, so broad-minded that he will speak candidly and discuss philosophical issues even with a 'low-caste' person like you. You must meet him!"

There are many so-called Dalits like me, who have successfully cast off the shackles placed on them by the caste system. This is the magic wrought by Babasaheb and the education that he put within our reach. Of course, that doesn't guarantee us cooperation or appreciation from others. So often we encounter people who think themselves cultured (and are often well intentioned), who remain imprisoned by the stereotypes of the caste system.

The plane was flying over majestic, mountainous terrain. I sensed the eyes of my father looking at me from the window. I pulled out the old, yellowing, palm-sized portrait. It was wrinkled and its corners were bent. Yet Bai and Dada still looked back at me from the picture. The struggles of their fight for survival had marked their faces, especially Bai's. Dada wore a stoic expression and looked completely at ease. But Bai looked stiff and uncomfortable, with a far-off expression in her eyes. I remembered being possessed by similar thoughts when, seventeen years ago, I was on a flight to America for my doctoral studies. I was then a recipient of a national scholarship from the government of India.

My father had wept then. His only words to me were that our ancestors had never even crossed the boundaries of our little village in India, and today his son was all set to cross the seven seas.

"I have got everything. I am ready to die now," he had said.

I wondered what Dada would have thought if he were alive today. My father would surely have wondered, in turn, what Babasaheb Ambedkar would have thought of my achievement. Then, inevitably, I thought of the story Dada had told a thousand times — the story of the first time that my brothers Janu and Dina had seen Babasaheb Ambedkar. Dada had taken them to a protest rally led by Babasaheb. They were terrified of the mob chanting slogans. Jostled and pushed, the children felt claustrophobic and our father shoved people away, making room for them, wading through the human sea. Young Dina clutched Dada's hand and whined that he wanted to go home.

Suddenly, they came upon a man in a blue suit, a tie, and a hat. He stood apart from the crowd, exuding self-confidence. It was Dr. Ambedkar. There was a hush as he began speaking.

After the speech was over, Dada clutched my brothers' shoulders and shoved them past everyone toward Dr. Ambedkar. They were terrified, but Dr. Ambedkar patted my brothers on the back, and asked my father, "Are these your sons, Damu? Send them to school . . . Give your sons a good education . . . They will surely rise to make big names."

Dr. Ambedkar got into his chauffeur-driven Studebaker and was whisked away. Dada remained silent all the way home. Once there, he gathered all the kids in the neighborhood to tell them the story. Excited, they vied with one another to sit close to our father. He told the story of Dr. Ambedkar and how he had gone abroad to a foreign university to get the highest degrees there. I was awed by the story.

Though I had not really understood how, I had an inkling that my family was different from the others in our community. I knew that I had to go to school and become like Dr. Ambedkar, carry a briefcase like him, wear a suit like him.

THE MILIEU

Wherever I go, I carry the small world of my childhood home in Wadala with me. Wadala is a suburb of central Mumbai, with a distinct identity of its own, a mix of old and new: Mumbai Port Trust quarters, Antop Hill, the Muslim shrine of Sheikh Misri Dargah, and a few other settlements. It was one big melting pot of communities: Muslims, Christians, north Indians, and south Indian construction workers (Kongatis), but the majority of people in Wadala were Dalits from Nashik and other places in Maharashtra.

The Dalit majority was mainly due to the Mumbai Port Trust. After independence in 1947, the Port Trust implemented a preferential policy in employing Dalits as a measure toward their upliftment. The MPT had staff quarters in Wadala, in chawls. Gradually, relatives and friends of MPT workers also settled in the Wadala vicinity and the community burgeoned. People who lived in Wadala even for only a year would swear that they could never live anywhere else. The atmosphere in Wadala grew on you in a strange sort of a way. So even after retirement, when they had to leave the MPT staff quarters, people huddled in small rented apartments nearby, refusing to move away.

Businesses took root. They were passed on from generation to generation, and eventually Wadala grew crowded and squalid. Yet nobody wanted to move out. Taking advantage of its insularity from the main city, thugs and gangsters from all over Mumbai drifted in, finding a safe haven, operating small and sometimes large criminal gangs.

My siblings and I spent the better part of our childhood in this neighborhood. The center of our world was, of course, our father—Damu—whom we called Dada.

Most children address their fathers formally, but Dada insisted that we call him "Baap," a colloquial yet earthy term that literally means "the one who sired me." Whenever someone tried to correct us, Dada had the choicest words. "Arre, call a spade a spade. Language, when spoken, should come alive with meaning. It should have flavor, like the pungency of spicy chutney of bombil fish. You and your refined saheb-like mannerisms can go down the drain. Your polite, bland language is as insipid as boiled potatoes."

Dada looked tough and ugly. He was of medium height, dark and with a chiseled face. Usually stern, his eyes lit up and his expression softened when he talked to children. Dhoti, white shirt, khaki jacket, and black cap were his usual garb, and the stick in his hand was more for intimidation than for support. Respectable middle-class fathers came home each evening from their "office," but Dada came home from "work." Though usually never one to fuss over or pamper his children, some evenings, on his way home from work, he brought us biscuits called naankatai, wrapped in crumpled yellow paper. I cannot to this day recall a better-tasting biscuit.

Dada had a pleasant manner but also an irascible temper. I was the sixth and youngest child. He would have been in his early fifties when I was born. What I remember about Dada from my childhood is that he had lost most of his teeth. So when he was angry, his toothless face twisted into ferocious shapes, and I would be petrified—especially when he screamed in anger, "Damblady biscuit." I had no idea what kind of biscuit this was. I assumed he meant, "I'm not going to buy you tasty biscuits anymore."

Only years later did I find out that he meant "Damn bloody bastard!" As I grew older, I finally asked him about the "damblady biscuit" and he said he had picked up the English abuse while working with a European saheb. He knew that it was a kind of curse but he was very proud of the fact that he had learned English "direct from a Gora saheb," and not from some desi upstart. Swear words were a part of that education, and he thought they went well with his personality.

Her name is Sonubai. Though she is our mother, we call her Bai, instead of the customary Aaee. We called our grandma Aaee instead. Contrary to Bai's real name, Sonu—or gold—she did not have an ounce of gold adorning her body. When I was old enough to understand, I realized that she had learned to find happiness in the rough way Dada addressed her—"Soney."

Bai and Dada were complete opposites. Bai was simple, her range limited to her immediate surroundings. Never mind the success and financial prosperity of her children; even today if I buy sweets on my way home, she asks, "Got paid today, did you?" She can't yet accept our having the freedom to spend money on sweets, except on payday.

Dada's broad-mindedness was all-encompassing and made up for Bai's narrow thinking. No wonder they squabbled. Their quarrels were a source of entertainment for the family, and sometimes just for the fun of it, I would spark arguments. I just had to goad Bai, "You are *so* fair and lovely. How did you marry a dark and ugly guy like him?" That was enough to get her started, "Arre, what can I tell you now . . ."

If I wanted to bait Dada, I would say, "Dada, this old woman nags you so much, why don't you find another wife?"

"Arre, before I knew it, they had tied this woman to me for life. Well, she was not so bad to begin with . . ." The next couple of hours passed in an entertaining duel. Of course, we all knew that these duels were mere sparring. There was intense love behind their lighthearted gibes.

Bai frequently went to Nashik. Dada pretended that he was

happy to get rid of her, if only for a few days. On the day of Bai's return, however, Dada was almost feverish, leaving for the station well before noon, even though her train did not come in until 4:00 p.m. Sure enough, the first thing they did on seeing each other as soon as she got off the train was find something to argue about.

Bai could never cope with the range of Dada's vision—and she knew that. But she always proudly proclaimed that her husband was one of a kind: out to do something different, and she supported him, although not without complaint. It was her nature to make Dada sit up and take notice that she was supporting him. Although it is the train's headlight that attracts attention, it's the unseen engine that does the work, and Dada would often tease her, "Our engine is good and dependable no doubt, but it makes a lot of noise."

Around 1950 we were living in Wadala, in a ten-by-ten-foot room on the ground floor of a two-story chawl, with a tiny kitchen that opened out into a common balcony running all around the building. The bathrooms were at the rear. We had to carry a kerosene lantern for light whenever we went to the bathroom. However, we had a dim electric bulb in the balcony outside. Nine of us lived in that tiny room: Grandma, Dada, Bai, four brothers, and two sisters. Janu, the eldest, was born in 1938, then followed Sudha, Dina, Leela, Trusha, and I. I was born in 1953. All of us were three years apart. Being the youngest, I was nicknamed "Chhotu"—little one.

Though Grandma was almost blind, she managed to maintain a strict vigil over all of us. How we would shiver when she raised her voice. She could be equally nice when she was in a good mood, and then she would come out with her hidden stock of sweets.

Janu went to Chhabildas School in Dadar, while the rest of us were admitted to the local Port Trust School. Most of our teachers were also Dalits; some of them had converted to Christianity. The teachers knew all the children and their parents personally.

There were many dangerous habits to pick up in the railway depot: alcohol, gambling, and stealing. But our teachers watched us carefully and taught us the importance of education even in those adverse circumstances.

Teachers were treated with great respect, almost revered, in our family. When a teacher dropped in to report on our progress, Grandma or Dada always gave them a good share of fruits or vegetables from Bai's stock, but Bai saw this as a loss in her business and disapproved.

There was little recreation for us. There was a lady welfare officer from the Port Trust, who often visited the chawl. Occasionally, she arrived in her Morris and took a bunch of kids for a ride. If we did well in school, we were given a towel and Lifebuoy soap. And those who topped their class also got to ride with her, as a special treat.

At home, we didn't even have a radio. When we finally got one in 1964, we invited friends over to "look" at the radio but refused to play it for long, saying that it would heat up. There was a welfare center run by the Port Trust close to our chawl. In the evenings, we went there to read. Initially, all I wanted was to sit there, flicking the pages of a book or magazine, peeping from the corner of my eye to see if someone was looking at me. I thought of myself as quite a prodigy, devoted to studious reading. By and by, however, I was hooked. Whenever new magazines arrived, we queued up to look at them. If we stayed late at the center, Bai and Grandma would get worried. Bai would be so afraid that something had happened to us that she would stand at the end of the lane, looking for us. Dada never worried. In fact, he encouraged us to read, insisting that his children had to know what was happening in the world.

Once, my brother Sudha was ill and not responding to medical treatment. It was feared that he might go lame. Bai persuaded Grandma to call a witch doctor. They put their plan into action when Dada was not around. The mystic healer came and laid out his paraphernalia in front of Bai, who sat with Sudha on her lap. At the end of the ritualistic puja, he went into a frenzied trance, chanting some mantras, gyrating as if possessed. Unexpectedly, Dada came home. For an instant, he was stunned by what was going on in his house. But the next moment, he seized the witch doctor and slapped him hard. The poor man jumped out of his trance and disappeared, leaving behind all his belongings! Bai stood shivering in fear. We thought he might hit her too, but he only admonished her and Grandma, and warned them not to try anything except medicine on his children.

My mother is the quintessential farmer's daughter. Without a care for the tiny quarters where we lived, she decided to raise chickens and tend goats. Every evening, she saddled us with polishing the glass lantern, cooping the chickens in a big basket, and tying up the goats to the balcony rail. Grandma walked around in tiny circles, supposedly supervising us when she could not even see very well. Bai was too busy selling produce to notice us. Her trade supplemented the family income, and we never had any shortage of fresh fruits and vegetables at home.

According to the Port Trust's rules, we were not allowed to keep animals, even pets, in the quarters. Bai raised goats regardless. One day, the inevitable happened and the officials took action. All our goats were taken into custody. Bai was sent a notice and summoned before a magistrate in the Small Causes Court. In local jargon, people referred to it as the "illiterate magistrate's court," because no one was allowed to present his case. Given the large number of small offenses for which punishments were standardized, it was impractical for the court to provide a detailed hearing. Bai had no idea what the court was like, as this was the first time she had been summoned there. She believed that she would be able to convince the "magister saheb" and he would give her a hearing and forgive her on humanitarian grounds. Her name was called out:

"Bai, did you keep goats in your home?"

"Yes, saheb."

"I fine you ten rupees."

"But we poor people need goats—"

"Fifteen rupees fine."

"Saheb, the children need milk—"

"Twenty rupees."

"But, saheb, what can we do—?"

"Twenty-five rupees."

Bai was astounded. She was shocked into silence. She thought, "That's what a saheb should be like. My children should become sahebs like this too." It would take many years for her dreams to come true.

In the evenings, all the children gathered in the balcony to study under the only electric lamp in the chawl. There was no one to help us out with our studies, since almost none of the parents had gone to school and knew very little reading or writing. The elder children stepped in to help the younger ones, and even grabbed the chance to whack someone under the pretext of teaching them. Although the parents in the chawl were uneducated, they were all greatly respected and feared. Any parent could discipline anybody else's child, and nobody would tell them to mind their own business. We were their collective responsibility.

All of us had our own ink pots and nibs and often it got messy, and our hands, feet, and clothes all became blue. We were not always to blame, though. Often the goats tied to the balcony would tug on their rope and jostle us, overturning an ink pot and walking all over our books dripping ink. This was often just the excuse we required to shut our books and get back to playing with the goats.

Grandma was not very sure what we did in school. She asked us each day what we had learned. Then we would show her a few pictures from our books, of a plow, farm implements, or fields of corn, and she would say, "What kind of school is this?" She could not understand why we had to go to school to learn about these things instead of going into the fields.

Later, she made a simple equation: first grade meant first book, and so on. Then she would ask all our friends, "How many books have you read?" She called math "counting," and she often advised Bai to learn some "counting" from us to help in her trade.

When we studied, we recited poems aloud, together. As we learned those poems, Bai and Grandma got to know them by heart too. So when any one of us was ill, Grandma would lull us to sleep, singing our textbook poem, "I only fall sick when it's school that I want to miss."

Dr. Babasaheb Ambedkar breathed his last within fifty days of our conversion. It took some time for many of us to adopt the Buddhist way of life, and many Dalit families continued to follow certain Hindu rituals. Several fairs and festivals dotted our calendar. Lord Khandoba's fair at Jejuri was the best of all, with different kinds of sweets distributed as prasad, and a huge feast of mutton curry marking the end. Khandoba was our family deity, and each year we did our best to save money to go to the jatra. Some devotees sacrificed a goat and distributed its meat, cured with salt and turmeric, as the Lord's blessed prasad. Even today, the very mention of this meat, called kanduri, makes my mouth water.

The ritual called "Return of the Gods" was immensely popular. The devotees carried out a procession of the Lord on a palanquin, with lanterns and torches burning on either side. It was a long walk, well outside the village boundary. In Mumbai too, a similar procession was staged in Wadala, which ended at a rock behind the Port Trust School. The devotees, who had returned from Jejuri, were considered truly blessed since they were lucky enough to have worshipped there. Ritualistically, they distributed prasad to the others, who had not been so fortunate.

Weddings, of course, were the other high point of our lives. Family elders arranged all marriages. The first meeting with the girl was a remarkable occasion. To determine the correct age of the prospective bride, her calves were examined, in the fashion of buying sheep and goats. She was then asked to walk, talk, and sing to ensure that she was not handicapped in any way. An equally important qualification was the girl's culinary abilities—could she make a perfectly round bhakri? Or did the bhakri turn out like a map? If a girl couldn't make tasty eggplant curry or dried fish chutney, her marriage prospects were bleak indeed.

Once the match was fixed, the trousseau and wedding arrangements took center stage. The bride's side and the groom's side had to buy clothes for each other. So "experts" from both families met in Dadar, an important shopping area in Mumbai. Nobody even thought it necessary to take the bride or groom along. Each family tried to outdo the other, and the shopkeepers made a killing. After hours of haggling, often accompanied by bitter complaints about the quality of gifts offered by the other side, the shopping expedition would end. Then the whole entourage, loaded with shopping bags and with half-asleep children, went to a nearby park. A few enterprising men bought sweets and savories such as ladoos, jalebis, and farsan, and it was soon a picnic.

The wedding ceremony was conducted with all the traditional Hindu rituals, even the sapta-padi, or the seven symbolic steps, which represented married life together. Instead of a Brahmin priest officiating at the wedding, some elder from the Dalit community would perform the rites. Salwe buwa, who often officiated, had a book called *Hindu Dharma Dipika*, which he guarded with his life. He said that he could even scare away a ghost with this book, and we kids believed him.

There would be many arguments in a wedding because relatives often came bent upon picking a fight, perhaps to add to the excitement. Many castes had a customary bride price, which the groom paid the girl's father, instead of the traditional dowry given to the groom for promising to take care of the girl. Another "progressive" custom, which prevailed until recently, was the financial assistance given to a bereaved family by all those coming to offer condolences.

Almost everything at the wedding feast was sweet, and after tasting two or three dishes, it would all taste the same. Some spicy side dishes were served just to give a break from the sweetness. The meal began with wheat porridge made of butter, jaggery, and roughly ground wheat. It was accompanied by a spicy moong usal, or lentil curry. Guests sat on the floor and ate off plates made from leaves tacked together. People usually asked for more servings than they could possibly eat at one go, and took back the rest, drying it in small cakes, so it would last them several days. Some particularly brazen guests brought their own large platters off which to eat.

All the people in the chawl had strong roots in their villages. Most went to their village as regularly as they could. Bai often went to Ozar with Grandma, but she was not often allowed to visit her own village, only hours away from Ozar. Surprisingly, Dada never encouraged us children to go along. He was too possessive of us and was afraid that we might pick up the laid-back habits of the village boys. Bai believed there were evil spirits and witches in the village who would cast a spell on children. Dada scoffed at this, but he was happy when Bai left the children with him when she went to Ozar.

Many relatives from the village would visit our Wadala home, and though compared to their village home we had only a tiny room, they thought we lived a life of luxury. We lived in "Mhambai," had proper meals every day, and ate a variety of vegetables. Besides, the coast ensured there was no dearth of fresh fish. When they returned, they took back bread and dried bombil fish, which we had to provide, for hadn't they brought us tender jowar or bajra cobs from their fields?

Dalits were still treated as untouchables in the villages even when city dwellers had started accepting them. In the villages, they were forbidden to wear shoes. So they carried their shoes in their hands from their houses up to the well outside the village boundary before putting them on. Even when they were in Mumbai, they were nervous about wearing their footwear, afraid that someone would scold them. They carried their footwear from our door until they were well past the Port Trust School. Once a matriculate Dalit had managed to find a house in a so-called upper-caste colony by concealing his caste. Then, one day, his mother-in-law came visiting. She had the old habit of carrying her chappals in her hands. Noticing this, the neighbors questioned whether he belonged to a "low caste."

All the Dalits belonging to a particular village held committee meetings in Mumbai. At the meetings, they discussed how they could help their village and their brethren. A membership fee of one rupee each would be collected, and this fund was to be used for minor repairs in the village or to help people in distress. Although it was a sacrifice for them to spare that rupee for the fund, loyal and committed, they unfailingly gathered the money. The age-old humiliation and scorn for their Dalit status, however, would come alive when they visited their villages. As they entered, the local teashop owner would shout sarcastically, "Get the silver cups out . . . the sahebs from Mumbai are here!" and the particularly unclean, broken cups used for poor Dalits would be brought out for them.

In 1955, the Port Trust offered Dada new quarters in another part of Wadala. Grandma and Bai were reluctant to move away from the old neighborhood because they feared that Antop Hill was a disreputable place where the children would fall into bad company. But Dada argued that the new house was larger, with electricity so the children could study. Dada was upwardly mobile before most men of his generation.

The New Colony at Antop Hill was a well-laid-out and self-sufficient community, much like a village. Its cultural center was the YMCA, which provided a study room, a playground, and even a gym. It also had a radio, which was a rarity in those days. The only other radio in our area belonged to a family who lived on the third floor of one of the buildings, and in the evening a crowd would gather on the road below, listening to the songs playing on it.

The doctor's dispensary was in the same area too. I think he gave the same red mixture to treat everything from a headache to cancer. But all the patients had great faith in "Dacter Saheb," whose hackneyed joke was, " 'Shake well before drinking' means shake the bottle, not the patient!"

In real life, it was difficult to demarcate the good and evil in our neighborhood. Crooks lived cheek by jowl with decent, law-abiding people who minded their own business. Such goondas and thugs were addressed as "ustaad," or chief. Gang wars were common occurrences. The thugs lived by the law of the jungle. Activities such as looting freight wagons in the Port Trust railway yards, brewing illicit liquor, and gambling went on openly and resulted in a vicious circle of fights, truces, and more battles.

The police rarely made their presence felt—except when they came to collect their own share of the booty, or hafta. Plainclothes policemen of the Special Branch were a little more feared but were equally easy to spot, for they tended to sport a uniform of their own—luxuriant, curled mustaches, arrogant looks, sturdy police boots, and white pantaloons folded down with clips to keep them clean. Occasionally, they made sudden raids. The gang leaders would temporarily feel threatened and the police would revel in their five minutes of fame. Usually, though, the gangsters never had any respect for the police.

Even in that jungle raj, there was a moral code of conduct. The thugs never harassed law-abiding residents as long as they were not police informers. In front of old and ailing people, the goondas maintained their own quaint decorum. All Wadala residents received protection without having to pay protection money, and they never had to fear the goondas.

But over the years, the goondas lost their hold on Wadala and fell on hard times. They had many talents that could have been groomed to benefit society, but that never happened. Given the right opportunity, perhaps many of them could have become successful entrepreneurs or could have won medals at the Olympics.

*   *   *

The story of the ugly duckling and its scornful brethren holds special significance for the Dalits. I wonder how many swans waste their lives thinking of themselves as ugly ducklings, trapped and punished by the inequities of our caste system. Countless Dalits were inspired to search for the swan within after Babasaheb Ambedkar touched their lives. Dada's vision ensured that my siblings and I became part of this wonderful quest.

LAYING A FOUNDATION

By the late 1940s, the whole sociopolitical environment was influenced and inspired by Babasaheb's ideas. He had completed his work on the Constitution of free India and was working in the Union Cabinet. The country had repaid its debt to Babasaheb by showering honors upon him. In Mumbai, the bastions of Ambedkar's ideology were Wadala, Naigaon, Sewri, and Matunga Labour Camp.

If Babasaheb was to address a meeting at Narey Park or Kamgar Maidan, people would come to hear him all the way from Wadala. Our colony in Wadala was always amongst those most receptive to his ideas. There was a great demand here for his fortnightly newspapers such as *Bahishkrit Bharat* and *Janata*. Every Saturday evening, all Wadala inhabitants waited eagerly for Appa Ghangale, who rode around on his bicycle selling Ambedkar's *Prabuddha Bharat* at thirteen paise a copy. Standing in groups on every corner and square in Wadala, reading Babasaheb's news and articles and discussing them, was an integral part of our lives.

Dr. Ambedkar's inspiring leadership had stimulated the rise of a whole army of local leaders and activists. All these men had two things in common—immaculately clean attire and impressive oratory. Their oratory drew on Babasaheb's concepts and teaching. Though most activists had only rudimentary education, fired by Ambedkar's ideology, they spoke logically and with great conviction. Their language was close to the rural idiom and hence went straight to the hearts of their listeners. It didn't matter if someone said "late India's prime minister" instead of "India's late prime minister." The audience was never pedantic. Those rough-and-ready speakers were one with their audience.

The activists financed their social work from their own pockets, strictly following Babasaheb's principle of probity in public life. They collected donations, however small, even four or eight annas, and walked everywhere to save on organization funds.

Dada assisted Upshum Guruji. We always saw Dada keep accounts of the donations, whether it was a rupee or two, or even less. He was in charge of the Matunga Labour Camp area and the Dalit concentrations around it. Through his own conduct, Dada taught us how a selfless social activist should behave. He would walk all the way from Wadala to Matunga, a distance of three miles, to save on funds. When someone suggested that he should temporarily borrow from the trust's funds to buy bidis when he was short of personal cash, they got the scolding of a lifetime.

Important events on our social calendar were Ambedkar's birthday and public meetings. Ambedkar's birthday brought a huge procession, and those who participated were dressed in their festive best. At its head, the procession had a massive photograph of Ambedkar on a bullock cart or a truck. There were firecrackers, and euphoric youths playing lezim—small, belled contraptions—and throwing colors in the air. If ever someone had the audacity to join the procession drunk, he was given a beating he would never forget. Women activists, dressed all in white, were an important part of the procession.

Election campaigns were occasions of great excitement. Babasaheb's movement created an awareness of political rights, and even illiterate people exercised their right by putting their thumb impression on the ballot. In the beginning, we had a ship as our election symbol. Then our party was allotted an elephant as its mascot. Parading massive cutouts of an elephant was a major part of campaigning, and the slogan was really simple—"Look, the elephant's here!"—and was especially effective when kids ran behind the procession shouting the slogan. We kids were happy that we could turn electioneering into a shouting match.

Before the actual meetings started, there were musical programs. People loved to hear martial songs presented by reputed shahirs, or folk poets, who played on a simple drum, called a duf, to accompany the songs. Later, these jalsas came to be replaced by bands. The bands did not play popular songs; their music was based on folk music, and it looked to Ambedkar's life and philosophy for its content, presented in the form of lilting songs. One of the chartbusters in Wadala went, "Bhimrao is my soul mate . . ." It was even played at weddings, and the listeners were spellbound every time they heard it.

By the time we had moved to the New Colony, all of us were studying at Chhabildas School in Dadar. This was another big change for us. During this time we learned to simultaneously inhabit two different cultural and emotional levels. On the one hand, we experienced the fiery movement inspired by Babasaheb, the struggle to gain rights of human dignity and to carve out an identity; on the other, we lived a respectable lower-middle-class life. We learned to speak mainstream Marathi without the accent of our dialect. We were overwhelmed by the excellence and idealism of our teachers, and education became an immensely enjoyable experience.

Almost unknowingly, our vision had widened. We became involved in the Boy Scout movement. For the first time, we had books bought for us that we could carry home. Babasaheb's writings were a staple, but there were others too. Dada was always concerned that the atmosphere at home should be conducive to study. He hung a framed photograph of Saraswati, the goddess of learning, on one wall. A glass panel with the motto "Where there is peace, there lives prosperity" adorned the living room.

The new house had a great facility—electricity at the touch of a switch. Janu would carefully arrange his desk on the balcony and study late into the night undisturbed. His table lamp could be seen from quite a distance. This inspired other parents to set a rule for their children: "As long as the Jadhav kids have their light on, you have to study as well."

Like all children, we loved new clothes, but we did not have the luxury of separate clothes for school and home. Our khaki shorts were made out of old coats that Dada would get from the Port Trust every year. Though Bai and Dada were thrifty about clothes, they insisted that we always wear shoes, which very few students in our school could afford. Our parents did not compromise in this regard.

Bai worked very hard to make ends meet with her small fruit-and-vegetable trade. Early in the morning, she would buy fruit from the wholesale market in Byculla, then sell it near the Central Railway Workshop in Wadala. Janu was responsible for keeping accounts and collecting dues on payday.

We had to get up early in order to walk the two-mile distance to school in Dadar. If we were late, the teacher caned us. Other Wadala children who also went to Chhabildas maintained a distance from us on the pretext that we mixed with the children of bootleggers and poor people. Our low caste was probably the main factor in keeping us apart. During the Ganapati festival, when we went to their house, we would be given prasad on our outstretched palms outside the door. They were careful not to touch us. Of course, some families made an exception to this practice and welcomed us to stay for the puja.

Janu passed the matriculation examination in 1956 with good grades. It was decided that he would go to Elphinstone College, since Babasaheb himself had studied there. Perhaps he was the first student ever to go to college wearing khaki shorts. When someone pointed this out to Dada, hurriedly he bought Janu four pairs of white cotton trousers but forgot the shirts. So Janu wore a different pair of pants every day, but he had to wash and wear his only shirt.

Janu was not happy at Elphinstone. He felt ignored and unaccepted by the other students, mostly from high-caste, well-to-do families. So he took admission in the Siddharth College started by Dr. Ambedkar, and was granted a government scholarship. One day, he used the scholarship money to buy lots of books. He thought that when he came home with the books, everyone would be happy that he had spent the scholarship money well. But Bai was angry. "What have you done? You could have brought the money straight home!"

Siddharth College gave Janu a new direction. He participated in debates and was a member of the mock parliament. The topic of all these writings and speeches was always Babasaheb and his Dalit movement.

Considering our financial situation, it was not possible for Janu to take part in extracurricular activities. That would have been a luxury. He knew that he had to earn money by doing whatever small jobs he could manage to get in order to help Dada finance our education. This was a common problem for all Dalits aspiring to rise. Accordingly, Babasaheb started morning college in Mumbai for the first time to help those learning while earning.

After the early morning lectures, Janu was free to take up a job during the daytime. He found a job as a clerk in the Customs Department, issuing permits. Once, an applicant was pleased at the speed with which Janu processed his papers and gave him a packet of suparis, betel nuts. Janu brought it home, thinking it would make Bai happy, since she loved them. Bai was certainly thrilled, but Dada was furious. He flung the suparis into the dustbin! That incident made a permanent impact on all of us.

When the annual examinations approached, Janu filed an application to get study leave. Whenever it was not granted, he simply resigned his job. By the time he graduated from college, he had been through seven or eight jobs. He applied for the prestigious Indian Administrative Service and was selected to join in 1963.

An old associate of Dr. Ambedkar's in Delhi, Dr. Shastri, was able to obtain Janu's results in advance. When he found out that Janu had passed the examination, he sent us a telegram, which read—"J. D. Jadhav passed IAS." The postman arrived with the telegram at the crack of dawn. Janu was away, and the only other person in our house who could read English was Dina. He was studying for his exams and had gone to sleep late the previous night. Awakened with a jolt when the telegram came, rubbing the sleep out of his eyes, he struggled to read the hazy lines on the telegram and mistakenly read, "J. D. Jadhav passed away."

"Janu *Bhau* is dead!" he screamed and fell unconscious. Pandemonium broke out. Neighbors gathered around. Since no one else could read much English, nobody attempted to read the message again. Besides, everyone was too overcome by grief to even think about the telegram.

A neighboring tenant from Tamil Nadu read it carefully, and declared, "Arre, this is good news! J. D. has passed the IAS!" Instantly, the atmosphere of terrible grief turned into one of jubilation.

When Janu was on his way to Mussoorie for training, Mumbai Central Station was almost overrun by residents of the Port Trust chawls. Among the people who had come to see Janu off, Dalits were a majority, but there were many of different regions and castes as well. There was a huge pile of garlands. They decorated the train compartment with flowers. Actually, most people there had no idea what IAS meant, but they knew that it meant something very important. Their celebration was selfless as they rejoiced wholeheartedly in Janu's success. He was fulfilling the shared dream.

As the train was about to leave, Dada took Janu aside and said,

"Maybe you don't remember—" Before Dada could complete his sentence, Janu knew what he was going to say. Many years ago, Babasaheb had told Dada, looking at Janu and Dina, "Give your sons a good education." Dada had obeyed Babasaheb's command and, in the process, Babasaheb's advice to his Dalit followers, "Win the seats of respect and power," had borne fruit.

At the time Janu was selected for the IAS, Dada was a Class IV employee with the Mumbai Port Trust. When Mr. Nadkarni, the chairman, heard that one of his workers' sons was in the IAS, he called Dada to meet him. Dada took Dina along. Dina sat down when Mr. Nadkarni invited him to do so, but Dada refused repeatedly, feeling it would be rude to sit in the presence of his superior. Only when Mr. Nadkarni said, "If you do not sit, I will have to stand too," did he finally, awkwardly, sit down.

"In the history of our organization, an employee's son has never been selected into the IAS. I am delighted that your son has won this honor."

"It's all due to blessings of people like you. And Babasaheb's inspiration."

"You encouraged your son to study, molded him. You have played a major role in his success. To celebrate this as an example for the officers and workers of the Port Trust, I would like to felicitate you."

"What can you do for me now? You can't promote me, because I am not qualified enough, sir. And even if you do promote me, I won't be able to do that work."

"How about if you are given an extension of a year in your present job?"

"I don't need that now, saheb. Two of my sons are working. The other two will finish their education soon. So I don't wish to work after retirement."

"You tell me what you would like . . ."

"Saheb, could you give a year's extension to someone else . . . whose children are still studying, and whose education would be affected by their father's retirement. Someone more needy than me should benefit."

Mr. Nadkarni was stunned. He shook hands with Dada and said, "You are indeed a great man."

When Janu left home to take up his job, all of us brothers and sisters were on the way up. Dina took boxing classes while studying in Siddharth College. The very first year, in the inter-college competition, his opponent proved too much for him: he punched Dina so hard that he had a broken nose and torn lips. Dina was more scared of our parents' reaction than the fact that he would have a disfigured nose. But contrary to his expectation, Dada comforted him. "Just as God doesn't get old if you miss one fair, a wrestler doesn't chicken out with the first defeat like this. Your wounds are your trophies. If a true boxer loses one event, he doesn't retire from the sport. You were beaten today. Doesn't matter. You should take it as a challenge and go on. Let's see what you can do." Dina persevered and went on to become a successful boxer.

INDOMITABLE DADA

We went to a Marathi medium school. The English language was offered only in middle school. But I knew some English even when I was in primary school, as my elder siblings used to study their English at home. One summer Janu taught me the Roman alphabet and made me practice scribbling the letters over and over again. It was a big challenge to decipher whole words by reading them letter by letter, and it became an absorbing hobby for me.

Once I had gone shopping with Dada near Wadala railway station. Across the road, there was a store named Panchsheel. The display board was written in large Roman letters, and below that the same name was written in smaller Marathi letters. I did not know enough English at that time to read the board. Dada saw me trying to read the board and said, "Chhotu, come on, read the board in English and you'll get a treat." I read the name in Marathi, and then pretended to struggle with each Roman letter as I read it haltingly for Dada's benefit. "Pansh . . . Pancsh . . . eeel, Panch-sh-eeeel," I stuttered. Dada was very pleased by my performance and said, "That's my Chhotu, the smartest of the lot. Come, I will treat you to a creamy lassi."

We sat in a restaurant, and the tall cool drink was served. I took a sip and almost choked on it. Dada kept asking me what the matter was. Finally, I confessed my deception and waited warily for a big spanking. Dada began to laugh instead. I was dumbfounded and sat staring at him. After a few minutes, sheepishly I asked, "Dada, I cheated you. Aren't you cross with me?" He started laughing again and he thumped me hard on the back with a twinkle in his eyes. "You are a first-class scoundrel, my dear, you even managed to fool your ustaad baap!"

Then he added, "Don't worry. I am not going to punish you. Your deception was a harmless joke, but you admitted it in the end and that proves you have a conscience. I am pleased by your honesty. I will treat you to your favorite naankatai." I was too scared to tell Dada that I had confessed to him less out of honesty than out of the fear of being found out. After that incident, he always called me a "first-class scoundrel."

Dada exemplified the newfound pride and awareness that Babasaheb Ambedkar had inculcated among Dalits. He learned to be fearless, and he raised us to be brave. He was never one to preach but always taught us by his own example. Once I had accompanied Dada to the rationing office to get our permit renewed. We were sent from one office to another, until we came upon two clerks, a young man and a woman. Dada and I stood near their table, waiting to be called. Even after about five minutes, both the clerks, who were supposedly there to "provide the highest service to the public," had no time for people like us. They were busy whispering to each other, while their feet flirted below the table. Dada cleared his throat and the man glanced up at us, but he did not think this dhoti-clad man merited any attention, and continued his banter with the woman.

Dada was furious. He walked out of the room and went to the senior manager's office. Outside his room, in a voice that would be heard in the entire section, he thundered, "Saheb, it looks like your office is a house of romance."

The astounded officer asked, "What are you saying?"

Dada then related the whole incident. I can never forget the look on those clerks' faces when they apologized to Dada in front of the whole office. The manager was apologetic too and personally attended to renewing our permit. Once we were out of that office, Dada said, "Chhotu, don't ever be afraid of anyone. We are law-abiding citizens and don't owe anything to anyone else's baap."

I was in secondary school and Dada was in charge of the Port Trust Railways cabin, adjacent to the Reay Road station on the Harbour Railway line. Sometimes Bai would ask me to carry him his lunch there. I would happily agree, excited about traveling by myself the two stations by train. But what I had an eye on was pocketing some money, as we were never pampered with pocket money.

Once when I had gone with his lunch as usual, I decided to buy a one-way ticket so that on my way home, I would buy a samosa and a naankatai with the remaining money. I was so excited that it probably made Dada suspicious because he asked, "Where's your ticket?"

I fished in my pocket and handed him the ticket. He looked at it and then asked me why I had not bought a return ticket. I coolly told him that I had forgotten. Dada's look told me all was not well. Indignantly, I said, "I am going to buy one now." I gave him his lunch and left. Hurriedly, I went to the platform, eager to walk home and buy the snacks. Realizing that Dada might be watching, I sauntered toward the ticket window. Once sure that I was out of his sight, I jumped onto the tracks and crossed over to the other platform, waiting for a train to Wadala. In about two minutes, Dada was miraculously beside me, from nowhere.

"Show me your ticket," Dada said.

I could not answer and smiled shamefacedly. Dada bought me a ticket and sent me home. Whenever I think of that incident, the memory of the beating I got when he came home in the evening sends shivers down my spine.

Dada was always watchful about our studies. If we didn't study enough and scored low marks, he did not hesitate to thrash us.

Though there was no effusive praise for a good report card, his face would light up looking at it. His eyes sparkled with such love and pride that we didn't mind his silent appreciation.

I passed the matriculation examination in 1969. Dada was overjoyed when he saw my marks. He was especially pleased with my marks in Sanskrit and the medal I had won in that subject. "The Brahmins never let us learn this language because it was the language of the gods. Now we have shown them."

So saying, he thumped my back in congratulation.

Dada took great pride in his work. In 1965, soon after Janu got married, he took his wife to see the railway cabin where Dada was in charge. Dada not only introduced her to all his colleagues but also showed her the work a cabin man had to do.

Dada was always enthusiastic about trying out everything. Intrigued by the skill with which the coconut sellers from south India wielded the sharp knives to skin coconuts, he tried it many times. The inevitable happened. Once he managed to cut open his thigh instead of the coconut, and only then gave up the idea.

Dada retired from service in 1970. Soon after that, he suffered a heart attack. He had smoked bidis until then. The doctor advised him to give up smoking. "How can I abandon a friend of forty years?" he retorted. So the doctor suggested he smoke cigarettes instead of the pungent and unfiltered bidis. Immediately, Janu bought him a packet of 555 State Express cigarettes.

That day there was a visitor from our village chatting with my father. Dada took out the pack of cigarettes. He fumbled to open it. When he lost patience, he simply tore it open. He took one cigarette for himself and gave one to his friend. Both lit up, took a few puffs, and shook their heads in disappointment. We were amazed.

Dina couldn't stop himself.

"Dada, these cigarettes are made by the order of the queen of England, and you say they are no good?"

Dada gave a very typical reply: "Don't tell me about the queen of England. Has she ever tried my Shivaji bidi? If she ever does, she will throw away these cigarettes!"

Time hung heavy on his hands after he retired. He did not find reading easy. Besides, since he had worked with his hands all his life, he loved "repairing" things—even things in perfect working condition did not escape his hands.

Early one morning he told me, "Chhotu, this clock ticks too loudly." Realizing his intent, I said, "It's working fine. The ticking is just the same as it was before. But if you want to repair it, go ahead."

He ignored my sarcasm, since he had made up his mind. He dismantled the clock and put it together after much polishing and cleaning. He had worked with watches years ago, but he was out of practice now. His eyesight too was not what it used to be. Not surprisingly, the clock stopped working. I couldn't help remarking, "Dada, you sure managed to stop the clock ticking!"

He felt bad. "They don't make clocks like they used to," he muttered. That made *me* feel bad. After that, all of us adopted a sporting attitude about his "repairs."

In his old age, Dada rarely lost his temper. Even if he did, he was no longer the terror he had been in our childhood. Instead, he would just sulk. He was always punctual, perhaps because he had worked with a watchmaker once. He insisted on adhering to a timetable even for his meals, bath, and tea. If his timing went awry, he grew displeased. Then he would sit silently, not speaking to any of us. Regardless of who had made him angry, it was my duty to placate him, perhaps because I was the youngest, and there was a special bond between us. The ploy that never failed was to go to him and touch his feet, asking forgiveness. He saw through the dramatic gesture, and soon he would be chuckling. And when he called me a "first-class scoundrel," I knew his anger had disappeared.

I shared a special closeness with him, especially in his later years, and I sometimes forgot the protocol of the father-son bond and became unusually frank, even impertinent. Once I said to him, "Dada, it's fortunate that you never believed in family planning."

He did not like this foray into his personal life and asked me gravely, "Why do you say that?"

"Dada, if you had stopped at two or three, I would never have been born!"

His gravity disappeared in an instant, and he laughed heartily, opening his toothless mouth, calling me a scoundrel before clapping my back.

After retiring from work, Dada began falling ill from time to time. He always chose to be admitted to Saint George's Hospital. He knew everyone there, from the ward boy to the doctors. His sunny disposition had made him friends there, and he even had nicknames for all the nurses—Darky, Fatso, Shorty—and they did not seem to mind.

Once the nurse he called Darky reminded him, "You are dark too."

Dada told her, "That's true, but I am not halfway dark like you. My color is so pure and strong—if it fades, money refunded!"

He underwent major surgery in 1972. One of his kidneys was removed. I went to stay the night with him in the hospital. When I arrived, I was stunned to see him surrounded by five or six nurses: one of the nurses was enacting a Marathi folk song for him. Such was his charm.

Before I got married, there was occasional discussion at home about finding a match for me. It was never serious, however, because everyone assumed, knowing my independent spirit, that I would make my own choice. A relative suggested, "Be sure to choose some poor girl from our community so an entire family can benefit." I did not have to reply to this. Dada fired back at him, "Aren't you smart? Does a man get married for the welfare of others? If he listens to you, one family might do well. But is he supposed to marry all the eligible girls in our community so that everyone benefits? He has to choose a life partner, be she poor or rich."

This argument went on for some time. Then suddenly Dada changed tracks and addressed me, "You think you are a social activist, don't you? Then why don't you marry a girl from the sweeper caste?"

"Dada, in getting married, should one choose a soul mate or a caste?"

He conceded my point.

"Yes, you are right. Think carefully before you choose your wife. If the two of you are not compatible, it is very difficult to get on in life. Just remember that whichever girl you choose, don't bother about what caste she is from."

I really did not worry about the caste factor. Vasundhara, who was my choice, was from a higher caste. Dada was a little upset when he found out. "These people want their girls to marry our good boys so that they can save on dowry—which they would have to pay one of their own caste."

I pacified him, "This family is not like that. But suppose even if they were, how does it matter to us? Were we going to accept dowry from anybody?" He seemed to accept my argument. He just wanted to check if we were really made for each other, as we thought, and then he gladly assented to our wedding. It was not as easy to win over some others in the family—especially Vasu's mother, Indubai.

"Over my dead body. You will have to walk out," she wailed, "to marry a low-caste Mahar."

"But he is well educated and, above all, he is a good man."

"Education has nothing to do with it. He may be good but he belongs to a low caste. If you marry him, our family's reputation and position in society will be reduced to nothing."

Things did not end with arguments in Vasu's family. One afternoon, I was called out of a meeting in my office in the Reserve Bank of India when a visitor insisted on seeing me immediately. I was shocked to see that the person waiting for me was Vasu's mother. Before I could gather my wits, she launched into her tirade—loud and clear—in front of all my colleagues. Nothing that I said pacified her but only sparked her fury further.

"What will it take for you to stop seeing my daughter?" snarled Indubai. "We come from a well-respected, conservative family. My daughter will marry one of our own caste. I don't want to see you with her again."

I was stunned into an embarrassed silence, as were my colleagues, who discreetly left us alone.

"You are a good man for being a Dalit—well educated and with a good job in the bank. Ask your parents to find you a Dalit girl but leave my daughter alone."

That evening, after much prying by Vasu, when I finally told her the reason for my silence, she was livid. She had not imagined the repercussions of defying tradition and caste-creed prejudices in choosing to marry a Dalit. Vasu's elder brothers and father were far more liberal than her mother and were open to persuasion. After endless discussions I finally won their support.

Indubai gave in after realizing that nothing would change our decision. She was silenced into agreement, but her dissent was apparent throughout. She remained listless, and halfway through our wedding ceremonies, she walked out of the marriage hall. To any sympathetic listener, she would narrate how her daughter's life was doomed. The few Dalit families in the hutments in their locality were examples enough for her to form her judgment of all low-caste people. Many of the men living there were compulsive drinkers and gamblers who often beat up their wives. They lived in poverty, helpless in their situation. How could I be any different? Indubai predicted that her daughter would return home in less than three months' time. "How can a girl raised in a cultured family adapt to the life of a low-caste family?"

A few years after our wedding, Indubai doted on me as her favorite son-in-law, and would chat for hours with Bai, my mother, who speaks in a crude dialect. They compare notes on recipes and traditions, and sing traditional songs for family functions. Bring up the issue of caste, and there is an uncomfortable silence. Indubai admits she was a victim of her ignorance, coupled with societal conditioning. Today, Indubai's closeness to my family has to be seen to be believed.

It was November, and we wanted to get married in a month's time. Vasu and I had set our hearts on getting married in the Vanita Samaj, a centrally located marriage hall, well known among the elite. All our friends and family told us that the hall is always booked six months in advance and it was impossible that it would be available for us.

"Which month is your wedding date?" the official at Vanita Samaj asked us.

"Any weekend in December is fine," I replied.

"We only take bookings six months in advance . . . you have come a year and a month ahead of time."

"No, I am talking about next month, December this year," I explained.

The officer started laughing and said that their hall was booked for the next five months. I tried persuading him to open up the register and let me look, but he did not even bother to bring it out. After a few minutes of convincing, the officer opened up the register for December. Most of the days were marked off in red, but there were two weeks that were blank.

I looked up at him questioningly, and perfunctorily he told me that it was the inauspicious time in the Paush month when there are no wedding muhurta available. I told him that I wanted the hall on the first available Saturday in December.

"That will not be possible." He looked shocked. "How can you get married at an inauspicious time? No priest will be willing to conduct your marriage ceremonies." I had to spend a lot of time convincing him that it was up to me to find a priest, or to get married without one. I counted out the deposit money and insisted that he give me a receipt after booking the hall in my name.

"Listen to me," the official said kindly. "You are young and I can understand that you are impatient to get married . . . but how can I allow you to do something that is against our tradition? Please listen to me. Go home and consult the elders in your family and then, if you want, I can book the hall for you. I can assure you nobody will book these days in the meantime."

I was exasperated and losing patience. I looked at Vasu and asked her if she had any objections to getting married on a day that others considered inauspicious. Vasu was apprehensive, yet she was willing to go along.

"Look, here is the money. We are the ones who have to get married and we do not believe in superstitions. Every single day is auspicious for us, and the day we choose to get married becomes even more auspicious, because we have chosen it. The hall is available, and it is your duty to book it in my name."

The officer was aghast at my bluntness. Nodding his head with helplessness, he counted the money. "Are you sure . . . ?" he asked with concern once again before he wrote us a receipt.

"If you don't find a priest or your elders object to this date, to claim a refund, you will lose ten percent of your deposit."

I grabbed the receipt and happily turned to leave, but I was curious to know what would happen to couples marrying on inauspicious days.

"Could you tell us why no one gets married in this period?" I asked. The old man had nothing to say and merely looked blankly at us.

"What will happen to us now that we have chosen this day?" asked Vasu.

"I can't say," the man answered dejectedly. Then he looked at me and sharply said, "What is the point in explaining the consequences to you? You have already made up your mind."

I shrugged my shoulders and thanked the old man, who looked

as if he was debating with himself. Finally, he said, "Look, if you want to tear up the receipt now, I will give you all your money back. In the sixteen years that I have worked here, never has anyone married in the Paush month. Why do you want to tempt fate?"

I insisted that he explain the consequences to us. Choosing his words carefully, he said that if the marriage took place during that period, the gods would be displeased and place a curse on us, and there could be a mishap in the family.

"What mishap? Please tell us clearly," I said.

His expression relaxed for the first time as he may have thought he would be able to convince us to change our minds.

"They say that Paush marriages bring forth doom, and one among the couple could die in a few months."

I was determined not to let this have any effect on Vasu, so I laughed out loudly and dismissed his superstitious beliefs.

"This is reason enough for us to get married in Paush. Let's see who dies . . ." I smirked arrogantly and left. Later, I was sorry that I was rude to the old man, who was talking to us out of concern for our well-being.

We were married in the year 1979 at Vanita Samaj on an inauspicious day, but we have remained happily married for over twenty-five years now. Our son, Tanmoy, was born the following year.

Repeatedly, Dada showed how liberal and progressive he was. None of the daughters-in-law in our house had gone out to work. Though none of my brothers opposed such a move, neither were they particularly supportive. But Dada believed that women should be independent and even go out to work if they so wished, and his enthusiasm knew no bounds when he heard that Vasundhara would teach in Siddharth College, the institution established by Babasaheb Ambedkar.

In 1981, the government of India awarded me a National Scholarship and I set off for the United States to earn a Ph.D. in economics. Thereafter, Dada suffered numerous heart attacks. But he did not give up. In 1984, he had such a severe attack that the doctors declared he might live a few hours at the most. Everyone despaired. But Dada told one of my brothers, "I am not going to die till Chhotu comes home."

Dina called me in the United States, and I came to Mumbai immediately. I went directly to St. George's Hospital from the airport. I didn't want him to lose heart, to hear that I had come all the way from America because of his condition. So I pretended that I was in India on some work for the Reserve Bank. My story did not convince him. "You are still a first-rate scoundrel. Why did you come back? I told you I am not going to die till you come back with your degree. Go, finish your studies."

It was indeed an honor and a surprise when my university declared me its Best International Student in 1985. I hurried home to tell the news to my wife and children. At that moment, my eyes filled up at the thought of Dada. I felt he was the one who really deserved this award. How I wished he were with me. I longed for his thump of wordless praise on my back.

I returned home after my doctorate in 1986. Dada was almost a shadow by then, but his mind was still as alert as ever. Right until the end, he amazed everybody with his perspicacity.

He asked me about my research. It is almost impossible to explain, in layman's terms, research in a subject such as economics, but I did my best. His next question was, "How will this help the common man?"

He had put his finger on the basic question that many economists overlook. I was stunned. He warned me, "If all that you study, all your research, is not going to help the man on the street, it's a big waste."

Dada called me one day, his demeanor grave. "When Babasaheb returned to India with his foreign degree, he could have got any government job that he wanted. He chose to unite our people and launch a social revolution. You have an American degree too. Then why do you work for the Reserve Bank?"

"Babasaheb was different. I am just an ordinary man."

"I don't agree. Educated young men like you should go into politics and serve the people."

Finally, just to end the discussion, I said, "No one is in politics these days to serve the people. Those days are gone. Today politics is peopled only by thugs and goondas."

Dada was never one to give up. "So what, you are a first-rate scoundrel too!"

I was speechless at that.

In 1988 I moved to Ethiopia. The Reserve Bank had appointed me financial adviser to the Ethiopian government. Though Dada had suffered numerous heart attacks, it was cancer that he finally succumbed to. When I heard how ill he was, I hurried home to Mumbai. Although struggling with this fatal disease, he still held on to his sense of humor. He said, "America could not make you light-skinned, and Africa has not turned you dark!"

I could not help laughing. "That's because my color is like yours—'guaranteed never to fade'!"

On January 14, 1989, Dada died in St. George's Hospital. All his children were around him. The peace and contentment on his face afterward was enviable. My father-in-law exclaimed, "Dada seems to have willed his own death. Nothing could be more fortunate than to pass away on an auspicious day like today, Makar Sankranti, the Hindu New Year."[24]

Dada would have scoffed at such ideas. But he had certainly fought death as long as he wanted to survive, and given in on his own terms. He left us an invaluable legacy of determination and courage. Dada was not only our father; he symbolized a philosophy, a way of life. When any of us needs strength, we search for a part of Dada in us.

IN THE WORLD OF BAI

Bai calls me Dhurva. No one else calls me by this name. By the time I was born, our family's fortunes had improved enough for her to stop her small trade in fruits and vegetables. But Bai always gives me the credit, saying, "Dhurva is my special one. He came into this world and released me from the burden of carrying that basket of goods." Armed with this special status, I would of course lord it over my siblings. Sometimes, even when I was at fault, and Dada or Grandma were yelling at me, Bai would say, "Dhurva is such a baby, why are you so hard on him? He may have wronged this one time, but he is my special one. He is the lucky one who has saved me."

As a young child, I remember Bai being always caught up in endless work. Her day began long before any of us woke up and continued late into the night. We would hear her moving around, working even as we were falling asleep. When I opened my eyes, howsoever early in the morning, I would see her by the stove, made out of a broken metal bucket. Industrious by nature, she had lined it with cow dung and mud. She would light that stove around four in the morning to make tea, and bhakris for breakfast and lunch. Sometimes the stove refused to light and emitted a lot of smoke. Then the whole household would be up, eyes smarting, coughing our guts out, but she would somehow manage to get the stove fired, and each day, unfailingly, we had fresh hot bhakris to eat before we left for school.

Bai's favorite pastime was talking about our past to whoever would listen. Sometimes she talked to herself when there was no one around. Often, she recounted an incident about my birth. In the hospital, in the bed next to hers, was a Punjabi woman who had given birth to twin daughters. She already had five daughters and had hoped to give birth to a son. Desperately, the woman wailed, "Now my husband won't take me back into the house." Then she had pleaded with Bai, "You take these girls, and take as much money as you want, but give me your son." She begged her endlessly. Whenever I was around when Bai narrated this story, she would draw me close to her bosom and lovingly say, "How could I give a piece of my flesh away? After all, he is a bit of this Sona." She referred to her name, meaning gold, and that I was a chip off the gold block. But whenever I misbehaved, Bai alluded to the woman in the hospital: "I know where she lives. If you carry on like this, I will send you off to her and bring her daughters home." I would quickly fall in line, terrified that she would abandon me to that strange woman.

When we were young, Bai regaled us with mythological stories of Krishna and his simpleminded companion, Pendya. She was an expert in bringing a story to life, interweaving it with songs. In turn, we kept pestering her to tell us the stories over and over again.

One of the most touching stories was that of baby Chilaya. The divine trinity of Brahma, Vishnu, and Shiva wanted to test the faith of a devotee, Changuna. They went disguised as sadhus to Changuna's house one morning, when she was playing with her baby, Chilaya. Changuna looked the picture of happiness, her maternal love overflowing as she gazed adoringly at her son with his beautiful black eyes and shining locks of hair and the way they cast a shadow on his translucent fair skin. Changuna paid her obeisance to the sadhus and beseeched them to bless her little one who was the center of her universe.

The sadhus said that they were hungry and if she would feed them she would truly be blessed. Changuna humbly bowed before them and said that they had only to ask and she would offer them whatever they wished to eat, for was it not the highest honor to offer food to the hungry priests? The sadhus said that their hunger would be appeased by one thing, and one thing only. But they did not trust Changuna to serve them what they wanted. Changuna reassured them that they had only to utter the request and she would set herself to it at once. The sadhus asked her to serve them the cooked meat of Chilaya.

When the story reached this point, no matter how many times we had heard it, and though we knew the outcome, we would all grow tense and uncomfortable, chewing on our nails or fidgeting, eager for the story to end happily. Bai, however, would have no mercy on us. She would keep going on and on, "They ordered her to pound the baby's head in a mortar . . ." and we would groan in disgust. Bai would continue, "The other condition was that Changuna's sacrifice would be void if she shed a single tear while she made it . . ." My eyes would start streaming. Janu, who had outgrown the story by then, would tease me and call me a sissy for crying. But I did not care what he said, and almost shook Bai's shoulder, urging her to continue.

"With a heavy heart, Changuna did as the holy men ordered. In her mind, she kept chanting Lord Krishna's name to save her from this calamity. She had decided to kill herself once she had appeased the sadhus. Without her Chilaya, what did she have to live for? Changuna's heart was crying wildly, but she did not shed a single tear. The holy men were convinced of Changuna's sincerity and asked her to go out into the courtyard and call out to her dead son. Changuna thought her heart would burst with grief if she did that. How could she beckon her own flesh and blood that she had just cruelly killed? But she did as she was told.

Changuna calls,

> "*Chilaya, my sweet little Chilaya*
> *Come little one, answer the call of my heart . . .*

The jingle of your bracelets won't leave my ears,
And my eyes can't even shed any tears.

"Baby Chilaya, come back.
My baby, my arms hurt to hold you,
My breasts ache to suckle you . . .
My baby, come to me before I die,
Don't torment me, Chilaya
Baby Chilaya, come back."

The jingle of his bracelets, the patter of his feet.
The gurgle of his laughter,
There appears Chilaya
Running and leaping,
Scattering his lovely curls.

That would bring life back into me as I breathed a heavy sigh of relief, and Bai would cuddle me, and tickle the wits out of me, calling me a softy for crying. Bai almost spoke the touching song in her flat off-key voice instead of singing it. But even today, the memory of Bai singing Changuna's song can make me see baby Chilaya running toward his mother in slow motion, his curls fluttering.

Years later, in America, as a student, whenever I felt homesick, I would find myself humming Chilaya's song, or other equally off-tune lullabies that Bai used to sing us, imitating Bai's style and dialect. Vasu would tease me, "You sing just as off-key as your mother does!" But the memory of those songs would wrap me in the warmth of my home and family.

I would get engrossed in the world of myths and legends that Bai's songs and stories would re-create. Bai continued to live in that world. She firmly believed that the earth is balanced on the mythical serpent Shesha's head. Whenever there was news about an earthquake, Bai would say that Shesha, burdened with the weight of the earth, was adjusting the position of his head. We had all given up trying to convince Bai otherwise. When Neil Armstrong set foot on the moon in 1969 and pictures of the earth taken from outer space were available, I showed the pictures to Bai and victoriously said, "Look, this is the picture of our earth. Now show me where is your Shesha."

She looked at the pictures, and gave me the look reserved for a complete idiot. Condescendingly, she explained, "Shesha Naag is a god, Dhurva, how come you are so silly? Do you think photographs by ordinary mortals can capture God?"

That day I truly gave up the folly of trying to enlighten Bai.

When groceries arrive, Bai unrolls the string on every packet and ties it carefully into a spool—"just in case we ever need it."

Bai gets a pension of three hundred rupees or so from the Port Trust. She calls it "pensal." Waiting for the postman to bring her "pensal" is a favorite pastime. Her pension makes no financial difference to us, but it has great significance for her. If the postman is late by a day, she becomes anxious. When he brings the pension, she rewards him with a meager fifty paise. She thinks that is a generous tip. I feel sorry for the postman. I waylaid him once and tipped him ten rupees, so he would bring Bai's pension on time. He pocketed the money, saluted me, and said, "Can I tell you something, sir? Your ten rupees can't match the fifty paise that Granny lovingly gives me!"

Bai always addressed Dada as "Jadhav." So many people thought it strange that she should call her husband by his last name that Dada often berated her with "Soney, you are still a nitwit!" But when he was in a rage, nobody, including Bai, dared say a word. Bai specialized in making indirect strikes. Even if she was angry with any of the children, she directed some comment at Dada too: "How can the soil be any different from the mine?"

The love between Dada and Bai was evident when they ate jalebis. That was their favorite sweet. It was a pleasure to watch them eating jalebis, always entreating the other to eat some more—the beauty of a love that had mellowed in the evening of life.

Dada and Bai enjoyed going to the doctor, though they always seemed unhappy with him. If the doctor prescribed a diet, Dada followed it. He trusted the doctor, even if he outwardly made fun of the poor man. Bai was the opposite. She firmly believed that all doctors lied to her foolish sons and led them on, to get ridiculously high fees. Once every few years, she seemed to enjoy a hospital stint because that brought all the relatives visiting, and she was able to reestablish contact with everyone.

It is difficult to gauge Bai's thoughts. When my book in Marathi was published, there was an article about it in *The Times of India*. I was thrilled to see the photo of Dada that accompanied the article. Proud and overjoyed, I showed it to Bai. Nobody could have predicted her reaction: "Don't tell me about your father! He was so dark and ugly."

Another time, a reporter from an English magazine, *The Week*, had come to our home to interview me regarding the book. He expressed a desire to interview Bai too. Since he did not speak Marathi, I had to be the interpreter.

He asked, "How would you describe Dada?"

Bai answered, "He was dark no doubt, but he was a good man."

The reporter wrote, "He was dark but handsome."

The next question: "What qualities did you like most about him?"

"He never drank, never abused me. Best of all, he never raised his hand to me."

It was a telling comment on the meager expectations of women of her generation.

Bai aged measurably after Dada passed away. She has taken to feeding the crows, talking to them. Apart from the color, there is no similarity between Dada and the crows, but she holds on to the traditional belief that Dada comes to meet her in the form of a crow. Every day, before she eats, she hurries to place tidbits for the crows, muttering, "Looks like Jadhav is here!"

I even suspect that she occasionally argues with the birds.

EPILOGUE

On my first visit to the shrine of Vithoba at the famous temple in Pandharpur, the entire management committee of the temple had gathered to greet me. I was a VIP performing ritual worship and the temple authorities were eager to welcome me. However, as my car approached the temple, I became a bundle of nerves, and my palms grew sticky with sweat.

I was after all an untouchable—I belonged to a caste that was denied entry into the temple. Even the shadow of an untouchable was not supposed to fall on any temple. And that day, there I was being escorted with honor into the Temple of Vithoba—the ultimate seat of Hindu temporal power.

This meant a lot to me—although I hated admitting it. Even though the untouchables traditionally looked upon Vithoba as their savior, they were told that they had sinned in past lives and were therefore ordained to suffer disgrace and dishonor in this lifetime. As penance for their sins, they would be at the mercy of the high castes. Their only hope, they believed, was Vithoba, whose divine powers could rescue them from the painful cycle of birth-life-death.

The chairman of the trust and the head priest welcomed me.

Bickering priests were vying to catch my attention. Each one wanted to be the one to help me perform the puja. They were the proxy middlemen who would help me chant the ritualistic mantras. It was hard to control my tears or to wipe them away. I was painfully aware that I did not belong there. I was the unwanted, unworthy untouchable. I fished out a wad of crisp hundred-rupee notes from my pocket and began handing them out to the priests, pressing them into their outstretched, imploring, touchable palms. They swooped upon me like eager hawks.

In the sanctum sanctorum, I went through the motions of the puja, mechanically. All I wanted was to be left alone, to face Vithoba and look Him in the eye. It was the first time that I had ever visited a temple.

I was humbled.

I had done it. I had crossed the caste lines. I had beaten the system. The high-caste priests were themselves obsequiously leading me to do puja! I had made the quantum leap from the lowest rung to the top. But I could not understand why I was weeping.

It was then that a tall boulder right outside the temple came into focus. Before I knew what I was doing, I had left the priests and rushed toward the boulder. I hugged it hard, prostrated before it, and clasped it, its ragged edges bruising my palms, as startled onlookers stood aghast.

This boulder was the boundary beyond which the untouchables were not allowed to step. I imagined all my untouchable forefathers, their plight—a long journey on foot over high mountains to arrive here.

Feet blistered, throats parched, fasting with empty stomachs, singing His glory, they would carry the saints' devotional writings in a heavily decorated palanquin resting on their shoulders. For here was Vithoba, their savior. But once they reached the temple precincts, God was out of bounds for them.

After the long journey, the devotees would separate like oil and water once they reached the temple. The touchables could enter the temple. The untouchables had only the boulder. Their boulder that stood rugged and alone, a few feet outside the temple. The boulder became their makeshift Vithoba—crude, buffeted by the elements, quite unlike the richly clad, bejeweled idol of the god within.

I hugged the boulder, and a sigh escaped me. Like my ancestors,

I clutched it, trying to understand what they had endured. I suddenly knew for whom I wept.

I felt a weight lifting off my shoulders and a sense of deep tranquillity. The spirit of God is to be found even in the smallest atom. The ornate idol and the rugged boulder are one, images of the same universal spirit. I no longer felt agitated by constant reminders of my so-called low caste.

A long-cherished dream was fulfilled recently when I took my son, Tanmoy, who is an adult now, to Wadala to show him where we had lived. I showed him our former home. We saw the dilapidated Port Trust School, and the railway yards. I took him for a ride in the engine of a freight train. I considered showing him how we used to cross the tracks under a moving freight train, but then I thought better of it.

When we were college students, we sat in a restaurant outside Wadala Station for hours, in animated discussion. My son and I went to the same restaurant. Seeing me after so many years, the owner, Shetty, took some time to chat with me, but then he exclaimed, "Wow, now you are a big guy!"

"But I am the same old guy for old friends."

He laughed heartily at that. I was amused to see that he still had one gold-filled gleaming tooth in his mouth. "It's not like it used to be in the old times. It was nice when you people came here."

I was surprised. I had imagined we were terrible customers, ordering a half-cup of tea each, and sitting there for hours on end, but Shetty felt differently. "I used to hear new and interesting things from you guys. Now it's mostly drunks who come here and bother me."

Roaming around Wadala, Port Trust Colony, and Antop Hill, I was trying to give Tanmoy a glimpse of my childhood. Day turned to evening. Squalor and crowds seemed to close in on us. There were many stumbling souls with reddened eyes babbling to themselves. There might have been many ustaads among them too. But among the children I saw there, I kept looking for that little Dhurva.

AN ADDENDUM

When my father asked me to write about my life, I was skeptical to say the least. How many varied and life-changing experiences do twenty-year-olds really have? A lot, actually, once you step back and think about it.

As my junior year at Johns Hopkins University draws to a fantastic finish, I can't help but think of trite clichés about how quickly time flies and how old I am getting. It honestly seems like two seconds ago that I was in high school taking my SATs, and now it is time to take my MCATs! I can see myself playing field hockey at age fifteen and getting into fights with the other teams, cheering till I lost my voice at boy-band concerts at age ten (now I wonder why), and deciding to conquer the world by curing cancer and AIDS and winning the Nobel Peace Prize, all at age five. Well, maybe not that much has changed after all.

Before I continue, a little recap about my life is a must. I was born in Indiana, of all places, in 1985 while my parents were at Indiana University. So when I was two years old, we returned to India because my parents wanted my brother and me to grow up in a family-oriented environment. About ten years later, my dad got an assignment at the IMF in Washington, and so we moved to Maryland, where I went to high school. Wanting to be a doctor ever since I was a little baby, the natural choice was to apply to Johns Hopkins; and so far, I have had the time of my life.

In Mumbai, life was great. No, I did not have a pet tiger, we did have electricity, and no, I do not know how to walk on hot coals, so I cannot teach you. Instead, I can point you to the best bookstore in the city with the most peaceful coffee shop; I can take you to the hottest nightclub with any kind of music from salsa to old-school hip-hop, or watch a play in any language. Along with its own share of poverty and corruption, life in Mumbai, you see, is like life in any big city anywhere in the world. From first grade on, just like any other kid, I was consumed by school, sports, and my 60 million relatives—not to mention the millions that haven't been discovered yet. I swear that every Indian is related if we all dig deep in our family trees. I have always been treated as the baby of the entire family and even received special attention from everyone older. Sure, now I have about fifteen nieces and nephews who are trying to steal my thunder, but still. My father's side of the family is Buddhist, while mother's is Hindu. So on special occasions at the Jadhavs', we would say Buddhist prayers, which consist of hymns and personal introspection, in Pali. My mother's side would be more upbeat, with forty grandparents, uncles, aunts, cousins, nieces, and nephews all singing in Marathi to the beating of cymbals and such.

I discovered that I was a Dalit when I was twelve years old. I didn't really know what that meant, and wondered if I was different from all my friends for some strange reason. There was a teacher in sixth grade who recognized my last name and asked, "Are you the daughter of Dr. Narendra Jadhav? The Dalit scholar?" I was proud of my father, but completely bewildered as to why he had to have that title attached to him. Why couldn't she just call him a scholar? Why add the Dalit tag? Innocently, I went home and asked my father what all the fuss was about. Almost anticipating this question at some point or another, he sat me down and explained the struggles of my ancestors as well as Dr. Ambedkar's efforts.

I went to a renowned school in Mumbai—a private Jesuit institution—with girls from all religions and backgrounds. I blossomed there from a shy, awkward little girl into a confident, outgoing woman. I remember when I was four years old, there was a Halloween-costume contest, which I wanted to parade around and participate in. My mother put off making this costume till the last minute—a quality I happen to have inherited—and hastily made a hideous sunflower costume. The judges voted for the best outfit, and needless to say, some annoying girl with a fancy tailor-made princess outfit won. I was raging mad at this and refused to settle for the consolation prize. Hell, I wanted my victory lap around the stage and fifteen minutes of fame. My father was ridiculously pleased with himself because he saw the same ambition in me that he possesses. Talk to him now, and he will say that was the moment he knew I was going to achieve great things in life and was, indeed, "Daddy's girl." The flip side of this, however, is that now he expects me to outdo everyone at everything I do, and achieve excellence and the best grades. Take one advanced organic chemistry course at Hopkins, Dad, and then maybe we can talk.

One thing I can definitely thank my parents for is that they never forced me to do anything that I did not want to do. A lot of my friends were put into classical Indian dance classes at an early age. I flatly refused to indulge in this dancing, and rather, wanted to run track just like my brother. So they did not drag me to kathak and bharatnatyam classes, but instead encouraged me to improve my running at the soccer stadium across the street. I ran every day with my brother, who gave me pointers so as to win the medal come Sports Day at my school. This was in the third grade, and turned out to be a big lesson in my life. My hundred-meter sprint was about to start, and I was as nervous as any eight-year-old could be. I gazed into the stands and saw my parents waving at me, cheering me on. I knew I could win this; I had worked so hard for it. The gun went off, as did the other seven girls. I took the lead immediately and ran as fast as my legs could carry me. Again, I looked up at the stands to smile at my parents, and waved. In the middle of all this, I lost my concentration and thus lost the race. Losing this race was crucial because it taught me the importance of concentration. I realized that I had all the effort and strength to become a winner, but all that is nothing without concentration.

At Hopkins, like any other undergrad, I have no concept of time as life just morphs into a routine of schoolwork, food, going out, and sometimes sleep. The beauty about college is that I have no reminders or even reasons for people to remind me that I am a Dalit here. I am in a sorority with barely any Indian girls, and conversations do not revolve around what caste I belong to and why. Instead, I am content with being just an Indian, who shares common food, music, and culture with the rest of the large population of Indian students at Hopkins. Recently, as the vice president of the South Asian Society there, I was involved in organizing an annual fall culture show. The beauty of the event was that people of all ethnicities came together and performed without any inhibitions. Asians, Hispanics, whites, and blacks all gyrated to Bollywood songs and dance sequences. Caste is definitely not an issue anymore; race, if anything, is. You hear about atrocious hate crimes committed against various ethnicities, especially in the wake of 9/11, and realize that that is the important question and problem in the world today. Race relations are of international importance, while caste and communal violence—such as the recent religious riots in Gujarat—should be an anomaly.

My ancestors carried the burden of being Dalits and bowing down to demeaning tasks even after Indian independence. I am not bowed down by caste or religion; I have bigger problems, dreams, and ambitions. The beauty of my ancestors' efforts is that they were not in vain. Here I am, getting the best possible education I can get, which is exactly what they would want me to be doing. Education, they thought, was the only way to completely dissolve the caste system in India. The fruits of their labor are seen also in my being regarded as a human being by others, not as some Dalit who has access only to terrible facilities and inferior education, but as a woman who is on her way with equal opportunities to attain her childhood ambitions of conquering the world.

As a child, I was always fascinated by minute details in life. I always asked my family questions such as "Who was the first person to sit in a car?" or "Who was the first person to eat butter?" Now my questions are more relevant and important: "Who was the first person to stand up against caste discrimination in our family?" The answer is simple: my grandfather. He refused to let circumstances dictated by the upper castes shape his life; instead, he decided to shape his own destiny. He accomplished this by enrolling his children in the best possible schools he could. His children, however, lead double lives of sorts. My father, for example, deals with foreign dignitaries on a daily basis, but the ghosts of his impoverished past still haunt him. He works in places such as the IMF and makes decisions that shape nations, yet comes home to a mother who does not even know where America is. My generation, however, is free from all this. My grandfather's and Dr. Ambedkar's efforts have been brought to fruition in my generation. I have no reminders of being a Dalit, or any reasons to think I am different from my peers. My ancestors worked hard to make my life just like that of any other girl in the world. I have the torch they have lit for me and nothing can stop me now.

—APOORVA JADHAV

NOTES

1. Eleanor Zelliot, *From Untouchable to Dalit: Essays on the Ambedkar Movement* (Columbia, Mo.: South Asia Books, 1996), p. 22.
2. Ibid., p. 39. A crore is 10 million.
3. Ibid., pp. 86–89.
4. The mythical history was recounted first by C. B. Khairmode in his Marathi book *Amrutnak,* first published in 1929. It has been quoted since by many scholars.
5. Excerpts from Dr. Ambedkar's speech are from Dhananjaya Keer, *Dr. Ambedkar's Life and Mission,* 3rd ed. (Bombay: Popular Prakashan, 1971), p. 71.
6. Dr. Ambedkar's declaration of social independence for untouchables at Mahad coincided with the declaration of the goal of political independence for India by the Indian National Congress (Keer, op. cit., p. 105).
7. Ibid., p. 92.
8. Ibid., p. 100.
9. The Prince of Wales (later Edward VIII) visited Mumbai soon after and was booed and met with slogans and demonstrations (Gopa Sabharwal, *The Indian Millennium, A.D. 1000–2000* [New York: Penguin, 2000], p. 461).
10. The Kala Ram Temple was constructed in 1782 at a site believed to have been inhabited by Ram, Sita, and Laxman during their exile. The temple received patronage from the Peshwas, who were Brahmins and leaders of the Maratha Empire, which then dominated the region. Every year, Lord Ram's birth is celebrated in the Kala Ram Temple. Hundreds of thousands flock to the procession, in which the idols are carried out in two chariots donated by the Peshwas.
11. The factual account of the protest here draws on details provided by Keer (op. cit., pp. 136–38) and Y. D. Phadke (*Ambedkari Chalwal* [Pune: Sri Vidya Prakashan, 2000], pp. 3–73; in Marathi).
12. *The Times of India* (March 8, 1930), also quoted by Phadke, op. cit., p. 9.

13. For details of the historic Round Table Conferences and, generally, for the evolution of Dr. Ambedkar's movement, see "Untouchability, Caste System and Dr. Ambedkar."

14. Keer, op. cit., p. 192.

15. Gandhi told Babasaheb that the Congress had spent 2 million rupees for the upliftment of untouchables. Babasaheb retorted that the Congress had done nothing beyond giving formal recognition to the problem. Had the Congress been sincere, it would have made opposing untouchability a precondition for becoming a party member. In that meeting, Babasaheb told Gandhi that his approach to the problems of untouchables, based on a "change of heart," was not viable. He said Dalits believed in self-help and self-respect and were not prepared to have faith in leaders and Mahatmas. History tells us that "Mahatmas, like fleeting phantoms, raise dust but no level," he said (Keer, op. cit., pp. 165–68).

16. As reported by Mahadev Desai, Gandhi's secretary (Phadke, op. cit., p. 35).

17. Keer, op. cit., p. 178.

18. The Indian National Congress had ended the civil disobedience movement. The British Parliament passed the Government of India Act in 1935, which provided for a constitutional relationship between the Indian states and British India on a federal basis. Accession of the states to the federation was provided for. The act also provided for legislatures at the federal and provincial level. Gandhi had given his consent to work within the framework of the act.

19. Keer, op. cit., p. 253.

20. Ibid., p. 255.

21. In the conference in Mumbai on May 30, 1936, Babasaheb spoke extensively to justify his decision to renounce Hinduism. "What good is a religion that deals with life after death? What about the quality of life itself? Only those who are well placed and prosperous in this world can afford to live in contemplation of life after death. But why should we live within the fold of a religion which has deprived us not only of basic needs such as food, water and shelter, but also of the dignity of being alive?" (Keer, op. cit., p. 274.)

22. Keer, op. cit., p. 238.

23. Ibid.

24. According to the Hindu calendar, Makar Sankranti, considered highly auspicious, is the day the sun enters the house of Capricorn, the tenth sign of the zodiac, beginning its journey toward the Northern Hemisphere. The Kumbh Mela is held on this day every twelve years, when millions of Hindus flock to the sacred rivers for a holy dip.

GLOSSARY

Aaee a term of address or reference to one's mother

aaji grandmother

Aba a term of address or reference to elders, including one's father

abhanga devotional songs

Aga a sentence opener, expressing reference to a girl

amar rahe "long live"

anna one sixteenth of a rupee

antarpaat cloth curtain

Arre a sentence opener

atma soul

atya father's sister

baba father

Bai an informal honorific, used to address a woman

baksheesh gift

baluta entitlements in kind

bhajan devotional song

bhakri unleavened Indian bread, patted into rounds and roasted on a griddle

bhakti devotion

bhau brother

bhelpuri a spicy-sour snack made with puffed rice

bidi cheap Indian cigarette; tobacco in a hand-rolled leaf

bombil a fish found off Mumbai; also called Bombay Duck

boondi   sweet nuggets made from chickpea flour
buwa   minor religious authority

Chaturvarna   the fourfold division of Hindu society
Chaitya Bhoomi   memorial to Dr. Babasaheb Ambedkar in Mumbai
Chambhar   an untouchable caste, usually working with leather
chanya   dried pieces of meat
chappals   sandals
charpoy   bed consisting of a frame strung with rope
chavadi   village hall
chawl   large sprawling apartment building of one-room homes
chillum   funnel-shaped clay pipe for smoking
chool   mud stove

dada   big brother
dal   lentils
Dalit   downtrodden, oppressed; typically refers to former untouchables
desi   indigenous
dharma   duty
dharmashala   charitable guesthouse/lodging at religious places
Dhor   an untouchable caste in Maharashtra
dhoti   traditional male garment; a length of cloth wrapped around the lower body
Diksha Bhoomi   place for conversion of ex-untouchables to Buddhism
durgah   Muslim tomb
Dussehra   festival celebrating the return of Lord Ram from exile

fakir   Muslim holy man
fauzdar   police officer

filewallah   worker who replaced old railway sleepers with new
 ones

ghat   mountainous terrain
ghee   clarified butter
ghongdi   blanket
goonda   scoundrel
Gora   white person
guru-bhakti   devotion to a teacher
Guruji   title used for a teacher or elder

idya   slang for idea

jaggery   by-product of sugarcane, used as a sugar substitute
Jai Bhim   Victory/Hail to Bhim (i.e., Dr. Babasaheb Ambedkar)
jalebi   syrupy spiral sweet made from chickpea flour
jalsa   musical program
jatra   village fair
Johar   a form of salutation

kaka   uncle
kaku   aunt
kamandalu   brass pot
karma   destined duty or fate
Khandoba   name of a god
kumkum   vermilion adorning a woman's forehead
kurta   shirt

ladoo   a round sweet
lassi   buttermilk drink made by churning yogurt with water

Maay-Baap   mother and father
Mahar   an untouchable caste in Maharashtra

Maharin Mahar woman

Maharwada Mahars' quarters

Mahatma great soul

mama maternal uncle

mamledar revenue official

mandir temple

Mang an untouchable caste in Maharashtra

mangalashtak composition of eight couplets chanted during a
   wedding ceremony to bless the couple

mantra spell used in meditation

Maratha peasant community of Maharashtra

Marathi language spoken in Maharashtra

Mariaai goddess of pestilence, especially smallpox, traditionally
   worshipped by Mahars

memsaheb madam

modak dumpling with sweet coconut filling traditionally
   offered to Lord Ganapati

moong type of lentil

moong usal moong curry

muhurta auspicious time

naankatai kind of cookie

nirvana ultimate attainable bliss in human existence

paan leaf filled with betel nuts and other scented ingredients
   including tobacco

padar long, flowing part of a sari used for covering the torso

paise plural of paisa—one hundredth of a rupee

Pathans tribe from Afghanistan

patil village headman

pav bread

Peshwas Brahmin leaders of the Maratha Empire

photowallah photographer

pir Muslim man of God

potraj   servant of the goddess Mariaai
Purnima   full-moon night
prasad   offering of food blessed by God
puja   display of reverence

ragi   a kind of cereal
Ram Navami   birth anniversary of Lord Ram
Ram Ram!   salutation used by villagers
rangoli   art of decorating the courtyards of Indian homes

sadhu   holy man
saheb   boss
salaam   salute
samosa   a small pastry filled with seasoned vegetables or meat
sari   length of cloth draped around a woman's body
Sarkar   literally, denotes government; colloquially, used to
   address a person of authority
sasubai   mother-in-law
satyagraha   nonviolent direct-action mass technique developed
   by Mahatma Gandhi
savadhaan   caution
seer   a measure, about fifteen pounds
seth   owner
sheera   semolina pudding
Shesha Naag   mythological king of serpents, believed to bear the
   earth on its hood
sivarai   old form of currency, one quarter of an anna
supari   betel nut mixture

tamasha   folk theater from Maharashtra
tonga   horse carriage

usal   a spicy lentil curry
ustaad   chief

Vaishakh the month covering parts of April and May in the Hindu calendar

Wah an expression of appreciation
watan piece of land

Yeskar duty village duties assigned to Mahars

ACKNOWLEDGMENTS

I have accumulated many debts of gratitude during my work on this book.

First and foremost, I would like to thank Scribner for bringing out this American edition of the book and in particular Alexis Gargagliano, Susan Moldow, and John McGhee for their painstaking work. This edition could not have seen the light of day without the initiative and follow-up of my agent, Ms. Candice Fuhrman, and her team.

I would like to thank Anand Chandavarkar and Deena Khatkhate. Both have been a treasure trove of wisdom for me, and I benefited immensely from frequent interactions with them while working on the manuscript. Anand's deep insights into the evolution of India's sociological landscape helped me a great deal in widening the scope of this book.

Thanks are due to several colleagues and friends. Dileep Padgaonkar, Kumar Ketkar, Bimal Jalan, Montek Singh Ahluwalia, Vijay Kelkar, Y. V. Reddy, and Rakesh Mohan were not only strongly supportive but also offered valuable guidance. I am grateful to Devesh Kapur and Pratap Mehta, who organized a seminar on the book at Harvard University, and Tuli Bannerji, who did the same at MIT, which provided constructive feedback. Useful comments were also given by A. Premchand, Arjun Dangle, Kamalakar Sontakke, Achala Joshi, Dinkar Gangal, Usha Mehta, R. D. Bangar, V. G. Jadhav, Amit, Shobha, and Dilip Chitre, Chanda and Ravi Athale, Jitendra Borpujari, Vikram Savkar, Chandra Shekhar,

Partha Ray, Sujan Hajra, Sangeeta Das, Arindam Roy, Sunando Roy, Pallavi Chavan, and Bharati Banerjee.

Deserving special mention are Himali Belwalkar, Sunny Macmillan, and Radhika Menon for their excellent editorial assistance. I also wish to acknowledge Asha Damle, Vinod Nand, and Yashodhara Maitra, who were associated with a part of the initial drafts. Enthusiastic secretarial assistance by Ravi Sundararajan, Suresh Gulati, Mohammed Miskin, Ratnamma Kartha, Nityanand Pai, Vasanti Panshikar, and Bhaskar Dekate is gratefully appreciated.

Special thanks are due to Olivier Betourne, Vaiju Narvane, and the staff of Fayard for their efforts in bringing out the French version of the book. I also acknowledge the valuable contribution of Krishan Chopra, Kalpana Joshi, and Ajanta Guhathakurta of Penguin (India).

Finally, I owe a great deal to my family. I am indebted to my brothers Janardan, Sudhakar, and Dinesh, and their affectionate spouses, and my sisters, Leela and Trusha, and their spouses for their love and unfailing support, which has meant a lot to me. My niece Sucheta was always ready to provide valuable suggestions at every stage. Last but not least, I would like to express gratitude to my loving wife, Vasundhara, and our two wonderful children, Tanmoy and Apoorva, for their patience with me. Apoorva played the role of a tough in-house critic, adding considerable value to the book. I would not have finished this project had they not stood by me throughout. The extent of the gratitude I feel for them is beyond words.

ABOUT THE AUTHOR

Narendra Jadhav, born in 1953, is a well-known economist, presently the principal adviser and chief economist (in the rank of executive director) of the Reserve Bank of India. He has several scholastic honors and professional distinctions to his credit. He has represented India at various international fora and served as an international civil servant during his various assignments abroad, including a four-year term as the adviser to the executive director (India) at the International Monetary Fund. He is also a well-known public speaker and social activist.

Dr. Jadhav studied economics at the University of Mumbai and Indiana University, where he earned his doctorate. He has authored seven books, including two award-winning works in English on economics, *Monetary Economics for India* (1994) and *Challenge to Indian Banking: Competition, Globalization and Financial Markets* (1996), and a multiple-award-winning book, *Dr. Ambedkar: Economic Thoughts & Philosophy* (1992), in Marathi and English. He has published around seventy-five research papers in a number of prestigious journals and edited volumes. *Untouchables* is based on a family biography that he wrote in Marathi in 1993, which remained on the bestseller list for twelve years. The English version of the book was written in 2002; this was then translated into French and Spanish and is being translated into all the major Indian languages.